The Good Project

The Good Project

*Humanitarian Relief NGOs
and the Fragmentation of Reason*

MONIKA KRAUSE

The University of Chicago Press   Chicago and London

MONIKA KRAUSE teaches sociology at Goldsmiths College, University of London.

The University of Chicago Press, Chicago 60637
The University of Chicago Press, Ltd., London
© 2014 by The University of Chicago
All rights reserved. Published 2014.
Printed in the United States of America

23 22 21 20 19 18 17 16 15 14   1 2 3 4 5

ISBN-13: 978-0-226-13122-1 (cloth)
ISBN-13: 978-0-226-13136-8 (paper)
ISBN-13: 978-0-226-13153-5 (e-book)
DOI: 10.7208/chicago/9780226131535.001.0001

Library of Congress Cataloging-in-Publication Data

Krause, Monika, 1978– author.
   The good project: humanitarian relief NGOs and the fragmentation of reason / Monika Krause
      pages: illustrations; cm
   Includes bibliographical references and index.
   ISBN 978-0-226-13122-1 (cloth: alk. paper) — ISBN 978-0-226-13136-8 (pbk.: alk. paper) —
ISBN 978-0-226-13153-5 (e-book) 1. Non-governmental organizations. 2. Humanitarian assistance.
I. Title.
JZ4841.K73 2014
363.34′8—dc23

                                                                        2013045371

Contents

Illustrations

ILLUSTRATIONS

Acknowledgments

This book has its origins in a series of seminars on humanitarian action, organized for the Social Science Research Council by Craig Calhoun and Michael Barnett, which I first attended in 2004. The seminar brought together academics and practitioners in the New York City area, and with that some of the finest minds in the field. It was a privilege for me to listen to their discussions. In the following years, relief workers in positions of considerable responsibility added to their already busy work schedule in order to make time to answer my questions. I thank my respondents for their generosity in sharing their time, experiences, and reflections.

Mentors and colleagues at several institutions provided the necessary context for this work. During my time at New York University, I have been incredibly fortunate to have had the guidance and encouragement of a set of advisers well worth emigrating for. Craig Calhoun never ceases to surprise—with the breadth of his knowledge, the precision of his thinking, and the many different things he seems to be able to fit into a twenty-four-hour day. He has been extremely generous in sharing his ideas and his vision, but also his time, understanding, and good judgment. This book and my approach to many other issues owe much to him. It has been an honor to be able to observe Richard Sennett think, write, and teach over the years. I am very grateful to have been able to count on his advice across two continents, and back. I thank Neil Brenner for his seriousness, enthusiasm, generosity, and encouragement. Eric Klinenberg, always challenging and always wise, has been a model adviser since my first week at NYU. Harvey Molotch has served as a model for perfect performances. I also owe thanks to Juan Corradi, David Garland, Jeff Goodwin, Steven Lukes, Mary Nolan, Chris Pickvance, Andrew Ross, Chris Shilling, Miri Song, and Judith Stacey.

Members of the Nylon workshop and other groups at NYU have been good friends and wonderful colleagues: I thank Melissa Aronczyk, Claudio Benzecry, Nandi Dill, Matthew Gill, Alexandra Kowalski, Noah McClain, Erin O'Connor, Olga Sezneva, Owen Whooley, Marion Wrenn, Grace Yukich, Sarah Damaske, Neal Caren, and Dorit Geva. A writing group with Samantha MacBride and Robin Nagle and ideas groups with Michael McQuarrie and Aaron Panofsky, and later with Claire DeCoteau and Isaac Reed, have helped me keep focus and inspiration. Aaron Major, Noortje Marres, Linsey McGoey, Daniel Menchik, Shani Orgad, and Lisa Stampnitzki are friends who have also read draft chapters and provided helpful comments. The book also benefited from conversation with Emily Barmann, Julian Go, John Mollenkopf, Iddo Tavory, Ann Swidler, and Susan Watkins. Aysen Darcan provided necessary knowledge.

I would like to acknowledge financial support from NYU's Graduate School of Arts and Sciences, the Academic Council of the UN System, the John F. Kennedy Library, and the Lyndon B. Johnson Library. I appreciate the assistance that I received from librarians, and I would like to thank, in particular, Regina Greenwell at the Lyndon B. Johnson Library, who was extremely generous when the most interesting document to have emerged out of weeks of research was not among my notes. Bev Skeggs chaired the Sociology Department at Goldsmiths during the time I finished the manuscript, and deserves some credit for all of the interesting things going on there. I am grateful also to Dominick Bagnato, Candyce Golis, and Jamie Lloyd, and to Jennie Munday and Simon Sharville, who helped prepare the final manuscript.

Two reviewers for the University of Chicago Press provided exceptionally thoughtful comments that helped me improve the manuscript. I am especially grateful to the reviewer who came up with the final title of the book. At the Press, I thank Douglas Mitchell for his interest in this project in particular and his vision in general, as well as Timothy McGovern and Marian Rogers.

I am grateful to my family and to the friends who have become like family away from home. I thank Jill Conte, Sarah Kaufman, Julia Loktev, Michael Palm, and Eric Robinson in New York, Tricia Lawler in Istanbul, and Will Davies, Susanne Hakenbeck, Javier Lezaun, and Ann Kelly in London.

I think I could and would have written this book without Michael Guggenheim. I am grateful to him for making me much happier than I ever imagined I could be; I am grateful to our daughter, Hani, for waiting to be born until just after I finished revising the manuscript, and for living with us now.

Introduction

"The crisis in Darfur presents a defining moral challenge to the world," reads an appeal by Save Darfur.

More than four years have passed since the start of the genocide in Darfur, Sudan. As many as 400,000 innocent people have been killed and more than 2.5 million more have been driven from their homes. These refugees now face starvation, disease, and rape, while those who remain in Darfur risk torture, death, and displacement. We must act quickly and decisively to end this genocide before hundreds of thousands more people are killed.[1]

This description of the crisis in Dafur emphasizes the large number of victims. The text also suggests suffering beyond comprehension and from which there is no escape. To impart this sense of entrapment to the reader, it provides two sequences of three different evils within one sentence: "starvation, disease, and rape" and "torture, death, and displacement." Yet amid the horrors of that description, there is something comforting and reassuring in the notion that "we must act." The "we" reminds the reader that he or she looks at this suffering from the outside, and suggests that he or she does not face this violence and suffering alone but rather as part of a community that shares his or her concern: "we, the international community," "we, global civil society," or "we, people from relatively well-off countries

---

1. "Help Stop the Genocide in Darfur," on Save Darfur's official website, accessed August 31, 2011, http://action.savedarfur.org/campaign/savedarfurcoalition (site discontinued).

who care." There is also something reassuring about the "we *must* act." If we must act, this might imply that "we can act." With the right values and the right information, we can do something to help.

The crisis in Darfur is only one of many situations that have become the basis of appeals like the one above in the last twenty years. If we think about the crisis in Kosovo in the late 1990s, the Indian Ocean tsunami in 2004, the earthquake in Haiti in 2010, or the AIDS pandemic, each of these complex and diverse social phenomena has been brought to our attention as an "emergency." The notion of an "emergency," in the analysis of Craig Calhoun, "is a way of grasping problematic events, a way of imagining them that emphasizes their apparent unpredictability, abnormality and brevity, and that carries the corollary that response—intervention—is necessary."[2]

Western governments today feel obliged to develop some kind of response to many—though by no means all—distant "emergencies," and members of the general public often feel motivated to give. But what does it mean to act on the suffering of people who are distant? It is not just geographical distance that separates "us" and "them." Various forms of social organization also stand in between and mediate; that is, they both link and separate in specific ways and in ways that show patterns, which we can analyze. The institutions of the news media constitute one such form of social organization, and scholars have analyzed the role of the media in communicating suffering in some depth in recent years.[3] Donors are also separated from and linked to distant suffering by markets, governments, the history of colonialism, different forms of knowledge and expertise, and different systems of meanings.

In this book, I address a specific set of organizations that stand between the constructed "we" and a variety of forms of suffering across the world: nongovernmental organizations (NGOs) in the area of humanitarian relief. Organizations like the International Committee of the Red Cross (ICRC), Doctors Without Borders/Médecins Sans Frontières (MSF), Save the Children, Oxfam, and CARE have come to play an increasingly promi-

---

2. Craig Calhoun, "A World of Emergencies: Fear, Intervention, and the Limits of Cosmopolitan Order," *Canadian Review of Sociology and Anthropology* 41, no. 4 (2004): 375; Calhoun, "The Idea of Emergency: Humanitarian Action and Global (Dis)Order," in *Contemporary States of Emergency: The Politics of Military and Humanitarian Interventions*, ed. Didier Fassin and Mariella Pandolfi (New York: Zone Books, 2010), 59–79.

3. Luc Boltanski, *Distant Suffering: Morality, Media, and Politics*, trans. Graham Burchell, Cambridge Cultural Social Studies (Cambridge: Cambridge University Press, 1999). See also Stanley Cohen, *States of Denial: Knowing about Atrocities and Suffering* (Cambridge: Polity Press, 2000); Lilie Chouliaraki, *The Spectatorship of Suffering* (London: Sage, 2006); and Suzanne Franks, "The CARMA Report: Western Media Coverage of Humanitarian Disasters," *Political Quarterly* 77, no. 2 (2006): 281–84.

nent role in global politics and in our thinking about global politics in the last twenty years.

These organizations are called on to respond to a variety of issues and problems, and an increasing amount of money is channeled through them. More and more aid from former colonial powers and the wealthier nations of the world to former colonies and poorer nations is disbursed as humanitarian aid rather than development aid. Official budgets for humanitarian relief rose sixfold between 1990 and 2012, from $2.1 billion to 12.9 billion.[4] More and more of this humanitarian funding is channeled through nongovernmental agencies, and a lot of this money passes through a relatively small number of large organizations.[5]

Many observers have celebrated these organizations and have tacitly assumed that all we need to know about them is their aims and their values and how much of their aims they have achieved. Others, more critically, have pointed at the role of money and power in these organizations, and in particular at the role of external interests, such as those of Western donor governments. Both the naive and the critical accounts are too simplistic, however, and do not engage the empirical questions concerning how these organizations actually do their work.

How do these organizations translate values—or interests, for that matter—into practice? How do these values translate into what aid workers do every day, and what they do not do? What are the practical constraints that make this translation possible, and what are the implications of these constraints? How, for example, does any particular organization decide which particular lives to save and which particular needs to service? How do they account for these decisions, to themselves and to others? How do different organizations interpret these values differently? And what do the answers to these questions tell us about the kind of mediation these organizations provide and the role they play? In this book, I will address these questions by examining how these organizations do their work, focusing specifically on the practices of managers in the largest humanitarian relief NGOs.

4. Development Initiatives, *Global Humanitarian Assistance Report, 2013* (Somerset, UK: Development Initiatives, 2013). The $12.9 billion already shows a slight downward trend, since a peak of $13.9 billion in 2012.

5. Abby Stoddard, "Humanitarian NGOs: Challenges and Trends," in *Humanitarian Action and the "Global War on Terror": A Review of Trends and Issues*, ed. Joanna Macrae and Adele Harmer, Humanitarian Policy Group Report 14 (London: Overseas Development Institute, 2003), 25–36. See also Peter Walker and Kevin Pepper, *Follow the Money: A Review and Analysis of the State of Humanitarian Funding*, Briefing Paper (Medford, MA: Feinstein International Center, Tufts University, 2007).

The Argument

I will argue that humanitarian NGOs have come to inhabit a shared social space. This shared social space produces both the assumptions that are common across agencies and the debates agencies have with each other about what it means to be a humanitarian. It is important to understand the practical logic of that space as an important aspect of what is standing between those who give, on the one hand, and "the suffering of the world," on the other hand; this practical logic mediates efforts to help those in need.

Drawing on in-depth interviews with desk officers in many of the largest Western relief NGOs, I develop two claims about this space. First, I argue that to understand the practices of humanitarian relief agencies we need to understand that relief is a form of production and has one primary output or product, which is the "project." Managers produce projects and strive to make good projects. This has important benefits. But the pursuit of the good project develops a logic of its own that shapes the allocation of resources and the kind of activities we see independently of external interests but also relatively independently of beneficiaries' needs and preferences.

Second, agencies produce projects for a quasi market in which donors are consumers. The project is a commodity, and thus those helped, the beneficiaries, become part of a commodity. The pursuit of the good project encourages agencies to focus on short-term results for selected beneficiaries. The market in projects also means that beneficiaries are put in a position where they are in competition with each other to become part of a project.

Considering humanitarian relief as a mode of governance, it is important to recognize that, in addition to the benefits for those in need emphasized by liberal observers, and the forms of direct domination highlighted by critics of humanitarian relief, there is also a form of indirect domination at play, which is mediated by the market for projects.

In contrast to accounts that analyze and critique "humanitarian reason" based on a reconstruction that attributes coherence based on ideas or interests, I argue that the pattern we see is rather one of a fragmentation of reason. In contrast to those who critique international aid as excessively planned and rationalized,[6] I argue that the current structure of humanitarianism is already shaped by the success of these critiques, and the consequences of this are not only positive ones.

6. E.g., William Easterly, *The White Man's Burden: Why the West's Efforts to Aid the Rest Have Done So Much Ill and So Little Good* (London: Penguin Press, 2006).

Not all humanitarian relief agencies are the same, of course, and I will explore the differences among organizations in what follows. When I say that humanitarian agencies share a space, this means that they are oriented toward each other in formulating their differences. I will map the controversies about what it means to be a humanitarian, and I will suggest that the diversity of agencies can form part of, rather than undermine, the market for projects.

Global Governance and Fields of Practice

It is now widely acknowledged that transnational links of all kinds are essential to understanding the social world and the political order of the present moment. But talk about the global political order after the end of the Cold War can still focus on abstract ideas, either celebrating the new power of universal values and concerns or critiquing new forms of imperialist ideology. Both optimistic accounts and critical accounts tend to portray global governance as rather coherent and unitary.

In order to fully understand the new forms of linkage that are created by globalization, I would suggest that we need to reconstruct our knowledge based on careful attention to *practices of linkage*. I would count studies that have looked at such practices among the very best studies of globalization. Yves Dezalay and Bryant Garth draw attention to the role of international lawyers in the politics of Latin American countries.[7] Saskia Sassen highlights judges' use of international law in national contexts.[8] Nicolas Guilhot makes an argument about a group of professionals acting as "democracy promoters."[9] David Mosse and Richard Rottenburg study networks of development experts.[10]

7. Yves Dezalay and Bryant G. Garth, *The Internationalization of Palace Wars: Lawyers, Economists, and the Contest to Transform Latin American States,* Chicago Series in Law and Society (Chicago: University of Chicago Press, 2002).

8. Saskia Sassen, *Territory, Authority, Rights: From Medieval to Global Assemblages* (Princeton, NJ: Princeton University Press, 2006).

9. Nicolas Guilhot, *The Democracy Makers: Human Rights and International Order* (New York: Columbia University Press, 2005). See also studies of professional economists by Johanna Bockman and Gil Eyal, "Eastern Europe as a Laboratory for Economic Knowledge: The Transnational Roots of Neoliberalism," *American Journal of Sociology* 108, no. 2 (2002): 310–52; and Marion Fourcade, *Economists and Societies: Discipline and Profession in the United States, Britain, and France, 1890s to 1990s,* Princeton Studies in Cultural Sociology (Princeton, NJ: Princeton University Press, 2009). For a theoretical discussion of the uses of field theory for studying transnational forms, and an application to states, see Julian Go, "Global Fields and Imperial Forms: Field Theory and the British and American Empires," *Sociological Theory* 26, no. 3 (2008): 201–29.

10. David Mosse, ed., *Adventures in Aidland: The Anthropology of Professionals in International Development* (New York: Berghahn Books, 2011); Mosse, *Cultivating Development: An Ethnography of Aid*

In response to rationalist analyses of organizations, some authors, especially in anthropology, and in science and technology studies, have insisted on the messiness and heterogeneity of practice in different fields, including international aid.[11] I agree with the emphasis on practice and on empirical observation, but I think it is important to ask not just about hybrid forms and contingent negotiations but also about patterns and about order. In the sociological tradition of differentiation theory, following the arguments of Pierre Bourdieu and others,[12] I want to examine the possibility of specific logics of practice in specific social worlds, or fields.

We have learned from previous work that organizations exist in a field with other organizations and can be shaped by reactions to a shared environment.[13] To this insight about organizations in the neoinstitutional tradition, Pierre Bourdieu adds a historical approach, a specific hypothesis for thinking about fields that are organized around high ideals, such as religion, art, or law, and an account of symbolic divisions among actors, which I will show are relevant for understanding humanitarian relief. By analyzing humanitarian relief as a field, I probe to see whether there is a social space of some shared taken-for-granteds and some shared interpretations, and whether there is a set of actors here who, in their disagreements, honor each other as relevant opponents.

Humanitarian relief NGOs have played an important role in linking the West to faraway places and to distant suffering in particular, and they have been central also to discussions about global civil society. We have a number of edited volumes addressing issues surrounding humanitarian relief NGOs,[14] and we have excellent studies of individual organizations

---

Policy and Practice (London: Pluto Press, 2005); and Richard Rottenburg, *Far-Fetched Facts: A Parable of Development Aid*, trans. Allison Brown and Tom Lampert (Cambridge, MA: MIT Press, 2009). See also Dorothea Hilhorst, *The Real World of NGOs: Discourses, Diversity, and Development* (London: Zed Books, 2003); and Läetitia Atlani-Duault, *Au bonheur des autres: Anthropologie de l'aide humanitaire*, Recherches Thématiques 8 (Paris: Armand Collin, 2009).

11. John Law, *After Method: Mess in Social Science Research*, International Library of Sociology (London: Routledge, 2004). See also, for example, Dorothea Hilhorst and Maliana Serrano, "The Humanitarian Arena in Angola, 1975–2008," *Disasters* 34, no. 2 (2010): 183–201.

12. See, for example, Pierre Bourdieu drawing on Weber in Bourdieu, *The Rules of Art: Genesis and Structure of the Literary Field*, trans. Susan Emanuel (Stanford, CA: Stanford University Press, 1996); and Howard S. Becker, *Art Worlds* (Berkeley: University of California Press, 1982). For a different version of this tradition, see Niklas Luhmann, "Differentiation of Society," *Canadian Journal of Sociology* 2, no. 1 (1977): 29–53; and Luhmann, *The Differentiation of Society*, trans. Stephen Holmes and Charles Larmore, European Perspectives (New York: Columbia University Press, 1982).

13. Paul J. DiMaggio and Walter W. Powell, "The Iron Cage Revisited: Institutional Isomorphism and Collective Rationality in Organizational Fields," *American Sociological Review* 48, no. 2 (1983): 147–60; and Neil Fligstein, "Social Skill and the Theory of Fields," *Sociological Theory* 19, no. 2 (2001): 105–25.

14. See Michael Barnett, and Thomas G. Weiss, eds., *Humanitarianism in Question: Politics, Power, Ethics* (Ithaca, NY: Cornell University Press, 2008); Richard Wilson and Richard Brown, *Humanitari-*

in humanitarian relief, most notably the ICRC and MSF. Among the best studies of individual humanitarian NGOs is the early and ground-breaking work of Pascal Dauvin and Johanna Siméant on MSF and MDM (Médecins du Monde), the works of Peter Redfield on MSF, and the work of Didier Fassin.[15] In this book, I want to look not at any specific organization but at the ensemble of Western humanitarian NGOs.

Humanitarianism: Practice, Ideas, Field

This book is based on a distinction between humanitarian ideas, humanitarian practices, and the field of humanitarian relief organizations. Humanitarian ideas—ideas that have been or could be claimed to be humanitarian—have a very long history, as evidenced, for example, by the parable of the Good Samaritan in the New Testament. We have evidence of humanitarian practices—practices that have been or could be described as humanitarian— in response to disaster, illness, and poverty dating back to antiquity. But for the longest part of human history, the meaning of humanitarian practices has been either subsumed within a more undifferentiated social whole or shaped within other spheres of social life such as religion, politics, and medicine. Humanitarianism as a field distinct from other realms of practice has a much shorter history, and it is this field that is the object of this book.

Beginning in the mid- to late nineteenth century, humanitarianism emancipated itself from other fields of practice and developed its own stakes that make competing claims to a humanitarian identity possible.

anism and Suffering (Cambridge: Cambridge University Press, 2009); Erica Bornstein and Peter Redfield, eds., *Forces of Compassion: Humanitarianism between Ethics and Politics* (Santa Fe, NM: School for Advanced Research 2011); Ilana Feldman and Mirian Ticktin, eds., *In the Name of Humanity: The Government of Threat and Care* (Durham, NC: Duke University Press, 2012); Didier Fassin and Mariella Pandolfi, eds., *Contemporary States of Emergency: The Politics of Military and Humanitarian Interventions* (New York: Zone Books, 2012).

15. See Pascal Dauvin and Johanna Siméant, *Le travail humanitaire: Les acteurs des ONG, du siège au terrain* (Paris: Presses de Sciences Po, 2002); Peter Redfield, "A Less Modest Witness: Collective Advocacy and Motivated Truth in a Medical Humanitarian Movement," *American Ethnologist* 33, no. 1 (2006): 3–26; Redfield, "Doctors, Borders, and Life in Crisis," *Cultural Anthropology* 20, no. 3 (2005): 328–61; Redfield, "The Impossible Problem of Neutrality," in *Forces of Compassion: Humanitarianism between Ethics and Politics,* ed. Erica Bornstein and Peter Redfield (Santa Fe, NM: School for Advanced Research Press, 2011), 53–70; Didier Fassin, "Humanitarianism as a Politics of Life," *Public Culture* 19, no. 3 (2007): 499–520; and other essays in Fassin, *Humanitarian Reason: A Moral History of the Present,* trans. Rachael Gomme (Berkeley: University of California Press, 2012). On organizations in neighboring fields, see also Stephen Hopgood, *Keepers of the Flame: Understanding Amnesty International* (Ithaca, NY: Cornell University Press, 2006); Hilhorst, *Real World of NGOs;* Michael Barnett, *Eyewitness to a Genocide: The United Nations and Rwanda* (Ithaca, NY: Cornell University Press, 2002); and Atlani-Duault, *Au bonheur des autres.*

Humanitarian NGOs are central to this history. In the second half of the nineteenth century, the ICRC established advocacy for a special status for humanitarian actors. In the 1970s, MSF established a position critical of the ICRC in the name of a more pure form of humanitarianism. Since the 1980s, the field has expanded and consolidated.[16] Common stakes have brought agencies closer together, and many of them are now part of shared conversations about ethical principles and technical standards as well as common training initiatives. Common stakes have also led to a more intense contestation about what it means to be a humanitarian.

I am concerned with practices within organizations that claim to be humanitarian NGOs, and I am concerned with the way humanitarian ideas are understood within these organizations. I do not mean to imply, however, that these concerns exhaust humanitarian practice or humanitarian ideas, which continue to be claimed by other types of organizations and in private charity.[17]

I focus on Western NGOs in this book, and this focus has some justification in the history of the humanitarian field. While compassion, generosity, and charity have a much broader history,[18] the field of humanitarian relief organizations has its origins in Europe in the nineteenth century, and its history includes the history of Western colonialism and of decolonization. Western agencies have been dominant in humanitarian relief from the 1970s through the 1990s and 2000s. It is important to note that this is now changing with increasing Asian and Middle Eastern funding for humanitarian relief,[19] and I hope the impact of this shift can be taken up in future work.

---

16. Barnett, "Humanitarianism Transformed," *Perspectives on Politics* 3, no. 4 (2005): 723–40; Barnett, *Empire of Humanity: A History of Humanitarianism* (Ithaca, NY: Cornell University Press, 2011); and Peter Walker and Catherine Russ, *Professionalising the Humanitarian Sector: A Scoping Study* (Cardiff: Enhanced Learning and Research for Humanitarian Assistance, 2010).

17. I am deliberately focusing on practices in NGOs in the field of humanitarian relief. A certain decontextualization is involved in this, but one, I would argue, that reflects the empirical decontextualization of these practices. For the theoretical benefits of the opposite move, a recontextualization of humanitarian practice, not just "on the ground" in emergency settings as is usually done, but in the complex range of practices that could be said to be humanitarian, see Erica Bornstein, *Disquieting Gifts: Humanitarianism in New Delhi* (Stanford, CA: Stanford University Press, 2012).

18. See, for example, Amy Singer, *Charity in Islamic Societies* (Cambridge: Cambridge University Press, 2008).

19. Jonathan Benthall and Jérôme Bellion-Jourdan, *The Charitable Crescent: Politics of Aid in the Muslim World* (London: Tauris, 2003); Jonathan Benthall, "Financial Worship: The Quranic Injunction to Almsgiving," *Journal of the Royal Anthropological Institute* 5, no. 1 (1999): 27; Jonathan Benthall, "Islamic Humanitarianism in Adversarial Contexts. In Bornstein and Redfield, *Forces of Compassion*, 99–121; Andrea Binder and Claudia Meier, "Opportunity Knocks: Why Non-Western Donors Enter Humanitarianism and How to Make the Best of It," *International Review of the Red Cross* 93, no. 884 (2011): 1135–49; and Kerry Smith, *Non-DAC Donors and Humanitarian Aid: Shifting Structures, Changing Trends*, Global Humanitarian Assistance Briefing Paper (Somerset, UK: Development Initiatives, 2011).

The Desk Officers

This book draws on a range of materials, including archival sources, reports, observations in trainings for relief professionals, and background interviews. I discuss my methods in more depth in the appendix. A particular aspect of my research design, however, is worth discussing here because it is key to the analytical focus I adopt in the book and is closely linked to the specific questions I am asking and to the answers I can and cannot give. To learn about how humanitarian relief agencies actually do their work, I interviewed people with a very specific role across different organizations and asked them about their everyday work practices.

I interviewed fifty desk officers and directors of operations in sixteen of the world's largest relief NGOs. The people I interviewed—the desk officers—are not representative of all relief workers, and I did not aim to construct a representative sample of all relief workers. Rather, I spoke to this particular group of managers because they occupy a position that is of great practical relevance. Their offices are only one site to investigate as part of the sociology of humanitarian relief NGOs, but they are both a very interesting and a strategic site for studying the field of humanitarian relief organizations.

I interviewed desk officers and directors of operations because they play a key mediating role between strategic planning in the organizations' headquarters and the day-to-day management of operations in the field. In a relief organization, the operations department usually oversees work across the world in liaison with the agency's country directors. It is the center of the organization's outgoing flows. Humanitarian agencies' operational departments are divided into several regions or "desks." A desk officer is in charge of operations in at least one but usually several countries. Decisions are prepared here, and the most detailed knowledge of internal structures and events is located here, not at the highest level in the organizational hierarchy. Decisions on this level also set the frame for implementation on the ground.

For my interviews, I chose a sample of organizations that would allow me to learn about the largest Western and most influential relief organizations, because most of the funding is channeled through them.[20] I also

---

20. See Walker and Pepper, *Follow the Money*; and Kang Zhao et al., "Assortativity Patterns in Multi-Dimensional Inter-Organizational Networks: A Case Study of the Humanitarian Relief Sector," in *Advances in Social Computing: Third International Conference on Social Computing, Behavioral Modeling, and Prediction, SBP 2010, Bethesda, MD, USA, March 30–31, 2010; Proceedings*, ed. Sun-Ki Chai, John J. Salerno, and Patricia L. Mabry, Lecture Notes in Computer Science 6007 (New York: Springer, 2010).

included organizations that would allow me to discover what might be different about smaller agencies, religious agencies, agencies from different countries, or technically specialized agencies.

I asked desk officers about their work, their everyday practices, probing for details wherever possible. I sought to uncover the shared practical knowledge and shared frames of interpretation of this group of managers. With this design, I stand in a specific tradition of interviewing experts.[21] In this tradition, the expert is not interviewed because his or her knowledge is "better," but because it is especially practically relevant and full of consequences, as he or she has decision-making power. The expert is not asked to give information about a subject area that he or she is knowledgeable about as an observer. Rather, his or her practical knowledge of organizational processes she or he is involved in herself or himself is the target of the investigation.

The people I interviewed took a variety of routes into humanitarian work. Many older workers had some initial background in development work and had moved into humanitarian relief because it seemed more immediately necessary and useful or because the emphasis of funders had shifted. Some of the younger workers had specifically set out to become professional humanitarians. Some had specific technical backgrounds as doctors, nurses, water engineers, or experts in nutrition; some had joined from management positions in the private sector; and some had joined from the military. When I met them, these workers were based in New York, Atlanta, London, Paris, Geneva, or Brussels, but they all had previous experience in delivering programs in the field, and they all still travel to visit the field in the Global South regularly.

The Organization of the Book

The object of this book is the field of humanitarian relief organizations. I argue that humanitarian relief NGOs inhabit a shared social space, and I seek to describe the logic of practice within that shared space. Chapters 1, 2, 3, and 4 discuss the components of that logic and their implications.

---

21. Alexander Bogner, Beate Littig, and Wolfgang Menz, eds., *Interviewing Experts* (Basingstoke, UK: Palgrave Macmillan, 2009); and Michael Meuser and Ulrike Nagel, "ExpertInneninterviews—vielfach erprobt, wenig bedacht," in *Qualitativ-empirische Sozialforschung: Konzepte, Methoden, Analysen,* ed. Detlef Garz and Klaus Kraimer (Opladen: Westdeutscher Verlag, 1991), 441–71. The expert-interview is also different from the life-history interview; for life-history research, see David Lewis, "Tidy Concepts, Messy Lives: Defining Tensions in the Domestic and Overseas Careers of U.K. Non-Governmental Professionals," in Mosse, *Adventures in Aidland,* 177–98.

The first chapter takes us into the headquarters of the world's largest humanitarian relief NGOs in order to discuss shared practices of project management. It examines how desk officers make decisions about where to go and whom to help. This allows me to show the routines and procedures that shape their work. Desk officers aim to help people, but they do so by producing projects. Their professional concern is to produce good projects, and I show how the pursuit of the good project develops a dynamic relatively independently of values, interests, and needs on the ground.

Chapter 2 looks at how the pursuit of the good project in humanitarian relief affects how desk officers imagine people in need. The role of the populations being served has often been ignored by economists modeling nonprofit organizations and has been misunderstood by theorists of civil society. Rather than being primarily "beneficiaries" or "clients," they are also part of the product being packaged and sold by relief organizations and labor for it.

Chapter 3 describes the management tools that make the project possible as a unit of planning and exchange. The logframe, a prominent planning tool, has introduced an emphasis on clear goals and evidence for results in foreign aid. In doing so, however, this tool has separated evidence of results according to very specific project aims from a conversation about the broader sets of effects an intervention might be having, and from conversations about the broader sets of effects the totality of interventions might be having.

Chapter 4 describes the symbolic divisions and differences within the humanitarian field. In developing their distinctive positions on questions of humanitarian policy, agencies draw on different intellectual and national histories, but diversity is also shaped by competition for a specific type of symbolic capital: humanitarian authority. Today, when we, as a donating public, confront distant suffering, our response is mediated by the two aspects of the logic of practice of the humanitarian field: the shared practices and routines of the field of humanitarian relief, and the reflexive position-taking and symbolic positioning within the field of humanitarian relief. While some field approaches posit a division between economic and cultural capital, I suggest we can map organizations along the dimensions of field-specific capital, on the one hand, and different kinds of capital dependent on other fields, such as the political field or the religious field, on the other hand.

My main aim in this book is to describe the practical logic of humanitarian relief and its implications in the present. But it is important to emphasize that this logic of relief has a very specific history and thus does not simply follow from either the content of humanitarian ideas or the fact that there is suffering or that there are disasters or civil wars. I take a specific approach to the tasks of writing the history of humanitarian relief and explaining how we got to the present moment. My aim is not, as is expected in some circles in the social sciences, to focus on one cause of change and then show that this cause is more important than all other causes. Nor do I simply aim to tell a story that situates the present moment in larger contexts and processes. My approach is rather to identify the elements of the logic of humanitarian relief, and then the conditions of possibility that have to be in place for relief to exist in the form in which it exists today. In this approach, analytical description and explanation fall together. When we ask what would have to be different for humanitarian relief to be different from what it is now, we approach the phenomenon like the missing piece of a puzzle; as we determine the conditions in its environment that codetermine its shape, we also get a better sense of this shape.

It is then possible to trace the history of the elements of the logic of humanitarian relief and their conditions of possibility. On a general level, this means being explicit about some of the conditions that we usually take for granted, as though they were an invariable part of human societies, and therefore do not consider as causes of humanitarianism in its present form, and that we therefore usually do not consider as possible leverage points for analysis and for political action. Histories of humanitarian relief often focus on the history of humanitarian ideas, and sometimes on the conditions that humanitarian relief currently responds to. But we also need to consider, for example, that large parts of the world population do not have access to basic provision and that this seems to matter to some Western funders some of the time.

The historical parts of chapters 3 and 4 discuss two other neglected conditions of possibility of humanitarian relief as it exists today. I emphasize the role of management tools in shaping the market for projects. In tracing the history of these management tools, we see a shift within Western states from development policies with broad goals and expansive yet nonspecific responsibilities assumed toward people to a regime of accountability for specific results on the level of the intervention. Efforts to make aid more responsible have resulted in the abdication of responsibility beyond very specific project aims. Chapter 4 traces the history of the authority specific to the humanitarian field. I show how humanitarianism has become a field in which symbolic position-taking makes sense.

By the end of chapter 4, my analysis of the different elements of the practical logic of the field of humanitarian relief and their histories will be complete. I then discuss in chapters 5 and 6 how resilient that logic is and how it interacts with ideas and institutional developments inside and outside the field. Chapter 5 discusses the most thoughtful and the most resourceful reform projects that have arisen from within humanitarian relief. This allows me to examine humanitarianism in its most recent form and, some would argue, at its best. I will show that the impact of these reform projects, too, is shaped and limited by the pursuit of the good project. Indeed, these reform initiatives end up becoming a part of the institutional structure of the market for projects—one approximating a standard for products in this market; the other, a fair labor standard, which seeks to contain the most extreme versions of unfair competition among agencies.

In chapter 6, I take up what is often hailed as the main ideological alternative to humanitarian relief in linking "us" to "them": the idea of human rights. I discuss the relationship between human rights and humanitarian relief and explore the role human rights has played in humanitarian relief. I show that the idea of human rights is not in itself a remedy for the shortcomings of humanitarian relief, as some claim. The impact of the idea of human rights is itself mediated by organizational practice, and this is true of the field of humanitarian relief as well as of the field of human rights.

In the conclusion, I return to the questions about global order raised in this introduction from the perspective of the sociology of fields of specialized practice. Having described the specific mediation that the humanitarian field provides between Western givers and distant suffering, I outline some of the implications for a politics we can develop vis-à-vis this mediation. I will argue that we need a politics not just of ideas or resources but of organizational practice.

ONE

In Pursuit of the Good Project

Every advance is a gain in particular and a separation in general. It is an increase in power leading to a progressive increase in impotence but there is no way to abstain. ROBERT MUSIL, *THE MAN WITHOUT QUALITIES*

Large humanitarian NGOs have much in common with other large organizations. But they also set themselves very specific tasks and employ very specific practices. Humanitarian relief organizations aim to save lives, relieve suffering, and service basic human needs. According to the principles they typically embrace, they are committed to serving people across national borders and without regard to race, ethnicity, gender, or religion.[1]

If we pause to think about this for a moment, this commitment means, practically speaking, that these organizations need to find some way to make choices in order to make their mission manageable. At any given moment, there is always a surplus of people that could be helped, something that some desk officers talk about very openly. "It is perhaps the most interesting thing about my job," one desk officer at a medical relief organization told me, "and the most difficult. I mean, if you have two patients, how can you choose? They are both sick, and you are a medical doctor. And the needs are everywhere, and you will not save the planet!"

1. International Federation of Red Cross and Red Crescent Societies, "The Code of Conduct," http://www.ifrc.org/Global/Publications/disasters/code-of-conduct/code-english.pdf.

These organizations face a version of the problem of triage.[2] The staff member quoted above draws on the analogy of a doctor practicing medicine, and it is in medicine that professionals have thought and written most explicitly about the problem of triage. If you are a doctor arriving at a battle scene or responding to an accident, for example, you can refer to a set of procedures that help you to decide whom to treat first; you will treat first those who need it most, but you will also try not to waste time on those victims who have little chance of survival.

But relief NGOs face the problem of triage in specific ways. A desk officers is not exactly a doctor deciding between two patients; rather, he or she is part of an organization deciding between two battlefields. Also, relief NGOs are understood and understand themselves as a response to the failures of other providers of services. As NGOs are global in reach, claiming to serve all of humanity regardless of race, creed, nationality, or location, the problem of triage poses a particular challenge to humanitarians' self-understanding. Humanitarians are fierce critics of an international order that sacrifices some lives for others; yet they themselves must chose whom to save and whom not to save.[3]

This chapter will examine how managers in relief organizations deal with this challenge. How do relief agencies determine where to go, where to do what, and how much? How do agencies choose a country? How do they decide on an issue? How does any particular agency decide which particular lives to save? How do agencies compare the needs of patients with HIV/AIDS to the needs of those with malaria? The Central African Republic to Sudan? A flood to a civil war? And how does one choose whether to provide latrines or doctors? Tents or teachers?

These are important question in and of themselves: how humanitarian relief agencies confront these questions and how they resolve these dilemmas have important implications for who does and who does not get help. In the context of this book, asking these questions also has a second, more strategic purpose: studying how desk officers in relief agencies make their environment manageable and reduce its complexity is a good way to examine the internal structure and everyday practices of agencies, and it is a good entry point for an analysis of the characteristics of these organizations and this field of organizations.

What I found in discussing these questions with people in very dif-

---

2. Guido Calabresi and Philip Bobbitt, *Tragic Choices: The Conflicts Society Confronts in the Allocation of Tragically Scarce Resources* (New York: Norton, 1978).

3. See Peter Redfield on triage as a challenge for MSF in "Sacrifice, Triage, and Global Humanitarianism," in *Humanitarianism in Question: Politics, Power, Ethics*, ed. Michael Barnett and Thomas G. Weiss (Ithaca, NY: Cornell University Press, 2008), 196–214.

ferent organizations is the basis for my claim about shared practices and assumptions in the field of humanitarian relief organizations. I will argue that humanitarian relief agencies share a set of practices and taken-for-granteds that help them select relevant information. These routines take some things out of the realm of conscious decision-making and guide and frame the decisions that are being made.

Studying how decisions about relief are made is also the basis for the specific argument about the form of this logic of practice, which I develop in this chapter and the three chapters that follow. I argue that humanitarian relief is a form of production, transforming some things into others. Agencies produce relief in the form of relief projects. As the unit of production is the project, managers seek to do "good projects." The pursuit of the good project develops a logic of its own that shapes the allocation of resources but also the kind of activities we are likely to see—and the kind of activities we are not likely to see.

These practices and assumptions have a specific history, which I will discuss in chapters 3 and 4. There are practices and assumptions that are shared across humanitarian organizations, be they secular relief NGOs or religious ones, NGOs with narrow or expansive agendas, independent NGOs or government contractors. All NGOs strive to produce good projects—in some sense or other—and this and its implications is the subject of this chapter. Where NGOs differ is in the content of their ideas of what a good project is and in the conditions under which they are willing to do their work. I will return to discussing these differences in chapter 4.

Before I return to the desk officers and the problem of triage, I will briefly discuss this problem in the context of previous thinking about humanitarian relief, and I will develop some of the presuppositions for asking this book's questions in the sociology of practice and the sociology of fields.

Two Views on International NGOs

Our thinking about global civil society has been shaped by a back and forth between two diametrically opposed approaches, each with very different implications with regard to what humanitarian organizations are understood to do and the role humanitarian organizations are thought to play. One approach focuses on stated ideas or values; the other on hidden interests. NGOs are either said to serve human dignity and channel the voices of the oppressed, or they are described as a tool of the interests of donor governments or imperialist systems of domination.

A large share of the scholarship on NGOs has taken for granted that they pursue their stated aims and values. The tendency to focus on stated aims is particularly strong among observers of international humanitarian NGOs.[4] From this perspective, the only questions left to answer about these organizations are questions about their history, the resources they mobilize, the strategies they use, and, most crucially, the extent to which they achieve their stated aims.

In this camp, the exclusive focus on values is maintained even if it is acknowledged that values are diverse and sometimes in tension with each other. Jennifer Rubenstein, for example, discusses a range of values that influence how decisions are made: the focus on need but also a commitment to minimizing harm, the goal of participation, a priority for victims of intentional violent acts. She does not, however, discuss any other considerations that might influence the distribution of relief and how they might be linked with these values.[5]

Critics in the humanities often share a focus on ideas with the authors discussed above but then suggest, in the mode of a critique of ideology, that they are the wrong ideas. Giorgio Agamben suggests, for example, that there is something problematic about humanitarian ideology in its reliance on the notion of bare life, which attributes a form of value to human beings while isolating them from their political context.[6] Critics in the social sciences tend to argue that ideas and values are either inconsequential or a cover for underlying interests. These interests could be conceptualized as those of the actors or organizations involved or those of the government. But scholars also apply class-based or systemic theories of imperialism to humanitarian action.

Earlier forms of humanitarianism and philanthropy, such as, most prominently, the anti-slavery movement but also punishment reform as well as the temperance movement, have been hotly debated by scholars along these lines,[7] and these debates are echoed in debates about inter-

4. Margaret E. Keck and Kathryn Sikkink, *Activists beyond Borders: Advocacy Networks in International Politics* (Ithaca, NY: Cornell University Press, 1998); and Thomas Risse, Steve C. Ropp, and Kathryn Sikkink, eds., *The Power of Human Rights: International Norms and Domestic Change* (Cambridge: Cambridge University Press, 1999).

5. Jennifer C. Rubenstein, "The Distributive Commitments of International NGOs," in Barnett and Weiss, *Humanitarianism in Question*, 215–35.

6. Giorgio Agamben, *Homo Sacer: Sovereign Power and Bare Life.* trans. Daniel Heller-Roazen (Stanford, CA: Stanford University Press, 1998); and Slavoj Žižek, "Against Human Rights," *New Left Review* 34 (July/August 2005).

7. See David Brion Davis, *The Problem of Slavery in the Age of Revolution, 1770–1823* (Ithaca, NY: Cornell University Press, 1975); Thomas Bender, ed., *The Antislavery Debate: Capitalism and Abolitionism as a Problem in Historical Interpretation* (Berkeley: University of California Press, 1992); Thomas L. Haskell, "Capitalism and the Origins of the Humanitarian Sensibility, Part 1," *American Historical Review* 90,

national NGOs. Sociologist James Petras, for example, referencing the role of churches in colonialism, writes: "In recent decades, a new kind of social institution emerged that provides the same function of control and ideological mystification—the self-described Non-governmental organizations."[8]

In discussions of aid, the relevant outside interest has long been assumed to be that of donor governments.[9] Petras, for example, continues: "The NGO are significant worldwide political and social actors operating in rural and urban sites of Asia, Latin America, and Africa frequently linked in dependency to their principal donors in Europe, the US and Japan."[10] This kind of critique has gained currency partly because Western states have increasingly used humanitarian rhetoric, sometimes in a way that did seem to directly serve their interests abroad.[11] Such criticism has been precipitated in particular by the role of Western NGOs in the US-UK invasion of Iraq and Afghanistan, a context in which then US secretary of state Colin Powell himself described NGOs in 2001 as "such a force multiplier for us, such an important part of our combat team."[12]

The division between values and interests has a long and complex intellectual history; in the more recent history of the social sciences, this division is exacerbated by investments in a specific linear notion of causality, where "values" and "interests," or "culture" and "political economy," become constructed as "variables" at the expense of each other.[13] The division takes a specific form in politics and international relations, a discipline in which many of the scholars who initially noticed the important role of humanitarian NGOs were trained. The orthodoxy within the

---

no. 2 (1985): 339–61; and Haskell, "Capitalism and the Origins of the Humanitarian Sensibility, Part 2," *American Historical Review* 90, no. 3 (1985): 547–66.

8. James Petras, "NGOs: In the Service of Imperialism," *Journal of Contemporary Asia* 29, no. 4 (1999): 429.

9. Finn Tarp and Peter Hjertholm, eds., *Foreign Aid and Development: Lessons Learnt and Directions for the Future* (London: Routledge, 2000); and David Hulme and Michael Edwards, eds., *NGOs, States, and Donors: Too Close for Comfort?* (New York: St. Martin's Press, 1997).

10. Petras, "NGOs," 429.

11. Frank Furedi, *The New Ideology of Imperialism: Renewing the Moral Imperative,* Pluto Studies in Racism and Imperialism (London: Pluto Press, 1994); Noam Chomsky, *A New Generation Draws the Line: Humanitarian Intervention and the "Responsibility to Protect" Today* (Boulder, CO: Paradigm Publishers, 2012); and Chomsky, "Humanitarian Imperialism: The New Doctrine of Imperial Right," *Monthly Review* 60, no. 4 (2008).

12. Secretary Colin L. Powell, "Remarks to the National Foreign Policy Conference for Leaders of Nongovernmental Organizations," October 26, 2001, in *September 11, 2001: Attack on America—A Collection of Documents,* The Avalon Project: Documents in Law, History and Diplomacy, Yale University Law Library, http://avalon.law.yale.edu/sept11/powell_brief31.asp.

13. See Andrew Abbott, "Transcending General Linear Reality," *Sociological Theory* 6, no. 2 (1988): 169–86; and Ernst Mayr, *The Growth of Biological Thought: Diversity, Evolution, and Inheritance* (Cambridge, MA: Belknap Press, 1982).

discipline established during the height of the Cold War emphasized the self-interested behavior of actors, either as an inherent feature of states or as a result of the anarchic nature of international affairs.[14] When a new generation of scholars in a different political climate wanted to make a case for the role of shared understandings and values, they chose to focus on human rights and humanitarian NGOs to argue their point. This agenda led them to focus on humanitarianism in a very selective manner: humanitarianism was interesting to that discipline because values played a role. In a next step humanitarianism became defined by its values.[15]

The Indeterminacy of Ideas and Interests

The problem with both of these accounts—the one emphasizing values and the other emphasizing interests—is that they seem to have already decided what relief NGOs are and what they do. Because the theoretical debate is shaped by these extremes, texts that intervene somewhere in the middle often circle around this problematic and rarely fully open the empirical questions that arise about these organizations: Neither a focus on interests nor a focus on values directs us to look more closely at what these organizations are up to in practice. What do people do inside these organizations? What does a normal day in the office look like? What organizational procedures do they use? What kinds of jobs do people have? How do they see the world? How do people come to know what they know?

I want to circumvent this debate from a perspective oriented toward practice. It is clear that neither values nor interests alone determine decision making in humanitarian relief. The point here is not just to say that both matter somehow, as has been noted within the sector,[16] but first to rethink the dualism of ideas and interests, and second to specify concretely how ideas and interests get translated into practice.

In the division between ideas and interests, between celebration and cynicism, the debate on relief has been very similar to debates on science, art, and religion. In each of these fields, some point at the highest values—

14. Hans J. Morgenthau, *Politics among Nations: The Struggle for Power and Peace* (New York: A. A. Knopf, 1948); Kenneth N. Waltz, *Theory of International Politics* (Boston: McGraw-Hill, 1979).

15. Keck and Sikkink, *Activists beyond Borders*, 1; and Chomsky, "Humanitarian Imperialism."

16. James Darcy and Charles-Antoine Hofmann, *According to Need? Needs Assessment and Decision-Making in the Humanitarian Sector,* Humanitarian Policy Group Report 15 (London: Overseas Development Institute, 2003); and Guenther Fink and Silvia Redaelli, *Determinants of International Emergency Aid—Humanitarian Need Only?,* Policy Research Working Paper 4839 (Washington, DC: World Bank, 2009).

truth, beauty, god, or morality—while others point at the self-interested behavior of individuals or explain how these values are exploited for the reproduction of some unfair state of affairs. In these fields, as in thinking about human rights and humanitarianism, the normative clout of the highest value, and the rebellion it inspires, have initially made it difficult for a sociological perspective to emerge.

For the investigation of humanitarian relief we can learn from what has been said in the philosophy and sociology of science about indeterminacy. Philosophers of science in the first half of the twentieth century have pointed out that the scientific interpretation of data is always underdetermined by evidence; that is, evidence allows for various interpretations.[17] If evidence does not entirely determine scientific production, neither do scientists' values. "The pursuit of truth" is just too vague to provide much guidance on how to collect data or conduct one's experiments.[18] This insight has directed attention, for some currents in the sociology of science, to the practices and assumptions that fill this space of indeterminacy.

In the same way, the needs or problems on the ground allow for various interpretations and responses. Neither proclaimed values nor imputed interests can exhaust the content of the everyday practices of humanitarian relief agencies. If humanitarian relief workers wanted to simply follow their values, this would not tell them what to do. Any given practice is necessarily underdetermined by values like "to ease human suffering according to need" and by interests like "to enhance the image of the USA abroad." It is not so much that values or interests are not real, but that in and of themselves they tell us very little about actual practices.

The problem with the most common ways in which "cultural" explanation is practiced is that its proponents do not pay attention to the level of practice. The problem with the most common ways interest-based explanation is practiced is the same. That does not mean that meanings do not matter or stakes or perceived advantages or disadvantages do not matter, but that these are situated in contexts that need to be explored closer to the ground.[19]

The question thus becomes, Which social institutions and technolo-

17. Willard Van Orman Quine, *Word and Object* (Cambridge, MA: MIT Press, 1960).
18. See Bruno Latour and Steve Woolgar, *Laboratory Life: The Social Construction of Facts* (Princeton, NJ: Princeton University Press, 1986).
19. See the debate between Theda Skocpol and William Sewell in Skocpol, *States and Social Revolutions: A Comparative Analysis of France, Russia, and China* (Cambridge: Cambridge University Press, 1979); William H. Sewell Jr., "Ideologies and Social Revolutions: Reflections on the French Case," *Journal of Modern History* 57, no. 1 (1985): 57–85; and Skocpol, "Cultural Idioms and Political Ideologies in the Revolutionary Reconstruction of State Power: A Rejoinder to Sewell," *Journal of Modern History* 57, no. 1 (1985): 86–96.

gies help to decide how interests are interpreted and how values are translated into the real world? We could examine these institutions on various scales. My focus here is on the meanings and practices shared on the level of the field of humanitarian relief organizations. The practical logic of the field of humanitarian organizations mediates between several external factors—problems in the world, human needs, and outside interests—and what agencies end up doing. It also mediates between values and principles actors hold and what is implemented on the ground.

Practicing Relief: The Particular Logic of an Organizational Field

What do humanitarian relief organizations actually do? To move beyond idealized conceptions of international NGOs, some recent work on transnational NGOs has usefully drawn attention to what relief organizations share with all other organizations, including for-profit firms. Alexander Cooley and James Ron have developed a model from the perspective of a political economy of organizations, which they test for the case of relief organizations as well as organizations providing prisoner-of-war monitoring and for-profit organizations providing economic technical assistance. They emphasize the "organizational insecurity, competitive pressures and fiscal uncertainty that characterize the transnational sector."[20] They find that "nonprofit INGOs respond to contractual incentives and organizational pressures much like firms do in a market."[21] Similarly, Johanna Siméant has found that relief NGOs have internationalized in order to maximize access to resources, much as for-profit organizations did in the same period.[22]

While it has been useful to compare relief NGOs to for-profit organizations, to understand relief work better we need to know more about what is specific about the practices of relief organizations. In particular, we need to understand how these practices link them to donors on the one hand and beneficiaries on the other.

20. Alexander Cooley and James Ron, "The NGO Scramble: Organizational Insecurity and the Political Economy of Transnational Action," *International Security* 27, no. 1 (2002): 6.

21. Ibid., 7; see also Aseem Prakash and Mary Kay Guggerty, "Advocacy Organizations and Collective Action: An Introduction," in *Advocacy Organizations and Collective Action*, ed. Aseem Prakash and Mary Kay Guggerty (Cambridge: Cambridge University Press, 2010), 1–29.

22. Johanna Siméant, "What Is Going Global? The Internationalization of French NGOs 'Without Borders,'" *Review of International Political Economy* 12, no. 5 (2005): 851–83. See also Mark Lindenberg and Coralie Bryant, *Going Global: Transforming Relief and Development NGOs* (Bloomfield, CT: Kumarian Press, 2001).

Neoinstitutional analyses of fields have directed our attention to a meso level of analysis, between interactions and large-scale structures.[23] Focus on a specific field of practice complements insights about single organizations and models designed to show what relief organizations share with all organizations. A field of practice most broadly is a realm in which actors take each other into account.[24] We expect a field of practice to be a space of shared taken-for-granteds and interpretations, or, to use Pierre Bourdieu's term, *doxa*.[25] We expect that the field of practice mediates between ideas, values, and problems on the ground, on the one hand, and outside interests, on the other.

Observers of the aid world have long noted that this world is to some extent self-referential; that is, it is to some extent driven by its own concerns.[26] I want to establish the fact that these factors internal to humanitarian relief matter empirically, and, going beyond this, I seek to make an argument about the specific logic of the field of humanitarian organizations. I specify a particular logic on the particular level that is my empirical focus, which can then be examined further in terms of how it interacts with different aspects of the social world.

Sociologists are only beginning to assemble material for a comparative analysis of the logics of practice of particular fields of organizations— organizations concerned with particular objects of practice, operating in particular environments. Among the reference points for comparison are John Thompson's study of academic publishing, which offers a strong claim about the explanatory power of the logic of a field, and the work of Dallas Smythe, which recasts our understanding of the media by pointing at the role of the audience commodity.[27]

23. Paul J. DiMaggio and Walter W. Powell, "The Iron Cage Revisited: Institutional Isomorphism and Collective Rationality in Organizational Fields," *American Sociological Review* 48, no. 2 (1983): 147–60; Walter W. Powell and Paul J. DiMaggio, eds., *The New Institutionalism in Organizational Analysis* (Chicago: University of Chicago Press, 1991); and John W. Meyer and Brian Rowan, "Institutionalized Organizations: Formal Structure as Myth and Ceremony," *American Journal of Sociology* 83, no. 2 (1977): 340–63.

24. Powell and DiMaggio, *New Institutionalism*; and Neil Fligstein, "Social Skill and the Theory of Fields," *Sociological Theory* 19, no. 2 (2001): 105–25. For a similar point regarding producers in a market, see also Harrison C. White, *Markets from Networks: Socioeconomic Models of Production* (Princeton, NJ: Princeton University Press, 2002).

25. Pierre Bourdieu, *Outline of a Theory of Practice*, Cambridge Studies in Social Anthropology 16 (Cambridge: Cambridge University Press, 1977).

26. See, for example, Tony Waters, *Bureaucratizing the Good Samaritan: The Limitations to Humanitarian Relief Operation* (Boulder, CO: Westview Press, 2001); and Philip Qarles van Ufford, Dirk Kruijt, and Theodore Downing, eds., *The Hidden Crisis in Development: Development Bureaucracies* (Amsterdam: Free University Press, 1988).

27. John B. Thompson, *Books in the Digital Age: The Transformation of Academic and Higher Education Publishing in Britain and the United States* (Cambridge: Polity Press, 2005); and Dallas W. Smythe, "On the Audience Commodity and Its Work," in *Media and Cultural Studies: KeyWorks*, ed. Meenakshi

I will argue that relief is organized around a set of shared practices. These are practices of production—they transform materials and labor into something new. The primary product of relief agencies' practices is the "project." It is an organization's main unit of planning and income, and it lends a certain coherence to what are otherwise quite disparate activities. The practices of project management are largely taken for granted by those in and close to the sector; they are "how things are done." They form part of a professional's practical knowledge, which is then combined with technical expertise and ethical orientation.

The Desks, the Project, and the Program

Humanitarian agencies today employ staff in a variety of roles at their headquarters offices. Many are employed in roles that are not at all specific to relief—for example, as receptionists, canteen staff, fund-raisers, accountants, and human resources managers. Someone in the headquarters office is maintaining the printer and orders paper clips when they run out. Someone is greeting visitors, and someone makes sure the website is working. Many staff use generic skills for a specific purpose, such as media spokespeople and staff working in advocacy. Others draw on skills especially relevant to relief work, such as technical expertise in nutrition, water engineering, or infectious disease, combined with experience and training in project management.

In one of the agencies I visited, I was given a tour of the headquarters offices by a head of region of a medium-size religious relief agency. The agency occupies a nondescript four-story office building in a suburb of London. It employs about three hundred staff at its headquarters, comprising a fourth of its total staff. Staff are organized into departments that mediate between various parts of the outside world and the organization itself. On the ground floor is the reception, the canteen, and the stationery store (see fig. 1.1). "This is our fund-raising department, connecting us to our supporters here in the UK," my guide said of the third floor. "This is our international office," he said of the fourth floor, "connecting us to our staff abroad."

An organization's outgoings flow through the operational department. The director of operations reports to the president and the board of the organization and oversees work across the world. Humanitarian agencies' operational departments are divided into several regions or "desks."

Gigi Durham and Douglas M. Kellner, KeyWorks in Cultural Studies 2 (Malden, MA: Blackwell Publishing, 2006).

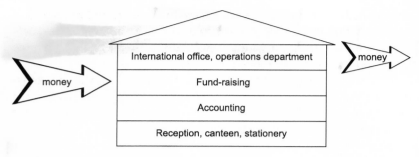

1.1   The headquarters building of a relief agency

A desk officer is in charge of operations in at least one but usually several countries.

The director of operations and the desk officers are served by a number of support departments. They draw on the expertise of technical experts, such as nutritionists, public health experts, and water engineers. They also work with policy advisers, fund-raisers, and a human resources department. The desk officer has a key mediating role between the field officers and country directors, on the one hand, and headquarters executives, on the other.

The desk officer manages projects and project staff in cooperation with donors and other agencies and communicates this work. A recent job advertisement for a position as Senior Desk Officer for Eastern and Southern Africa with Malteser International described the role as follows:

·   Initiate, plan, support and evaluate health and relief projects in the region
·   Assure the financial and operational back-stopping as well as co-ordination of programs in close co-operation with the teams in the field
·   Co-ordinate and ensure proper budgets and plans for the region
·   Ensure good relations and co-operation with major national and international institutions and donors for Humanitarian Aid and Development
·   Responsible for donor project application and reporting
·   Identification and recruitment of project expatriate staff
·   Contribute to public relations and lobbying for the organization.[28]

One desk officer with a medical relief agency described his work to me as follows: "My role is to define the objectives of our projects in my coun-

28. "Vacancy: Senior Desk Officer for Eastern and Southern Africa," on ReliefWeb's website, accessed November 9, 2008, http://www.reliefweb.int/rw/res.nsf/db900SID/OCHA-6TVE7S?OpenDocument (site discontinued).

tries, to make sure the appropriate means are in place and to manage it month after month in liaison with the project managers in the field. It is my job to design the project and to follow up and to adapt our activity or objective according to the changing context."

Note that the key unit of production is the project; the sum of an organization's projects is its "programming." What precisely is a project? A training manual on project management used in the nonprofit sector explains:

Large or small, a project always has the following ingredients:
—specific outcomes: products or results
—definite start and end dates: dates when project work begins and when it ends
—established budgets: required amounts of people, funds, equipment, facilities and information.[29]

The project has an important enabling role. It lends coherence to a set of quite disparate activities, which could include, for example, collecting data, hiring staff, ordering supplies, booking planes, and writing reports. It connects diverse materials and tools, such as food, office equipment, paper, and means of transport. It links a certain budget to certain established goals. It also links what different people are doing in different places, and it integrates activities across a specific time frame. Moreover, a project is also a story that can be told about the coherence of these activities, tools, and people; a story that can help internal and external communication.[30]

The project is the primary unit of planning interventions and of helping people. For those organizations that receive funding from institutional donors—either from government agencies such as USAID (United States Agency for International Development) and the United Kingdom's DfID (Department of International Development) or from intergovernmental agencies such as the European Union's ECHO (European Community Humanitarian Office) or the United Nations' OCHA (Office for the Coordination of Humanitarian Affairs)—the project is also the primary unit of fund-raising. The initiative for a project can come from the

29. Felisa Tibbitts, "Project Development and Management for the NGO Sector," Human Rights Education Associates, accessed November 10, 2009, http://www.hrea.org/index.php?base_id=336; also in Stanley E. Portny, *Project Management for Dummies*, 2nd ed. (Hoboken, NJ: Wiley Publishing, 2006), 10.

30. Richard Rottenburg, "Accountability for Development Aid," in *Facts and Figures: Economic Representations and Practices*, ed. Herbert Kalthoff, Richard Rottenburg, and Hans-Juergen Wagener (Marburg: Metropolis Verlag, 2000), 143–73.

donor, through a call for proposals, for example. It can come from the agency, when agency staff make the case to a donor for relief in a specific setting. Donors pay for projects based on a proposal, and they expect a report detailing what has been achieved according to the terms of the original proposal. These funders pay for specific projects with specific aims in specific fields of expertise and in specific places based on their preferences.

Managers distinguish different phases in the lifetime of a project, namely assessment, planning, implementation, monitoring, and evaluation. Together these phases make up the "project cycle." During assessment, the goal is to ascertain the need on the ground and justify the project. Planning establishes the ends and means of a project; it is here that managers specify what the goals of a project are and what means they will put in place to achieve it. During implementation, plans are put into practice. Monitoring means the collection of data during implementation that can be used to see if progress is being made, to adjust to changing circumstances, and to improve the project as it evolves. Evaluation involves data collection after the end of the project to assess whether the aims of the project were achieved and to produce reports for internal and/or external audiences.

A critical part of any relief project is a specified target population. Who exactly is benefiting from an intervention, and how, needs to be clear. Beneficiaries need to be identified and recruited; access to beneficiaries needs to be secured, and, to some extent, beneficiaries have to cooperate with the project.

Filtering Need

How do agencies decide where to start a project? How big will the project be? What kind of project will it be? How do agencies allocate relief? The official mantra is "according to need." This often provokes strong reactions, and there are voices that—from disappointment with the real, existing world of humanitarian relief—maintain that relief is a business like any other and that NGO values are just a front. But it is important to note that in the contemporary social world, most organizations do *not* claim to allocate resources according to need. Many resources are quite openly allocated according to purchasing power through markets. Some resources, such as jobs or educational titles, are claimed to be allocated according to performance or merit. If need matters, as in some welfare programs, access is usually restricted to those who are members of a specific social group or a specific political community.

Professional standards, professed values, and public expectations encourage professionals in NGOs to give first and foremost to those most in need regardless of nationality, creed, or race or ethnicity. This is a very distinct guiding orientation, and it would be hard to understand relief unless we take it seriously. However, while need is the guiding orientation, need alone does not guide decision making, and some of my respondents would add that perhaps it *cannot* do so. As a desk officer with a medical relief agency told me, "Needs are everywhere. That there is need is not enough for us to justify a project."

To become practically relevant, needs have to be known. The perception of needs is filtered through an agency's understanding of its mandate. All relief organizations focus on "emergencies," in itself a rather curious category that has come to encompass civil wars, refugee crises, the HIV pandemic, epidemics such as cholera or a measles outbreak, as well as natural disasters. As Craig Calhoun notes, the concept of an emergency emphasizes the brevity and the exceptional qualities of a situation.[31] The concept also directs attention to characteristics of an aggregate situation. According to the technical definition, mortality rates over 1 in 10,000 people or 2 in 10,000 children under five per day indicate a humanitarian emergency.[32] But a lack of government capacity to respond may also be required for the definition to be fulfilled. "If there is a hurricane in the US, are we going to respond? No! Because there is a government that is able or should be able to respond!" an officer at MSF France told me.

Some organizations focus exclusively on emergencies as opposed to development work. This is an important part of the self-definition of MSF, for example. Other organizations do only development work, while many agencies today do both types of projects in separate departments. Other than as a distinction between types of funding and the rhetoric of justification that comes with it, the distinction between humanitarian relief and development aid has become increasingly blurred. Development agencies respond to crises in areas where they are already working, and apply for "humanitarian" funding. On the other hand, many emergencies have become chronic, and emergency agencies may work for years in

---

31. Craig Calhoun, "A World of Emergencies: Fear, Intervention, and the Limits of Cosmopolitan Order," *Canadian Review of Sociology and Anthropology* 41, no. 4 (2004): 373–95.

32. Franceso Checchi and Les Roberts, *Interpreting and Using Mortality Data in Humanitarian Emergencies: A Primer for Non-Epidemiologists,* Humanitarian Practice Network Paper 52 (London: Overseas Development Institute, 2005).

one place. Pure emergency organizations such as MSF now have a separate "emergencies" department for new interventions, separate from the department for ongoing work.

The definition of an "emergency" affects the way needs come to the attention of aid agencies. Subspecialties among agencies also affect the interpretation of needs. Some are specialized according to their expertise: "We deal with some of that by saying we are a medical organization," a desk officer at MSF Switzerland explained to me. "In a way we make it easy for ourselves because we are saying we are focusing on children," a policy officer at Save the Children told me when asked how they deal with an apparent surplus of needs. Within its broad mandate, each agency has program priorities, which change and evolve. These could be specific technical areas, types of situations, types of problems, groups of beneficiaries, countries, or a combination of these. "War, poverty, and natural disasters are our three items," one desk officer at a Christian agency told me. "I try to fit everything I propose into one of these." Another agency focuses on HIV and AIDS and environmental sustainability. Indeed, HIV/AIDS, disaster preparedness, and climate change are among the most recent additions to agencies' areas of focus.[33]

Countries Matter

Parallel to all thematic concerns, issues, and technical areas of expertise runs a division according to countries of operation. The maps in the headquarters offices show that national borders and national boundaries matter for the allocation of aid. Populations are rarely compared directly by their need but are often considered as aggregates. Populations are usually compared as part of a crisis, a disease, or a country. The question for relief staff is, "Should we do something on AIDS?" or "Should we do something in Zimbabwe?"

Political factors on the national level are important determinants of suffering. The location of populations in need matters for humanitarian relief. When potential recipients are compared, different national standards of living are taken into consideration. "If you were doing it solely according to need, would you be giving everything to the Somalias and Central African Republics? Surely the needs are greatest there. But would

33. See Maia Green, "Calculating Compassion: Accounting for Some Categorical Practices in International Development," in *Adventures in Aidland: The Anthropology of Professionals in International Development,* ed. David Mosse, 33–47 (New York: Berghahn Books, 2011).

then nothing be going to the Kenyas?" asked a water engineer whom I met during a professional training event.

For humanitarian agencies, national boundaries also play an important role in determining the conditions for the production of humanitarian relief. Crises often attract attention under national labels. Government aid agencies like the United States' USAID or the United Kingdom's DfID structure their aid according to "regional strategies" and "country strategies." These strategies may reflect foreign policy interests; they also reflect a simple recognition that it is useful to think about suffering in its social context. The nation is seen as an obvious way to think about social context, and it is assumed that national organization is key to "stability."

Many agencies have a list of priority countries, and they think carefully about which countries and how many they work in. When agencies decide whether to start a project in a new country, this is a decision about need, but it is also a decision about risks and opportunities and a decision about investment in future production versus downscaling operations.

There are reasons to limit the number of countries one works in. One manager at a Protestant agency in the United Kingdom told me the agency had been trying to "slim down our portfolio." "So we're probably working in more than sixty countries worldwide," he said. "We've got this vision for moving down to these thirty-five countries or areas." The main reason for reducing the number of countries is cost-effectiveness. As he explained, "You need a certain management structure to manage any program. And if you're spreading your current resources very thinly over a large number of countries, you can potentially get quite a high overhead." The more an agency concentrates its efforts, the more it can achieve with a limited amount of resources. In order to help with this process, the agency was using a software program called SPIT (Strategic Poverty Identification Tool), which selects priority countries based on objective indicators, such as the number of people living on less than one US dollar per day, or the incidence of disasters.

In many ways, it is more efficient for NGOs to concentrate their efforts on a small number of countries. However the number of countries ought not be kept too low; agencies prefer to have a range of countries in their "portfolio." "There are donor constraints that steer you towards being an organization that has a number of outlets for your work," one director of operations at a US agency observed. He explained further:

Most of the funding available to us is tied not only to particular kinds of activities but also to geographic areas. So to be really simple, the USAID has a lot of money in its American bureau with a budget for Latin America. We could say, "We've got the best program in the world in Bangladesh, give us another hundred million dollars," and they'd say, "Well, we're not giving you our Latin American money." So if we want Latin American money, then obviously, we're going to work in Latin America.

Within each region, certain countries might be accorded strategic priority because they are the poorest country or of interest to donors, and a presence in these countries would allow an agency to take advantage of other opportunities in the region. The director of operations added: "If you weren't working in Haiti today and you wanted to work in the Americas, you probably want to work in Haiti." This interview was held well before the 2010 earthquake. Haiti was known as a vulnerable country, and it was thus a good starting point for developing expertise in an area and demonstrating that an agency could work under difficult conditions.

It was also explained to me that being present in too few countries is bad practice in terms of risk management. One desk officer with a French agency analyzed some of the trade-offs as follows:

From a purely administrative or financial point of view it would be much more cost-effective to have only four but bigger missions, instead of the twenty we have today. But it would also be much more risky. So we have to find a kind of balance. Darfur, Chad, Somalia, Ethiopia—the biggest needs are in those four countries. Everybody agrees on that. We could increase, increase, increase, and increase those missions but then we run the risk that if one of those missions has to stop in one week because the authorities are saying, "Okay, guys, get out," or because of security or political issues and so on, then it's not right. We cannot afford losing one quarter of our activity. We would have to dismiss all these people; it's just not manageable, and we have to find a kind of equilibrium and to have big missions and smaller ones with less security risk.

In the conversation I just reported, the desk manager emphasized the risks in terms of the conditions for his agency's operations: the security situation and the relations with political authorities.

But an agency may also have a reputation to lose if it focuses its efforts too much. One manager I spoke to told me that there had been a debate within his agency as to whether it would not be better to focus exclusively on Asia and Africa. He was of the opinion that it might hurt the agency to be seen as an exclusively Asian or an exclusively African organization. It might be—and this is my interpretation—that at some point, an agency loses its humanitarian, universalist status if it becomes too closely associated with a particular country or region.

Adding Value

When asked what considerations go into starting a project somewhere, all respondents emphasize the importance of "making a contribution" or "adding value": "First of all we need to think about whether we have the skills and the capacity to really make a difference," one desk officer told me.

Of course, this makes a lot of sense. The point, these managers suggest, is not to spend money as though this was an end in itself. The point is, rather, to actually achieve something. It is very hard to argue with that. However, when values are translated into "making a difference," the real world enters the picture. To achieve something, money and resources are needed. To achieve something, the characteristics of both the giver and the recipient matter.

When managers begin thinking about "making a contribution" or "adding value," a number of factors enter the equation. Generally speaking, resources are necessary, and an important resource is money. "It is a mixture between need and resources really. We have only a certain amount of money that is coming from private donations, so for most projects we need to also consider the preferences of institutional donors," one desk officer told me. Resources depend on donors' priorities and media attention. "It is a mixture between needs and media attention, frankly speaking," another respondent told me and recalled the 2004 Indian Ocean tsunami, a crisis during which, in his view, agencies received more donations than the situation on the ground merited.

But whether or not an agency can make a contribution, and thus whether or not an agency will help, also depends on the more mundane logistical issues that arise in the planning of projects. To make a difference, access to the population in need has to be secured. That means visas for expatriate staff need to be obtained from the receiving government. Other forms of government support also make it easier to operate in a country, such as free movement across the territory (which cannot be taken for granted with a visa) and protection.

The resource "safe access" creates many dilemmas for humanitarian NGOs because it implies some level of cooperation with the state or the security forces controlling a territory. If an agency is working in Chechnya, for example, and accepts the protection of the Russian army, this raises questions about the agency's independence. MSF does not seek the consent of governments for its operations; this means it makes itself independent of government support. Yet MSF has strong criteria of its own as to the conditions under which its medical teams work. MSF will not begin or continue projects if it sees the independence of its medical teams compromised by restrictions on their movement or when its staff would require armed protection. Consequently most sections are currently not working in Afghanistan, Burma, Somalia, or North Korea.

Security is an important factor to be considered, and most respondents say it has become increasingly important. One desk officer told me: "In Iraq, Afghanistan, Somalia, yes for sure, those three countries, there is no question, there are needs. But nobody is working there. We can't work there. . . . They are shooting everywhere in that space." This is a difficult judgment that involves principles and values, as one desk officer of a Christian organization explained to me: "Any decision we take regarding security is a value judgment about the risks that are worth taking, about the relative costs and benefits regarding our presence there, the security for our staff on the one hand and the benefits to the population on the other."

The contribution an agency can make depends on what the organization itself has done before and is able to do. A head of emergencies at one agency put it this way: "So if it is in a country in which we have no contacts, no history, no experience, we will go in there much more cautiously or maybe not go in there at all, compared to if it's somewhere where we're well established, have lots of contacts, have a long history of engagement. There are issues in terms of organizational strategy if we go somewhere completely new. So in terms of scaling up somewhere where you are that is easier to do."

In the wake of the Rwanda crisis, institutional donors have emphasized the need for coordination, and managers are encouraged to think about need in relationship to what other agencies are doing, and to identify a gap in services.

Material factors on the ground, including characteristics of the populations being served, will determine how much value a project can add. A desk officer for eastern Africa with a French agency drew a map to take me through the considerations involved in one particular case in Cameroon. His organization had conducted an assessment there because they had received reports of an influx of refugees from central Africa:

People were very spread out, in a very high number of locations with very few people in each location, maybe a hundred people here, a hundred people here. To open a mission in this country, in such an underdeveloped area with no road, nothing, it needs a high, high, high level of logistical means to go there and get to and reach

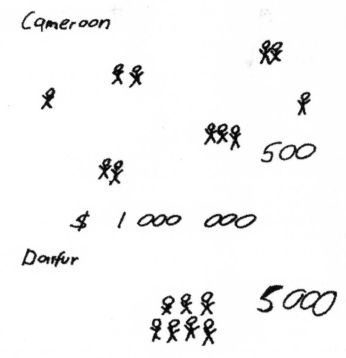

1.2 Logistical dilemmas in humanitarian relief

these people. This means it is very costly and at the end, it's only—I don't know, I don't have the figures—maybe five hundred people or children in the end within two or three months that we could reach and treat. For that it would be, say, one million, around one million US dollars or Euros, okay? . . . These one million dollars I would prefer to use in Darfur, in a big camp, and there we could maybe reach five thousand people in the same time with the same amount of money, which is ten times more.

The desk officer drew me an image like the one in figure 1.2. They decided against the project: "So at the end it's sad, but you have to make this balance, and you have to make this calculation. That's the balance between that and that."

In the theory of project management, needs assessment is a stage prior to and separate from project planning. I took part in a needs assessment simulation during a training for staff of humanitarian relief agencies where the trainer kept reminding us to assess the needs on the ground thoroughly before we considered what we might do about them. However, even the most purist assessment will make mention of road access and other important considerations for the response. As one water engineer working as a consultant remarked,

There is an incentive to help those that are easy to help. If there is some place where people have never gotten anything, but it is harder to get to, it is very hard for you to launch a project, as donors will say to you, "But your competitor is doing this much for that many people much cheaper elsewhere."

The conditions of production contain not just prohibitive but also facilitating factors. Some projects are carried out because the site meets certain requirements. A desk officer with a French agency told me about a project in Mongolia he had inherited from his predecessor: "I reviewed the data and went to a meeting with all the technical people here, and I said: 'Guys, are you sure that we should continue to put such an amount of money, energy, and so on in this country with this impact?' It was quite a strong meeting for hours and hours saying, 'Yes, we should continue,' 'No, we shouldn't,' and so on and so on. In my mind we should stop—and a lot of other people think we should continue."

Ten months later the project continues:

We have agreed that we are going to use this country as a kind of pilot project country. It's not an operational problem anymore, it's more the research department trying to find out how we could use this country as a pilot project country; we try to do scientific research, is that right? You can do that there because the authorities are very welcoming. There is no trouble at all with the authorities, security is perfect, people can stay in the country for three years instead of six months in Darfur. So there are very good conditions that can help us to stay there for three, four, five, ten years. If we want to stay there for ten years, we will still be welcomed by the government, and so we can put in place some pilot projects and then use the results of this project in other places and duplicate them in other countries.

In this specific case, there has been a subtle shift in the goals and the justification of humanitarian activity: the primary goal here is no longer "relief to those who need it most," and this is what my respondent was concerned about. Other considerations are "doing some useful work," "learning something for the future," and "employing staff." Of course, the assessment of the case is complicated by the fact that there are people with needs in Mongolia—and for any given project it can seem callous or cynical to say it should not be done. My point here is not to diagnose a betrayal of humanitarian principles and priorities but to point to the mixture of considerations that come into play when values are translated in the real world, including not just material concerns but also different kinds of values.

The Project's Limits

A project delivers positives: latrines, doctors, teachers, tents. But it delivers specific positives to specific populations within a certain range of budgets. It is important to understand the implications of the project's boundaries both in terms of its specific outputs and in terms of its specific target population. When some things are done, others are not done. When some people are helped, others are not helped.

The focus on added value, on an agency's sense of what it has to offer, creates a logic that is relatively independent from what recipients may want or need. Consider the following story that a desk officer shared with me:

In 1998 when I was in Sudan the people said: "Thank you for the food and for the drugs. But in two months we will be in the rainy season. By then the river will be completely full, it is a river full of fish. But we are naked, we have nothing. So just if we could have some hooks and some fishing nets for us it will be . . ."—so I came back here [to headquarters] and said: "Can I get €10,000 for 10,000 hooks and 100 nets?" They said: "No, we are not fishermen without borders. We don't bother." So it was refused by the director of operations. So sometimes I have seen completely stupid stuff like that.

Though this desk officer expresses his frustration, it is important to note that this is not an unusual case. It is not an exceptional case, nor is it necessarily a case of bad or heartless management. Rather, the decision made by headquarters reflects the normal practices and assumptions of professionalism, which also operate in many domestic contexts. A professional doctor is not usually available to teach or feed the hungry; as a professional, she uses her specific skill within certain organizational frameworks and procedures that are deemed to enhance the overall efficiency of the health-care system. She treats within the procedures of the hospital. Similarly, an academic also does not just teach everyone he meets, but operates within a system that protects his professional standards and access to his services.

Each relief project delivers positives to a specific set of beneficiaries.

Agencies try to identify those who are most in need, but the boundaries do not always make sense to those who implement them. "What if those around the people most in need still lack the most basic things for survival?" one trainer of humanitarian personnel remarked to me with some frustration. "Everything is always about those who are part of the project, never the others." Aid workers often come across this problem when they provide services to refugees and displaced people. The boundaries of the project are often drawn around some group of internally displaced persons when local populations themselves lack basic services. A project for people displaced by a crisis fits the definition of an emergency intervention, promising short-term results, when general poverty may be an unattractive target for funders.

The pursuit of "good projects" helps to make sense of the strategy of "humanitarian containment" found in some areas. According to a report on relief for Darfur, "The strategy among some international groups interviewed was to expand only when minimum standards had been achieved in their current program. . . . Agencies may play safe and keep their programs small, manageable, and risk-free in order to ensure that they will have the best possible evaluation."[34]

We can see why agencies might do this—they are in a situation where they are held accountable and have to show results, but they are held accountable only for their own specific project. This introduces a logic of "performing to the test." This is a classic phenomenon described by the sociology of organizations. It was first analyzed perhaps by Peter Blau, who found that when an employment agency began to be evaluated in terms of its placement rate, it began to prioritize the candidates it thought it could more easily place, at the expense of those harder to place.[35]

It is important to note that this dynamic does not just depend on how close-minded and inflexible donor agencies really are. All that is required is that agencies *think* that donors take the test of project results very seriously. One of my respondents recalled, for example: "We were discussing possible sites for a project and my project managers said of a location, 'We won't go there. It is impossible to deliver up to our professional standards there, and the donors won't like it.'"

34. Helen Young et al., *Darfur: Livelihoods under Siege* (Medford, MA: Feinstein International Center, Tufts University, 2005), 117.

35. See Peter M. Blau, *The Dynamics of Bureaucracy: A Study of Interpersonal Relations in Two Government Agencies* (Chicago: University of Chicago, 1963); and Michael Lipsky on creaming in Lipsky, *Street-Level Bureaucracy: Dilemmas of the Individual in Public Services* (New York: Russell Sage Foundation, 2010), 107–8.

Conclusion

I began this chapter by asking how relief agencies decide where to go, whom to help, and how. I have suggested that neither values nor interests determine decision making, nor do needs alone guide decision making. Values, interests, and needs cannot by themselves tell a manager what to do; they are indeterminate—that is, they are compatible with (and in tension with) many different kinds of practices and outcomes. Rather, I have argued, humanitarian relief agencies share a set of practices and taken-for-granteds that help them select relevant information and make the complexity of their environment seem manageable. These practices and taken-for granteds are shared across humanitarian organizations, be they secular relief NGOs or religious ones, NGOs with narrow or expansive agendas, independent or government contractors, These practices form the backdrop of discussions about different kinds of relief and are applied to a wide range of social problems on the ground.

I have suggested that humanitarian relief is a form of production transforming some things into others. Agencies produce relief in the form of relief projects. As the unit of production is the project, managers seek to do "good projects." The pursuit of the good project develops a logic of its own that shapes not only the allocation of resources but also the kind of activities we are likely to see—and the kind of practices we are not likely to see.

When disparities of aid are discussed in the public realm, the focus is often on donors' strategic priorities and the bias of the news media. As the cases of US willingness to support NGOs in Iraq, and the Indian Ocean tsunami, show, both of these factors certainly matter. But there is also an inequality in the distribution of aid that is the result of the mundane practical logic of relief operations. Some recipients are easier to help than others, and those who are hardest to help often receive no help at all.

If we imagine NGO relief functioning as some sort of insurance against disasters and violence, we are mistaken. There is no coverage for all affected, and it is important to note that relief NGOs do not provide half an insurance or an incomplete insurance either. Notwithstanding shared universal values, the particular logic of project management creates a material appearance of an insurance that may actively be in the way of actually providing one. Allocation of resources via projects also entails that some of the poorest populations in the world compete against each other instead of against elites in their own countries or elsewhere.

The humanitarian field is of course diverse. Agencies and individuals vary as to what they value about a project. Ideas about what a good project is change, and our knowledge about what works and what does not on a project level might improve over time. That is the purpose of extensive amounts of research for evaluations and the gray literature of the sector. Many humanitarian agencies are very reflective and self-critical. But the logic of project management itself, with its implications for bounding rationality, is rarely challenged in a sustained way in this field.

The pursuit of the good project changes the way managers think about partner organizations and about populations in need. Analysis of the selling and buying of projects requires us to rethink the role of the populations being served. Their role has often been ignored by economists modeling nonprofit organizations and has been misunderstood by theorists of civil society. Rather than being primarily "beneficiaries" or "clients," they are part of the product being sold, and they labor for it. It is to this aspect of humanitarian NGO programming that I turn in the next chapter.

TWO

Beneficiaries as
a Commodity

I told him that at any given moment realizing attracts me less than the unreal-
ized; and I don't just mean that of the future but also that of the past and that,
which has been missed.   ROBERT MUSIL, *THE MAN WITHOUT QUALITIES*

The previous chapter argued that humanitarian relief NGOs
form a space of shared practice. I have begun to examine the
nature of these shared practices, and argued that practices of
project management help managers reduce the complexity
of their environment and make their choices manageable.
Managers consider the world with a set of possible interventions in mind, interventions within a certain range of time
frames, and within a certain range of budgets. These practices are largely taken for granted and mediate between the
values of NGOs and what they do, and thus between those
who delegate their response to distant suffering to these
organizations, and populations in need. These practices are
applied to a wide range of social problems on the ground.

In this chapter, I will further explore the logic of practice
in this field, examining in particular what the shared practices of the field mean for the role populations in need play
in humanitarian relief. The role that populations on the
ground play in humanitarian relief is usually not analyzed
in much detail because observers adopt one of two positions. They either posit populations in need as entirely separate from NGOs. People on the ground are then seen as part
of the environment that agencies respond to or intervene
in. Or they posit populations in need as entirely the same as

NGOs. NGOs are then seen as a neutral conduit providing people with a voice within global civil society.

Humanitarian relief posits populations in need as the justification for its existence. For the managers I interviewed as well, populations in need generally speaking are part of the motivation and justification of relief. But, I will argue in this chapter, in the course of planning and delivering projects, two subtle shifts happen. First, while the rhetoric evokes populations in need in general or in a whole area, practically speaking only a subset of populations in need becomes relevant as potential or actual "beneficiaries"—that is as the chosen part of a population in need receiving services or said to be benefiting from an intervention. Second, while beneficiaries are an *end* of relief work, and managers work hard to provide good and appropriate services to beneficiaries, beneficiaries also become a *means* of delivering relief work. Beneficiaries are a necessary element of any successful project. In order to do their job, relief agencies need beneficiaries. Rather than being just "beneficiaries," "clients," or "citizens," the populations served are also part of the product that agencies plan and account for, if they work for institutional donors. I want to suggest that they are part of a commodity being sold to donors in a quasi market.

Let me clarify what I mean when I suggest that we can usefully think of projects—and populations in need as part of projects—as commodities. I am not suggesting that relief projects are things. I am not suggesting that relief projects are interchangeable and differ only in price per quantity, as some definitions of a commodity would have it. In that sense relief projects are not like grain, water, oil, or salt.

Projects are not things, and projects are not easily comparable to each other in monetary terms. Each project has its specific history and context, and most importantly, its specific aid workers and beneficiaries. That said, I do wish to examine the ways in which projects can be *treated* as things that are potentially comparable to each other, and the ways in which they *are in fact* compared to each other when allocating scarce resources. The concept of commodity highlights the way projects are produced, paid for, and involve labor, including in this case also the labor of beneficiaries. The producers in this market are not maximizing profits but, to the extent that they work with institutional donors, they produce with an orientation to exchange relief projects for money.

Consider as an analogy the argument Dallas Smythe has made about the news media. In an important article, "On the Audience Commodity and Its Work," Smythe points out that in the news media, what is bought and sold is not primarily content for audiences, but audiences for adver-

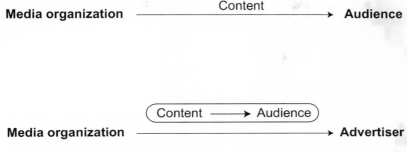

2.1 Smythe's rethinking of the product in media production

tisers.[1] That does not mean that the content does not matter or should not matter. But to explain patterns in what news organizations do, and to think about how we might influence it, the recognition that it is not just audiences who pay for access to content, but advertisers who pay for access to audiences, that the latter is in fact the main source of income for news organizations, is very important (see fig. 2.1). Similarly, relief organizations hand out shoes and tents and medicines to beneficiaries, but at the same time they also sell projects including beneficiaries to donors (see fig. 2.2).

That "beneficiaries" are part of the commodity does not mean that they do not benefit. They receive resources, and at times those resources save lives. But, as I have noted in the previous chapter, some beneficiaries are easier to produce, and some are easier to sell than others, which leads to inequities in the allocation of aid.

Analyzing beneficiaries as part of a product being sold allows us to take this analysis one step further. When (some) populations in need are packaged as beneficiaries by relief agencies, some of the poorest populations in the world are put in a position where they are in competition with each other for resources—the beneficiaries who receive help are always only a subset of populations in need. This institutional arrangement can be contrasted with institutional arrangements that might foster competition of populations in need with elites in their own countries, for example, or with elites or others in the Global North.

It also means that value is being extracted in the process of helping them under circumstances over which they have very little control. That

1. Dallas Walker Smythe, "On the Audience Commodity and Its Work," in *Media and Cultural Studies: KeyWorks*, ed. Meenakshi Gigi Durham and Douglas Kellner (Oxford: Blackwell, 2001), 230–56.

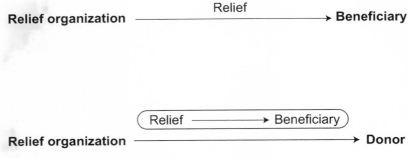

2.2 Beneficiaries as a commodity

value is partly economic and partly symbolic for relief agencies (as they receive not only money from institutional donors and the public but also authority to speak about suffering) and consists in moral and political authority for donors.

A number of conditions have combined to produce a kind of "market" in projects. These conditions include a lack of access to basic provision for large populations, natural disasters, civil wars, means for learning about suffering and providing relief,[2] the interest of Western governments and the Western public in the relief of suffering as well as in influence and stability, a loss of hope in development, the transformation of the state through competitive contracting to for-profit and nonprofit private actors, and a global scale of comparison for products. I will explain the history of some of these conditions of possibility in chapters 3 and 4.

The relationship with beneficiaries is an open wound within the relief sector; beneficiaries are continuously evoked in self-criticism and reflection. Instrumentalization of beneficiaries as I describe it here is not, however, the result of the attitude of aid workers or aid organizations. It is not a matter of choice for an individual program manager, nor is it only or directly the result of long-lasting colonial power relationships or racist ideology, as some suggest. It is the result of a market in beneficiaries that has been produced by states, aid agencies, and the media in recent decades.

Before I develop this argument, and its implications for our understanding of domination in the global order, I need to situate it in discussions about global civil society and in existing work in the sociology and economics of the nonprofit sector.

2. Thomas Haskell, "Capitalism and the Origins of the Humanitarian Sensibility, Parts 1 and 2." *American Historical Review* 90, nos. 2 and 3 (1985): 339–61 and 547–66.

NGOs as Entirely the Same as or Entirely Separate from Populations in Need

I have suggested that our understanding of the role of populations in need has been limited by the tendency to see NGOs either as entirely the same as populations in need or as entirely separate from populations in need. In conversations about issues to do with global civil society, abstractions evoking populations in need in general often stand in for the analysis of the role of local populations themselves. In fact, "global civil society," as a term, is sometimes used as though it in itself could stand in for populations across the globe. "Humanitarian principles," "democracy," and "politics from below" fulfill similar roles in discussions of global politics.

In a typical perspective, Manuel Castells, for example, defines global civil society as "the organized expression of the values and interests of society."[3] If NGOs are considered as part of global civil society in this sense, they are understood to express the values and interests of populations in need. Similarly, if NGOs are considered from the perspective of providing voice, access, or representation for groups or values excluded by the state or state-dominated international organizations, this does not direct our attention to the interaction and the possible friction between NGOs and populations in need.[4]

If sometimes populations in need are analyzed implicitly as entirely the same as "global civil society," some other genres of academic research analyze them as entirely separate. Consider the long history in anthropology of trying to study people as distinct communities in order to understand their "culture." In the context of the reports and semiofficial documents of relief, when populations in need are studied, they are mostly studied as an object separate from the relief system. Most often populations in need are studied as a potential object of intervention or policy. Studies in this genre consider what populations are lacking, and disregard previous intervention.

The critical literature in development studies has broken new ground by studying populations on the ground and aid interventions *at the same time.*[5] In the case of humanitarian relief, populations in need are still not

---

3. Manuel Castells, "The New Public Sphere: Global Civil Society, Communication Networks, and Global Governance," *Annals of the American Academy of Political Science*, 616, no. 1 (2008): 78–93.

4. Margaret E. Keck and Kathryn Sikkink. *Activists beyond Borders: Advocacy Networks in International Politics* (Ithaca, NY: Cornell University Press, 1998).

5. Stacey Leigh Pigg, "Investing Social Categories through Place: Social Representations and Development in Nepal," *Comparative Studies in Society and History* 34, no. 3 (1992): 491–513; Thomas

often studied as an empirical element of the relief system itself. Studies of aid or relief never analyze populations *not* served or needs *not* fulfilled as part of the actually existing system of relief. Populations not served are rather thought of as what relief is not, or *not yet.* This is part of a tendency to correct limitations of the present with a view to a better future. This tendency to correct the limitations of the present is, of course, entirely appropriate in a practitioner's search for "best practice": it enables people to focus on what they could do better in the future.

In writings that are, for better or worse, one step removed from practice, however, the stakes are a little different. To the extent that observers are writing and not acting, they should use the distance from current practice to analyze both aspirations, promises, and assumptions and real existing practices and distributions as part of the same reality. If we think of populations in need as part of existing humanitarian relief, and if we include the populations served and those *not* served, the needs fulfilled and the needs *not* fulfilled, we can see the exchanges in this field in a new light.

The Debate about the Nonprofit Sector

Economists have long done research on charities and nonprofit organizations, and we might want to look there for models of what this field of practice looks like when material constraints and the role of exchanges are taken seriously. But even though economists have used the metaphors of firms, prices, and markets, there has been no consistent account as to who the buyer is, and what the product is—that is, what the market is a market *in.*

The contribution of the discipline of economics to an understanding of the logic of practice of these particular firms (charities and nonprofit organizations) has been limited by two factors. First, economists' research has been shaped by problems arising from within economic theory rather than from an engagement with empirical reality. Second, there has been a division between research on charitable giving and research on nonprofit firms. Research on charities and giving has largely ignored the role of organizations; research on nonprofit organizations has not fully examined the implications of the fact that income comes from donations rather than from the selling of conventional goods or services.

Bierschenk, Jean-Pierre Chauveau, and Jean-Pierre Olivier de Sardan, *Courtiers en développement: Les villages africains en quête de projets* (Paris: Karthala, 2000); David Mosse, *Cultivating Development: An Ethnography of Aid Policy and Practice* (London: Pluto Press, 2005).

Economic research has traditionally focused on the supply of private charity by individual donors. Charity emerged as a category of interest to economists because according to the assumptions of economic theory it should not exist. If individuals and organizations can be assumed to act rationally and in a self-interested manner, how can the existence of charity be explained? To what extent can it be justified?

Economists look at charity as a response to market failures identified by economic theory. Charitable giving is predominantly seen as an altruistic response to the problem of public goods. A public good is a good that is nonrivaled and nonexcludable—that is, one person's consumption does not interfere with another's, and no one can be excluded from using such a good. These goods are difficult to provide according to market mechanisms. Any individual benefits from provision of a public good or suffers from its absence regardless of whether they contribute or not.

Assuming that most people would prefer to live in a society where there is some alleviation of poverty, a classic line of arguing is that some people will give "altruistically" to help provide public goods.[6] Other economists try to explain giving by pointing at benefits to the donor that are usually overlooked, such as the warm glow of giving[7] or the effect of signaling wealth.[8]

Economists researching charitable giving apply the market metaphor in a way that makes it very clear that it is the donors who are the consumers. For example, we have learned much about how the level of donations might be affected by the "price" of charity as influenced by tax exemptions. But in research on philanthropic giving or donations to charity, organizations have been seen largely as neutral conduits of funds between donors and the provision of public goods. In the literature on giving, if organizations feature, it is as facilitators of giving or as fund-raisers.[9]

In the theory of the nonprofit firm, on the other hand, the implications of income from donations have not been fully developed. The

6. Robert A. Schwartz, "Personal Philanthropic Contributions," *Journal of Political Economy* 78, no. 6 (1970): 1264–91; Gary S. Becker, "A Theory of Social Interactions," *Journal of Political Economy* 82, no. 6 (1974): 1063–93.

7. James Andreoni, "Giving with Impure Altruism: Applications to Charity and Ricardian Equivalence," *Journal of Political Economy* 97, no. 6 (1989): 1447–58; Andreoni, "Impure Altruism and Donations to Public Goods: A Theory of Warm-Glow Giving," *Economic Journal* 100, no. 401 (1990): 464–77.

8. Amihai Glazer and Kai A. Konrad, "A Signaling Explanation for Charity," *American Economic Review* 86, no. 4 (1996): 1019–28.

9. James Andreoni, "Toward a Theory of Charitable Fund-Raising," *Journal of Political Economy* 106, no. 6 (1998): 1186–213; Kieran Healy, "Altruism as an Organizational Problem: The Case of Organ Procurement," *American Sociological Review* 69, no. 3 (2004): 387–404. In the comparative elements of his analysis, Healy moves beyond the focus on the facilitation of donations, see Healy, *The Last Best Gifts: Altruism and the Market for Human Blood and Organs* (Chicago: University of Chicago Press, 2006).

	Mutual	**Entrepreneurial**
Donative	Common Cause National Audubon Society Political clubs	CARE March of Dimes Art museums
Commercial	American Automobile Association Consumers Union* Country clubs	National Geographic Society** Educational Testing Service Community hospitals Nursing homes

* Publisher of *Consumer Reports*
**Publisher of *National Geographic*

2.3   Four categories of nonprofit enterprises. Redrawn from Hansmann, "The Role of Nonprofit Enterprise," 842.

prevalence of nonprofit organizations in itself presents a puzzle to economists in the neoclassical tradition. By agreeing not to distribute profits inside the organization, a nonprofit organization limits the incentives for its members and staff. Why do people work for nonprofits, and why are such firms able to compete with for-profit actors?

According to Henry Hansmann, nonprofits arise in areas of contract failure, when public goods are at stake or the buyer is not the receiver. Relief NGOs are donative and nonmutual in the analytical grid developed by Hansmann (fig. 2.3);[10] their income comes from donations, and the

10. Henry B. Hansmann, "The Role of Nonprofit Enterprise," *Yale Law Journal* 89, no. 5 (1980): 835–901.

services do not benefit primarily members. But what are the implications of the fact that the buyers are not the receivers?

In classic attempts to determine how nonprofits compare to the neoclassical model of the for-profit firm in terms of efficiency, the product has been assumed to be the one given to clients or beneficiaries.[11] Economists of health have provided the concept of "third-party buying" to take more fully into account that the buyer may not be the receiver. This concept helps us understand certain problems in the provision of services entrusted to third parties. When an employer provides health insurance as part of a negotiated contract, or when a landlord is legally required to hire an exterminator for a building, for instance, perverse incentives might arise for the producer. The market may reflect preferences of buyers more accurately than the preferences of the end consumer.[12]

In the case of charities, however, additional problems arise. There is no legal or contractual framework that links buyer and receiver. The donor does not just choose between products—like an employer choosing health insurance for employees—but also between recipients. Here the concept of third-party buying would obscure what the consumer is buying, suggesting the product remains "food," when it becomes "an opportunity to provide food for the needy."

In this separation of literatures in economics, there is a missed opportunity to consistently perform a shift in perspective: donors are consumers, the buyers of a service. Once we recognize that donors are buying something, we need to examine the product in those terms. What is being consumed by donors are not pots and pans or tents or food, but the act of giving. This should invite us to rethink our expectations about the organization's process of planning, production, and marketing.

The Project as a Product

We have seen that the project is the primary unit of helping people. But it is also the primary unit of fund-raising. Agencies raise funds to do projects, but they can also do projects to raise funds. They have good reasons for doing that: only by bringing in money can the agency continue to

---

11. Mark V. Pauly, "Nonprofit Firms in Medical Markets," *American Economic Review* 77, no. 2 (1987): 257–62; Joseph P. Newhouse, "Toward a Theory of Nonprofit Institutions: An Economic Model of the Hospital," *American Economic Review* 60, no.1 (1970): 64–74.

12. Arthur L. Stinchcombe, "Third Party Buying: The Trend and the Consequences," *Social Forces* 62, no. 4 (1984): 861–84.

exist, and only by continuing to exist can the agency provide relief to the needy.[13]

All work is planned in projects. The link between money and project is quite formalized when money is received from institutional donors—and most organizations receive most of their funds from institutional donors. Institutional donors pay for specific projects with specific aims in specific fields of expertise and in specific places based on what they think is important. Donors thus pay agencies for projects. They pay so that something is done, and they pay for the opportunity to be able to say they supported that something was being done. Sometimes donor agencies quite literally insist on their flags being displayed in the field—a request that is not always welcome among humanitarian NGOs. Officials in donor agencies in turn use reports about funded projects to explain to politicians and taxpayers what they have done.

When donations from the general public are used, funds and beneficiaries are not as directly linked, but they can be linked via specific campaigning devices or via the image of an organization. Fund-raisers often do try to make the link between donation and beneficiary seem as direct as possible. The classic example is child-sponsorship, where an individual child is advertised as an opportunity to give, often with the added promise of photos and letters written by that child. Advertisements like the following, taken from a campaign by UNICEF, also seek to make the link as direct as possible: "A gift of 30 pounds ($50) could provide three families in Haiti with basic water kits."[14] In the vein of these strategies, fund-raisers are experimenting with ways donors and beneficiaries can be linked online; we can imagine online auctions where projects are introduced to potential donors. In many cases donations to an organization are tied to a specific area or crisis as a result of a specific appeal.[15]

---

13. Tony Waters's insightful *Bureaucratizing the Good Samaritan* also makes the point that the product of aid agencies is not shoes and tents for beneficiaries and that the goal is not profit. He writes, instead, that the product is mercy and that, "rather, the product is measured in terms of what are in effect needs and 'good feelings' of a distant constituency" (41). Waters, *Bureaucratizing the Good Samaritan: The Limitations to Humanitarian Relief Operations* (Boulder, CO: Westview Press, 2001). I highlight the role of the project as the product, rather than the emotions of the donors. This reflects the fact that relief agencies want to help, and need to provide assistance in order to raise funds. Assuming the project as the product allows us to look in detail at important processes that mediate between need, motivation to help, and payment, and allows us to rethink our understanding of the assistance process itself to the point where it reaches the populations in need, not just the aspect of fund-raising.

14. UNICEF, "Donate to UNICEF's Haiti Earthquake Children's Appeal," accessed January 30, 2010, http://www.unicef.org.uk/give/index.asp?page=32 (site discontinued).

15. This is what creates the problem of overfunding for specific crises that are heavily covered by Western media, such as the 2004 Indian Ocean tsunami. This is a problem that has been informally and widely acknowledged by aid workers but has been exposed most publicly by MSF, which has alerted donors that their money might be used for other causes.

MSF and some religious organizations are able to attract significant amounts of untied donation, giving them more scope for making choices. Financial independence frees them to some extent from the pressure to develop an instrumental attitude toward beneficiaries.[16] Managers who can draw on public donations thus do not need to be so directly oriented toward consumer wants; but competitors raise the question whether they are oriented toward consumers via the detour of media attention and the desire to protect their brand—a possibility we will return to when we discuss diversity in the humanitarian field in chapter 4.

Beneficiaries and the Project Cycle

Let us look again at the practices of producing relief and what roles these practices entail for local populations. Project management distinguishes four phases of a project: assessment, planning, implementation, and monitoring and evaluation. From the earliest stages, managers seek to specify who exactly is receiving relief, what they are receiving, and how they will be better off for it.

We can see here the transition from "populations in need" to "beneficiaries," which is then forgotten in all subsequent discussion. Consider this excerpt from a description of a project:

On the 8th October 2005 an earthquake struck the Kashmir region of Pakistan, killing approximately 73,000 people and leaving an estimated 3.3 million homeless. The region historically suffers very harsh winters with night-time temperatures regularly falling below zero degrees. The risk of potential human loss due to hypothermia was significant. The main aim of the programme was to reduce suffering and the effects of winter for the earthquake-affected communities. At the start of their operation Tearfund set up a programme to supply emergency shelter as well as meet the water and sanitation needs of the communities in Bagh district Azad Jammu and Kashmir (AJK).[17]

The focus of the text, and the focus of the organization shifts from the 3.3 million homeless to specific beneficiaries served in specific villages.

16. There is some evidence to suggest that the funds from the public are not used very differently than those from official donors, see Development Initiatives, *Public Support for Humanitarian Crisis through NGO's Development Initiatives* (London: Development Initiatives 2009). However, it is important to note that not all the aspects that might matter are covered in this data. For an independent organization, what matters is not just the freedom, which crisis to spend funds on, but also the freedom to decide what exactly to provide, and how exactly to provide it.

17. Tearfund, *Accountability to Beneficiaries in Kashmir* (Teddington, UK: Tearfund, 2008).

Relief work begins with an assessment. The task is to find out "what people need in a specific geographic area in the context of a specific disaster." A population is thus identified as a population in need. Good practice includes an analysis of capacities and existing coping strategies; "good" practice is defined as "good" against the everyday pressures of organizational life. Populations are often identified by what they lack: their needs are emphasized, and their political aspirations or conflicts are deemphasized.[18]

Relief work is commonly divided into "sectors" according to technical expertise. Key sectors include, for example, water and sanitation, health, nutrition, shelter, and nonfood items.[19] A specified target population is an important part of the definition of a project. In planning a project distributing food or plastic sheeting, for example, managers need to decide how many people to provide for and how to select the people who will be receiving aid. Professionals in sectors that provide infrastructure like water and sanitation will chose between different sites rather than between different individuals or groups, but they still need to specify who exactly they think will be benefiting from this intervention.

During the implementation phase a specific subset of a population in need is then transformed into "beneficiaries" of an intervention. Here relief workers build latrines or dig wells; people receive tents, are treated in a hospital, or participate in hygiene training. Good managers constantly collect data to allow them to assess the progress being made, to revise planning, and to prepare for an eventual evaluation. This is called monitoring. Organizational records can serve as data for monitoring. For example, a project manager may look at the agency's own records to see how many tents were given out in a given time period or how many latrines were built. Ideally, though, data should be about beneficiaries. That means, instead of knowing that "so many tents have been handed out," managers would rather be able to say with certitude that "so many beneficiaries now have tents."

Evaluations assess the project after its conclusion and seek to provide lessons for the future. Evaluation reports may be based on monitoring

18. See James Ferguson, *The Anti-Politics Machine: "Development," Depoliticization, and Bureaucratic Power in Lesotho* (Cambridge: Cambridge University Press, 1990).
19. The Sphere Handbook 2011 lists water, sanitation and hygiene, food security and nutrition, shelter, settlement and nonfood items, and health action as technical areas. There are companion standards in education, life stock issues, and economic recovery. Sphere Project, *Humanitarian Charter and Minimum Standards in Disaster Response* (Geneva: The Sphere Project, 2011).

data, or donors may fund an external evaluation by independent consultants after the end of the project.

The Labor of Populations in Need

Beneficiaries are rarely simply benefiting in a passive way. They cooperate with and contribute to the project in various ways. In what follows I analyze this cooperation to show that if the project is produced and sold, beneficiaries are not just part of that product but also labor for it.[20] During the production of relief, cooperation is asked both from people who receive benefits and from people who do not. This cooperation is situated on a continuum. At a minimum, local people are asked to at least passively tolerate a project and the presence of relief workers. It is important that they are not too openly hostile or cause too much disruption. In many cases more active cooperation is required, such as answering questions or standing in line; at the other end of the continuum, projects rely on beneficiaries to provide labor in a form that would be called work in most other settings, work that could be done by others and could be paid, such as digging trenches and building latrines.

In the process of humanitarian relief some local populations are defined as "beneficiaries," for whom aid must be provided; in this act, all other members of the local population become part of the "environment" of relief work. For example, during its response to the floods in Pakistan in 2010 Catholic Relief Services selected seven districts in three affected provinces to assist with shelter, water and sanitation, and hygiene. With this targeting, some villages become beneficiaries, and others became part of the environment of the project.

As part of the environment of relief, some members of the local population are defined as potential threats to security, though the same people can be assigned both the role of beneficiary and the role of threat at the

---

20. There is a long Marxist and feminist tradition of highlighting seemingly invisible forms of labor; see, for example, Nona Y. Glazer, "Servants to Capital: Unpaid Domestic Labor and Paid Work," *Review of Radical Political Economics* 16, no. 1 (1984): 60–87; Tiziana Terranova, "Free Labor: Producing Culture for the Digital Economy," *Social Text* 63.18, no. 2 (2000): 33–58. Harold Taylor is to be credited for first comparing beneficiaries in development projects to workers from a critical management perspective. He diagnoses the dependency involved for both groups and notes some similarities, but he does not examine the implications of the fact that income is from donors for helping beneficiaries rather than from the sale of products or services; see Taylor, "Insights into Participation from Critical Management and Labour Process Perspectives," in *Participation—The New Tyranny?*, ed. Bill Cooke and Uma Kothari (London: Zed Press, 2001), 122–38.

same time. An evaluation report of the flood relief project in Pakistan in 2010 notes a good response from both beneficiaries and nonbeneficiaries in targeted villages but also notes "growing security risks for partner and CRS staff, such as threats received from landlords and neighbouring, unserved union councils."[21]

"Security" as used in this context is security for agency staff and property in the field. The "security" of agency staff is conceptually distinct from the security of the local population, which is thematized under the heading "protection." "Security" is a precondition of production. "Protection," the physical safety of local populations, has been of increasing concern to aid workers since the 1990s, but it remains a separate question from security. We will return to the question of protection in chapter 6.

Beneficiaries and nonbeneficiaries are expected to comply with the orderly delivery of aid. A key element of security according to aid agencies is "acceptance." The discourse of "acceptance" acknowledges the active role played by local populations before and beyond any aid being received. As Abby Stoddard explains it, "Acceptance entails the agency becoming a familiar and trusted entity by the host community and the beneficiary populations, cultivating a network of contacts and intermediaries to maintain open lines of communication and reception from the key (often belligerent) parties."[22]

To put this definition in words that bring out the labor of local populations more strongly: beneficiaries are asked to be familiar with the agency, trust it, and serve as a network of contacts and intermediaries to facilitate communication and reception.

More tangible cooperation by populations in need begins with the assessment phase well before any benefits are actually obtained. Agencies typically send out a team of experts to assess needs on the ground. Assessments are done partly to improve planning, but they also take on a dynamic of their own: assessments have become part of the response repertoire of humanitarian relief, and not all assessments lead to actual relief projects. Assessments rely on a variety of forms of data—including observations, reports, and statistics—but they also use interviews and conversations with people on the ground. Sometimes relief workers interview individuals; sometimes they hold group discussions.

For aid agencies, assessment thus brings with it the problem of recruit-

21. Catholic Relief Services, "Real-Time Evaluation of CRS' Flood Response in Pakistan: Jacobabad and Kashmore, Sindh" (Baltimore: Catholic Relief Services, 2010).

22. Abby Stoddard, Adele Harmer, and Katherine Haver, "Providing Aid in Insecure Environments: Trends in Policy and Operations" (London: Center on International Cooperation/Overseas Development Institute Humanitarian Policy Group, 2006).

ment. At times, aid workers find people are quite willing to report on their needs. A relief consultant and trainer with experience in water and sanitation explained it to me: "Often people are actually left with very little to do through a disaster. They are happy to talk to you." Recalling an experiment with workers in a factory from the classic era of scientific management, he explained further: "It's like when they did that experiment where they tried various things to see what would make workers more productive. They found that workers are very motivated by the fact that people are interested in them."

Researchers in the Hawthorne plants in the 1930s had found that whatever changes they made to the factory setting, productivity increased, which led them to discover that it was the fact of being studied that made workers work harder. Similarly, it is suggested, people in emergency settings sometimes respond positively when outsiders show an interest. But at other times, it can be difficult to recruit informants, especially when several different organizations pass through the same area. Experts from different technical sectors, such as water and sanitation, health, or food may visit the area separately—and there is no guarantee that an assessment will lead to relief being delivered.

This problem is now widely acknowledged in the field. The guidelines of the Red Cross for emergency assessment explain the problem as follows: "The people are frustrated because they are expected repeatedly to answer the same questions, often with no obvious result. They lose patience with 'humanitarian assessments.' Under such circumstances, an assessment is unlikely to produce useful information."[23]

When local populations are not willing to answer questions or to participate in surveys or group meetings, they exhibit what relief workers call "assessment fatigue." During the Indian Ocean tsunami of 2004 for example, the international evaluation found that some people had been "assessed to death."[24] There are now efforts to better coordinate assessments and formalize data collection techniques. The United Nations tries to coordinate agencies that work in the same sector through the Cluster approach, so that ideally data in each sector is collected only once; but the initial experiences show that the problem of duplication continues to be one that has to be managed.[25]

23. International Federation of Red Cross and Red Crescent Societies, "Guidelines for Emergency Assessment" (Geneva: International Federation of Red Cross and Red Crescent Societies, 2005).

24. Claude de Ville de Goyet and Lezlie C. Morinière, "The Role of Needs Assessment in the Tsunami Response" (London: Tsunami Evaluation Coalition, 2006).

25. See, for example, Soma De Silva et al., "Real-Time Evaluation of the Cluster Approach—Pakistan Earthquake: Application of the IASC Cluster Approach in the South Asia Earthquake" (Geneva:

During the delivery of relief itself, labor by beneficiaries takes different forms. Distributing usually requires at least an orderly crowd—some agencies in some contexts will drop off food during the night or early in the morning to avoid disruption. In order to receive food in a camp, for example, it is often necessary for refugees to register. Receipt of relief—be it tents, nonfood items, or food—usually requires waiting and standing in line. As Michael Lipsky described for domestic settings in his classic book, *Street-Level Bureaucracy*, "Even the most ordinary queuing arrangements—those designed to provide service on a first-come first-served basis in accordance with universalistic principles of client treatment—impose costs."[26]

An emergency feeding program may require a mother to provide special care to a sick child. This special labor is not always a trivial issue for participants. One manager in a medical agency told me about a project, for example, where mothers were somewhat reluctant to take on this job, given their own understanding of their responsibilities as mothers to all their children and as women with responsibilities within a larger family. In this case, most of the women were eventually enrolled in the program.

Some projects are delivered in the form of training. This is especially prevalent in the human rights field and in development work but also has its place in humanitarian relief. Hygiene projects, for example, usually require people to take part in educational meetings, where they learn about how to use latrines safely, how to use water safely, and how to minimize the risk of the spread of disease. The point here is not to imply any criticism of these types of intervention, as someone writing from a libertarian or Foucauldian perspective might. I am sure behavior modification can have important roles to play—I just want to note for the moment that they involve time also on behalf of beneficiaries.

Agencies usually expect beneficiaries to maintain facilities like latrines, but sometimes they simply provide materials and expect beneficiaries to build the infrastructure themselves. In cases where the work could be done by others, which is true for latrine building but not for hygiene training, the participation of beneficiaries looks most like work in other settings.

IASC, 2006); Riccardo Polastro et al., "Inter-agency Real-time Evaluation of the Humanitarian Response to Pakistan's 2010 Flood Crisis," DARA International, 2011), http://daraint.org/wp-content/uploads/2011/03/Final-Report-RTE-Pakistan-2011.pdf.

26. See Lipsky, *Street-Level Bureaucracy: Dilemmas of the Individual in Public Services* (New York: Russell Sage Foundation Publications, 2010), 95.

Partnership as Subcontracting

The aid agencies that are the face of humanitarian work in the West work with a variety of other organizations on delivering the project— including suppliers, local government,[27] and other NGOs. More specifi- cally, some agencies work with local partner organizations to deliver the project. These organizations might be local churches or local community initiatives. These local partner organizations serve a triple role.

First, they are a partner agency, and the staff of the partner agency are fellow relief workers. Some agencies take this relationship very seriously and invest time and resources to make it meaningful for both sides. Chris- tian agencies have a long tradition of working with local churches—the UK agencies CAFOD (Catholic Agency for Development Overseas) and Tearfund, for example, work very hard to establish meaningful partner- ships. Organizations with a background in development also have a long record of working with partners and also take care to establish good rela- tionships.

Second, the partner agencies are also an important element of the product of relief; they too are marketed to donors as worthy beneficiaries that are being helped. "Capacity building" has become more prominent since the 1990s,[28] and it is through this term that working with partners can be sold to donors as an added value of a project. In development aid, a related discourse of good governance turns supporting other NGOs into a possible result of aid work.[29]

Third, for an agency the question of whether to work with partners or not is in part a labor question. Working with partners is generally cheaper than delivering services directly to beneficiaries. Expatriates flown in from the West or other countries in the region are more expensive than local workers. In working with partners, agencies are also able to delegate the responsibilities and risks regarding parts of their labor force. If local workers are hired directly this means risks are the agency's; if local work- ers are hired by a partner agency, the risks are delegated.[30]

27. Paul Harvey, *Towards Good Humanitarian Government: The Role of the Affected State in Disaster Response*, HGP Report 29 (London: ODI, 2009).

28. See also Ian Smillie, *Patronage or Partnership: Local Capacity Building in a Humanitarian Crisis* (Bloomfield, CT: Kumarian Press, 2001).

29. Läetitia Atlani-Duault, *Au bonheur des autres: Anthropologie de l'aide humanitaire* (Paris: Armand Collins, 2005).

30. For a critical discussion, see Stoddard, Harmer, and Haver, "Providing Aid in Insecure Environ- ments."

Participation and Accountability as Labor

In development work, donor agencies and aid organizations have long insisted on beneficiary "participation," especially since the mid-1980s. In humanitarian relief work, given how it has been shaped by the metaphor specifically of medical emergencies, this is a newer phenomenon. But as humanitarian relief has become institutionalized, some development agencies have moved into relief work, and some humanitarian projects have run over a long period of time, some relief agencies have also begun to emphasize the need for local participation.[31]

Scholars and practitioners in development have offered some incisive critiques of this trend.[32] It is open to debate whether real participation is achieved in the context of project management. Scholars have also raised interesting questions about the impact of participation in NGO projects on the legitimacy of local political institutions. Let me just emphasize here the one aspect raised by these critiques that is most relevant to the current argument: these initiatives also increase the labor involved for beneficiaries.

The latest phenomenon following on and adding to earlier discourses on participation is that of accountability. Since the 1990s relief NGOs have become more and more concerned with the "quality of relief." Among many other reform projects, perhaps the most far-reaching and radical is the Humanitarian Accountability Partnership (HAP). It is also the project that most explicitly tries to change the role beneficiaries play in relief. Agencies participating in this initiative are ready to accept the criticism that agencies tend to cater to the preferences of those with resources, or, as they would put it, are "more accountable to donors rather than beneficiaries," and are in the process of implementing procedures that are meant to address this imbalance. Unlike other reform initiatives, this initiative foresees a process of formal certification for agencies that comply with a set of agreed-on standards.[33] We will return to HAP in

31. David Mosse, "The Making and Marketing of Particpatory Development," in *A Moral Critique of Development: In Search of Global Responsibilities*, ed. Philip Quarles van Uffard and Ananta Kumar Giri (London: Routledge, 2003), 43–75.

32. E.g., Bill Cooke and Uma Kothari, eds., *Participation—The New Tyranny?* (London: Zed Books, 2001); especially Heiko Henkel and Roderick Stirrat, "Participation as Spiritual Duty; Empowerment and Secular Subjection," ibid., 168–84; David Mosse, "People's Knowledge,' Participation and Patronage: Operations and Representations in Rural Development," ibid., 16–35; Mosse, "Making and Marketing of Particpatory Development."

33. HAP Editorial Steering Committee, "HAP 2007 Standard in Humanitarian Accountability and Quality Management: Adopted by HAP on 30th January 2007" (Geneva: Humanitarian Accountability Partnership International, 2007).

chapter 5 when we consider the origins and the impact of projects that seek to reform humanitarian relief. Here we focus on what it entails with regard to the labor of beneficiaries.

HAP introduces forms and mechanisms that require work from beneficiaries. Beneficiaries are expected to absorb information, give feedback, and fill out forms. Agencies are genuinely interested in beneficiaries' feedback, but only a specific kind of feedback speaks to their work—feedback that works within the existing mandate and specifically the existing program design.

As populations in need are transformed into beneficiaries, recipients have to be socialized into this very specific role. They have to bridge the gap between their own needs and wishes, on the one hand, and agency reality, on the other. A manager at an agency involved with HAP explained to me: "You do actually need to explain to people the whole principle and help them understand, you know, why we would want your complaints and why is it good for you to be critical against this—but actually, there are limits to your criticism."

Relief as an Exchange

In chapter 1, I argued that relief agencies produce projects. I described some of the effects of organizational practices and material constraints on the allocation of aid. That analysis pointed at the inequities this logic produces *among* potential beneficiaries. Some people get help, while others do not. This has as much to do with the contingencies of logistics and expertise than with an objective difference in need.

In this chapter, I have argued that beneficiaries are part of the product of relief and labor for it. This allows us to analyze the implications of thinking about relief as a form of production in terms of power not only among potential beneficiaries but *between all the actors* involved in relief. The issue is not just about who gets relief and who does not but also who benefits from a system where some people choose to pay for projects, whereas others either become part of a project or are left to their own devices.

Beneficiaries receive life-saving resources. But relief is not a one-way transfer of resources. Rather, it is an exchange, and more specifically it is an exchange under conditions of competition and inequality.

The classic resource for analyzing gifts as a form of exchange is the work of anthropologist Marcel Mauss. When one person gives another a gift, it seems that resources flow only one way. But, as Mauss points out,

2.4 Mauss's rethinking of exchange

the giver also benefits (see fig. 2.4). He accumulates obligations owed to him. By seemingly wasting or destroying material goods he accumulates symbolic credit.[34] This analysis can be applied to the development context, where the gift travels from the individual donor, to the NGO, and sometimes through various partner NGOs, until it reaches the recipient; recipient then owes the donor.[35]

But in analyzing humanitarian relief we need to consider that these exchanges are different than the ones Mauss is analyzing in that they are mediated by a market and involve labor. In Mauss's analysis we have individuals exchanging gifts *with each other* in a community. In the case of humanitarian relief, we have a set of specialized producers, who have a professional interest in encouraging gift giving and gift taking. We also have to consider the context in which these exchanges take place, specifically that the gift concerns basic needs of the recipients. And we have to consider that only a small share of those who might be said to need help actually receive help, that there is thus a competition among gift receivers but that those who do not receive also give.[36]

For these reasons, we can't just draw on the analogy to the gift exchange as analyzed by Mauss; we also need to compare the exchanges in humanitarian relief to the exchange of labor for a wage as analyzed by Karl Marx (fig. 2.5).

This analysis started out as a questioning of a seemingly fair exchange between worker and employer. Workers give their labor power. Workers receive a wage on which their livelihood depends. Indeed, workers need and welcome employment. But, for Marx, this is only the surface of the

34. Marcel Mauss, *The Gift: The Form and Reason for Exchange in Archaic Societies* (London: Routledge, 1990).

35. Roderick L. Stirrat and Heiko Henkel, "The Development Gift: The Problem of Reciprocity in the NGO World," *Annals of the American Academy of Political and Social Science* 554 (1997): 66–80. See also Benedict Korf et al., "The Gift of Disaster: The Commodification of Good Intentions in Post-tsunami Sri Lanka," *Disasters* 34, no. 2 (2010): 60–77.

36. Pierre Bourdieu also aims to bring Marx and Mauss together and takes the analysis of gift as a basis for analyzing specifically modern exchanges. But he uses Marx's vocabulary in a metaphoric way and does not actually look at production, labor, and the role of organizations as a relatively independent dimension of social life. See the discussion by Ilana F. Silber, "Bourdieu's Gift to Gift Theory: An Unacknowledged Trajectory," *Sociological Theory* 27, no. 2 (2009): 173–90; John Beasley-Murray, "Value and Capital in Bourdieu and Marx," in *Pierre Bourdieu: Fieldwork in Culture*, ed. Nicholas Brown and Imre Szeman (Lanham, MD: Rowman & Littlefield, 2000), 100–119; John Guillory, "Bourdieu's Refusal," *Modern Language Quarterly* 58, no. 4 (1997): 367–98.

2.5 Marx's rethinking of exchange

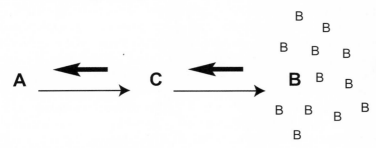

2.6 Exchange in the market for relief projects

phenomenon. Marx urges us to look beyond the tangible good outcomes (wages) at the overall exchange. Marx urges us to examine the conditions under which workers accept and welcome work. First, a large part of the population have had to be separated from the means of subsistence to enter this exchange. They have lost access to the land and have to earn money to eat. The means of production are privately owned and in the hands of a few, and workers have to compete against each other for jobs. Under these conditions, employers are able to extract a surplus value from workers. Building on this analysis, Marx was also able to express reasoned worries about the long-term consequences of these exchanges between unequals.

Donors do not give directly to beneficiaries. Donors give money to humanitarian agencies in exchange for projects with suitable beneficiaries (fig. 2.6). Agencies "source" beneficiaries within a pool of crises and need, package them, and sell them to donors. This means that populations in need are put in a position where they are in competition against each other, rather than against comparatively better-off groups, in their regions, countries, or globally.

This way of distributing relief allows donors to choose projects. There has been a debate in development studies about the relative power of donor agencies vis-à-vis NGOs,[37] and such power is likely to vary. As soci-

37. Michael Edwards and David Hulme, "Too Close for Comfort? The Impact of Official Aid on Nongovernmental Organizations," *World Development* 24, no. 6 (1996): 961–73; John Farrington

ologist Emily Barman has shown, it is important to consider this not only as a one-to-one relationship, but as part of an institutional framework, in which both donors and NGO are affected.[38] In this case, we need to consider this relationship between donor and NGO as part of the global market for projects, where several donors faces several agencies. There are of course many different consumers of relief, with different interests, values, and political visions. But their preferences are not random, and their variation is structurally limited. They have resources, and their preferences become relevant according to their purchasing power. They will likely not chose projects that offend them or are likely to threaten their resources in the future.

This way of distributing relief allows donors to accumulate status, and NGOs to accumulate money and status. Populations in need—whether they really are beneficiaries or are simply evoked as beneficiaries or potential beneficiaries—lend authority to agencies and donors under circumstances over which they have very little control. Representations of beneficiaries by agencies under these circumstances might make it harder for people to represent themselves.

Beneficiaries receive goods and services that are often useful and often life-saving. Food, water, and health care are necessary things. Latrines and tents reduce mortality in disasters. Of course relief does help recipients and is often welcomed by recipients. But recipients also give something in return: consent, time, and labor, for example. They give this labor under conditions over which they have very little control.

Donor agencies give money and receive the symbolic benefits of having helped. Relief agencies receive money and the symbolic benefits of having helped. Beneficiaries, even those who do not receive anything, lend themselves as a source of authority for those who help.

To say that beneficiaries are in competition with each other does not necessarily mean that populations actively participate in this competition—though there is evidence from the anthropology of development that they sometimes do participate, and especially that middlemen do so on their behalf.[39]

---

and Anthony Bebbington, *Reluctant Partners? Non-governmental Organizations, the State, and Sustainable Agricultural Development* (London: Psychology Press, 1993); Dorothea Hilhorst, *The Real World of NGOs: Discourses, Diversity, and Development* (London: Zed Books, 2003), 192.

38. Emily Barman, "An Institutional Approach to Donor Control: From Dyadic Ties to a Field-Level Analysis," *American Journal of Sociology* 112, no. 5 (2007): 1416–57.

39. Bierschenk, Chauveau, and Olivier de Sardan, "Courtiers en développement"; Davis Lewis and David Mosse, eds., *Development Brokers and Translators: The Ethnography of Aid and Agencies* (Bloomfield, CT: Kumarian Press, 2006). Clifford Bob also focuses explictly on the active role of insurgent groups, in looking for support for the case of advocacy groups, see Bob, *The Marketing of Rebellion*

It is fair to say that there are certain preconditions for participating in this game for both populations in need and local NGOs in terms of conforming to expectations. An individual beneficiary or a group of beneficiaries needs to be, first of all, "civilian"—that is, not overly engaged in their own political projects.[40] They also need to be willing to accept the agency on the terms it is willing to offer.

A local NGO needs to be impartial and nonpolitical, and it needs to have acceptable financial reporting mechanisms. Partner agencies are encouraged to professionalize in terms of acquiring technical expertise recognizable to Western organizations. They are also encouraged to specialize.

Donors encourage acceptable practice with agencies and will provide training to that effect. Agencies in turn encourage acceptable practice with local partners and populations themselves. Donors or relief agencies have few formal ways of punishing those who do not conform; but there are always other people who can be helped instead. In this way, some of the poorest populations, and local organizations, are pitched against each other in a race for resources. A director of operations at a large US agency explained to me: "You might have a lot of mountainous communities, and you might have in one state a very good local organization that could really benefit from some help, and in another state two or three organizations fighting with each other. Well, you probably wouldn't go to the second state."

Conflict is here seen as a sign of trouble; it is perhaps a sign of being unworthy, and at the very least a concern regarding efficient implementation.

A desk officer at a Christian agency in the United Kingdom, explained to me when I asked how they decide on which projects to support: "We are sitting here in the UK, and my partners are in Zambia, for example. They get very caught up in what is going on, and driven, then, by the need. And sometimes they are so busy trying to meet the need that they will begin to think, you know, where they have expertise in agriculture, they'll think that it would be a good idea for them to start doing HIV public health education. And you think, yeah—it is definitely a need, but is it your area? And should you be doing that?"

(Cambridge: Cambridge University Press, 2005); Bob, "The Market in Human Rights," In *Advocacy Organizations and Collective Action*, ed. Aseem Prakash and Mary Kay Guggerty (Cambridge: Cambridge University Press, 2010), 133–55.

40. Compare here to Clifford Bob's *The Marketing of Rebellion*. The differences between his observations and mine seem largely to be explained by differences between the market for rebellion and the market for human rights, on the one hand, and the market for relief projects, on the other hand, but this might be explored further.

In this story, the local agency wants to respond according to the needs of the community—HIV seems to be a problem in the area. However, at headquarters it is felt that the agency would do better focusing on its own area of expertise.

Direct Domination and Indirect Domination

Critics of humanitarian relief evoke populations in need as subject to power. It is important to be precise and ask what kind of power is found here. The form of power usually implied is that of direct domination. Populations in need are understood to be dominated either directly by the aid worker or the relief agency, or they are understood to be dominated by a system of which the aid agency is just another arm. The system might be called "global capitalism," "imperialism," "(neo)-colonialism," "neoliberalism," or "empire."[41]

In humanitarian relief forms of direct domination no doubt do exist. Aid workers do have power over beneficiaries. Aid agencies do exercise power in that sense, for example, when they control access to resources and services in a refugee camp. It is this kind of power that Tony Vaux, an experienced relief worker and manager with Oxfam, reflects on in his powerfully honest account in *The Selfish Altruist*. Vaux writes about his experience of arriving in northern Mozambique in the 1980s: "As the officials stepped forward deferentially to shake my hand, I felt pleasure in the reassuring sense of control over their lives, especially since I had been scared about my own. Slowly, I reminded myself of who I was—a person with power, more power here in war-torn Mozambique than I could dream of in my own life in a village in England. I was here to decide whether people received life-saving aid and whatever I chose they had to accept."[42]

This power can be abused, as Vaux himself is very aware of. Abuses are extreme cases, but precisely as such they reveal something about the underlying structure and potential of the situation. The incidents in camps in Liberia, Sierra Leone, and Guinea, where, according to a report by the United Nations High Commissioner for Refugees (UNHCR) and

---

41. David Chandler, *From Kosovo to Kabul: Human Rights and International Intervention* (London: Pluto Press, 2002); Noam Chomsky, *The New Military Humanism: Lessons from Kosovo* (Monroe, ME: Common Courage Press, 1999); Frank Furedi, *The New Ideology of Imperialism: Renewing the Moral Imperative* (London: Pluto Press, 1994).

42. Tony Vaux, *The Selfish Altruist: Relief Work in Famine and War* (London: Earthscan/James & James, 2001), 94.

Save the Children, hundreds of children were forced to exchange sex for services, can be understood in this context.[43]

But, I would argue, there is another dimension to the way populations in need are incorporated into humanitarian relief. Drawing on a contrast between direct and indirect domination developed by Moishe Postone, we can say that populations in need are also subject to a specific form of indirect domination, which is mediated by the market for projects.[44] We cannot fully understand the significance of these forms of domination if we do not examine the distinctive logic of the market in projects, and by implication in beneficiaries. This market mediates between beneficiaries (actual and potential) and the aid agencies. The logic operates before a given person receives relief, and relatively independently of how the delivery of the relief is designed. It affects those who receive and those who do not receive.

There may be some continuities between this market in projects and earlier, colonial forms of rule. The images the market in projects produces resemble to some extent those of its colonial predecessors. They continue familiar motives of Africans or refugees as helpless, dependent, and in need of intervention,[45] while emphasizing new themes of state failure and security.[46] Yet even if it may be old wine in new bottles, it is important to analyze the new bottles—the distinctive mediating institutional mechanisms.

I would add a note on the literature on governmentality here. A Foucauldian analysis, for example, of the way a relief agency disciplines beneficiaries certainly has insights to offer. Jennifer Hyndman's study of UNHCR examines the everyday practices that produce desired behaviors in the camp. She argues that power is exercised through both coercive and disciplinary means. "The use of particular reporting practices by UNHCR and other agencies," she observes, "are reminiscent of colonial practices that aim to standardize, control, and order the fields from which they were generated."[47]

43. Save the Children, *From Camp to Community: Liberia Study on Exploitation of Children* (Monrovia, Liberia: Save the Children, 2006); Corinna Csáky, "No One to Turn To: The Under-Reporting of Child Sexual Exploitation and Abuse by Aid Workers and Peacekeepers" (London: Save the Children, 2008).

44. Moishe Postone, *Time, Labor, and Social Domination: A Reinterpretation of Marx's Critical Theory* (Cambridge: Cambridge University Press, 1993).

45. See, for example, Heike Haerting, "Global Humanitarianism, Race, and the Spectacle of the African Corpse in Current Western Representations of the Rwandan Genocide," *Comparative Studies of South Asia Africa and the Middle East* 28 (2008): 61–77; Prem Kumar Rajaram, "Humanitarianism and Representations of the Refugee," *Journal of Refugee Studies* 15, no. 3 (2002): 247–64.

46. Mark Duffield, *Development, Security, and Unending War: Governing the World of Peoples* (Cambridge: Polity Press, 2007).

47. Jennifer Hyndman, *Managing Displacement: Refugees and the Politics of Humanitarianism* (Minneapolis: University of Minnesota Press, 2000), xxviii; see also Ole Sending and Iver B. Neumann, "Governance to Governmentality: Analyzing NGOs, States, and Power," *International Studies Quarterly* 50, no. 3 (2006): 651–72.

But I depart here in two ways. On the one hand, Foucauldians too often overemphasize the coherence of governmentality, as Pat O'Malley and colleagues have also argued.[48] Of course the tradition, in theory, emphasizes the dispersal of power, but authors very often end up attributing a hidden coherence to the sum of dispersed elements of power.

Second, governmentality is usually conceived of as a form of direct domination. Though Foucault begins precisely with a critique of approaches that imagine power primarily as negative,[49] governance is primarily seen as a constrainer, not as a (failing) provider. Because he tries so hard to avoid essentialism, Foucault builds his critique on libertarian assumptions; in his attempts to avoid making assumptions about subjects, he does away with everything that links people to people, and that makes people dependent on each other, such as needs and desires. This makes it hard to understand one person's needs as another person's source of power; it leads scholars in the governmentality tradition to consider only the power imposed on those who are intervened upon, not the power created by a mixture of intervention and neglect.

Eigensinn and Contradictions

"Populations in need" are not only populations in need—they might not necessarily see themselves as primarily in need. And populations in need are not naturally beneficiaries. They appear as such through the eyes of the relief agency. The transformation from populations in need to beneficiaries has to struggle against the *Eigensinn* of the recipients and is never fully successful or complete.

Eigensinn (literally, "proper meaning"; also translated as "obstinacy") refers to the way subjects interpret their own needs, the way they interpret the situation, the way they make decisions and act.[50] Analyses, especially from the left, often oppose compliance and resistance as though there were nothing in between. Consequently, *eigensinn* has either been overlooked in objectivist analysis or celebrated as resistance. In the first approach it is assumed that people are entirely compliant because they

48. Pat O'Malley, Lorna Weir, and Clifford Shearing, "Governmentality, Criticism, Politics," *Economy and Society* 26, no. 4 (1997): 501–17.

49. Michel Foucault, *Discipline and Punish: The Birth of the Prison* (New York: Pantheon Books, 1977).

50. See Oskar Negt and Alexander Kluge, *Geschichte und Eigensinn* (Frankfurt am Main: Zweitausendeins, 1981).

do not do exactly what the (critical) observer wants them to do. In the latter approach, observers often imply a unified object, a single logic of domination, that one might resist against, thus suggesting a unity of interest and of interpretation between observers and observed.[51]

Eigensinn is not necessarily a form of resistance. It is a more basic form of nonidentity. Consider the two meanings of the term "willful." On the one hand, it has been interpreted as "having more will than necessary, or rational, or allowed" by conservative interpreters or read as resistance by critical approaches; on the other hand, it simply means that the subject has a will of its own that cannot be reduced. The concept, in this latter sense, alerts us to possible contradictions when seemingly abstract logics meet concrete subjects. It is an open question how contradictions come to the fore or are temporarily resolved—if at all, and with which means. This concept is more in line with findings in development studies about the actions and reactions of populations vis-à-vis the development apparatus, than with the concept of "resistance."[52]

Populations are not always ready or willing to cooperate with aid agencies. We can see this in the case of the assessment teams that struggle to find informants. The "assessment fatigue" discussed earlier is a reflection of an alternative analysis of the situation that can be based on past experience and can be quite accurate—namely that perhaps the informants stand nothing to gain from participating in an assessment. Early on during my research I met a young aid worker who had been with the military and then returned to take a graduate degree at Columbia University's School of International Public Affairs to make a difference with aid organizations rather than the military. He shared this story with me of one of his first assignments: "I was on a need assessment in Somalia, and these people have nothing. There is the problem of drought, a lot of the income came from fishing, and people lost their boats in the tsunami. And the leader of the village brought all the people together and was very angry. He said: 'Nobody gives us anything, nobody cares about us, you just drive through here: why should we answer your questions?'"

51. The debate between the tradition of critical theory and new audience studies, on the consumption of cultural goods, takes this form. In De Certeau's and Scott's analysis of everyday practices of resistance the sympathy also goes beyond analytical respect for people's subjectivity toward assuming a shared agenda against oppression. Michel de Certeau, *The Practice of Everyday Life* (Berkeley: University of California Press, 1984); James Scott, *Weapons of the Weak: Everyday Forms of Peasant Resistance* (New Haven, CT: Yale University Press, 1985).

52. E.g., Bernadetta Rossi, "Aid Policies and Recipient Strategies in Niger: Why Donors and Recipients Should Not Be Compartmentalized into Separate 'Worlds of Knowledge,'" in Lewis and Mosse, *Development Brokers and Translators*, 27–50.

For the young aid worker this was quite a tricky situation, but he managed to diffuse the tension. He explained to the villagers that his work was important and that his report was necessary in order to tell other people about their situation. As we sat over coffee, he added rather sheepishly that when he returned from Somalia to the United States he submitted a report to his agency, but that report never resulted in a project.

During implementation, recipients' *Eigensinn* can also get in the way of the smooth delivery of projected outputs. One relief worker recalled: "We were delivering goods to a camp for Afghani refuges in Russia, and every time we came back what we had given them had disappeared and the refugees said: 'We don't have anything.' We had given them clothes for the children, and the babies were again without clothes. That leaves you in a very awkward position when the donor comes and wants to see what happened to the money."

It has long frustrated aid workers to see goods they distribute being exchanged for money rather than being used. Recipients also redistribute aid among themselves; food aid is often shared within families. If malnourished children are targeted, I was told, people may keep their children malnourished to obtain food rations to share with the whole family.

Populations can be "aid aware," as some aid workers call it—that is, they have previous experience of NGOs and try to work with what they have learned. This can be exacerbated by the fact that some crises are really cyclical and part of the normality of life in a certain area, and because agencies' resource allocation follows a logic of its own and can cover the same areas repeatedly.

When agencies responded to the 2007 floods in Mozambique, for example, they encountered a population that had some experience of refugee camps in Malawi supplied by the World Food Programme (WFP) during the civil war, and some experience of flood relief in 2001. According to an evaluation report, "The populations in the cyclone affected area had shared in the relief items bonanza that followed Cyclone Eline in 2000. . . . The distribution of aid after the 2001 floods was quite generous, as many agencies had large stocks of relief items that had arrived too late for distribution to those affected by Cyclone Eline in 2000."[53]

Beneficiaries' experience with the aid system can make it hard to obtain accurate information. In Mozambique, the interagency evalua-

53. John Cosgrave et al., "Inter-agency Real-Time Evaluation of the Response to the February Floods and Cyclone in Mozambique" (New York: United Nations Office for the Coordination of Humanitarian Affairs, 2007).

tion notes that "beneficiaries, in their effort to maximise the potential aid flows, misrepresented what they had lost, or what they intended to do. . . . When asked why they needed blankets they replied that they had lost them in the flood. After further discussion the interviewees acknowledged that they had not had any blankets and that they brought all their household possessions with them when they fled the low lands."[54]

The interview teams were often told by beneficiaries that the whole population intended to settle at the resettlement site. At some sites, this was clearly true, as people had already begun to invest in the sites by constructing assets such as granaries and birdhouses. However, at other sites many of the shelters had grass growing in them or had unrepaired damage to them, showing that they were used only occasionally or had been abandoned. This demonstrated that the population had already returned, either to the lowlands or to the neighboring villages.[55]

Agencies in turn have developed a repertoire of strategies to outsmart beneficiaries in order to deliver projects according to plan. Procedures have been developed to prevent people from registering for aid twice or in multiple camps. If at all possible, if they have the staff, I was told, agencies should try to hold registration in multiple camps at the same time so people cannot move between camps to register multiple times.

These strategies of planning with and against beneficiaries' *Eigensinn* include what could be understood as "preventing abuse." But at times they go much further than that. A country director for a Christian agency in Afghanistan told me about a project his agency had designed. The plan was to deliver latrines. Local people confronted the agency with some demands. "People are often very smart about how this whole thing works," he explained to me. "They knew we had to deliver these latrines, so they told us: 'You can build these latrines, but you must pay us for the labor'; well, we had kind of thought we would provide the materials, and they would do the labor for free." Here, local people refused to accept the agency's project on the agency's terms. They refused to simply be beneficiaries, and in particular they refused to labor for free for the agency, and instead demanded a wage.

In this particular case, the country director reported, the agency got around the problem and improved the project design: "We decided to do it differently the second time around; we started with some education projects; teaching women about hygiene. At the end of which they

54. Ibid., 47.
55. Ibid.

said, 'We need some latrines.' So we said, 'Well, we think we can help you out with materials if you could help with the buildings.' And then they got the guys to do the work. That is what I mean by community development!"

Conclusion

Populations in need are an end of humanitarian relief but also a means to an end. Managers' relationship to beneficiaries is not only an instrumental one but it is *also* an instrumental one. They value the opportunity to do good and have an impact. But managers also have a project to deliver. In the case of international humanitarian relief a project is produced for exchange in a market, where it is compared to other projects from other producers on a global scale.

I have tried to bring out a role that populations in need play in humanitarian relief that is not often considered. Populations in need are part of the product being promoted and sold in this market, and they labor for it.

Much debate about relief has understandably been about content and design on the level of a specific intervention. Observers ask: How relevant are services to the affected populations? How efficient is an operation? How participatory are an agency's planning processes?

These discussions certainly have a place. But in addition to such discussions, we also need a discussion about relief that moves beyond the content of relief toward its form. However good the content and design of a specific intervention, its form as a commodity in a global market in beneficiaries shapes its overall effect. It is a product within a limited range of possible products, given consumer preferences of those with resources, and it pits those helped against those not helped.

I will now examine how we got to where we are today. How did populations in need become beneficiaries? One could imagine many different histories of humanitarian relief: one could write this history as a history of humanitarian ideas;[56] one could also write this history as a history of the crises that relief responds to. Or one could imagine this history told as a history of the fortunes and conflicts of the most prominent relief organizations.

56. For an interesting account in this tradition, see Vanessa Pupavac, "Between Compassion and Conservativism: A Genealogy of Humanitarian Sensibilities," in *Contemporary States of Emergency: The Politics of Military and Humanitarian Intervention,* ed. Didier Fassin and Mariella Pandolfi (New York: Zone Books, 2011), 129–53.

I will take a different approach. In the next chapter, I will attempt to chart, instead, a history of the organizational infrastructure of the response to human suffering, in order to write a history of the market for relief. I will do this by writing a history of the "logframe," an influential management tool in the field. The logframe is a tool that helps managers plan projects. It is through this tool that projects became the unit of humanitarian relief, and it is also through this tool that projects became comparable.

THREE

The Logframe and the History of the Market for Projects

With a word, between spirit and life there is a complicated settlement in which spirit gets paid at most one half of any thousand of its demands and, in exchange, is decorated with the title of an honorable creditor. ROBERT MUSIL, *THE MAN WITHOUT QUALITIES*

The first training for relief workers I attended was a three-day workshop on "needs assessment," the first step of the project cycle. We were a group of ten people, meeting at a conference center in a village in Sussex in England. The group was a mixed group in terms of experience. It included a young logistician on his way to his first relief assignment in Malawi, a Dutch relief worker with more than twenty years of experience with a large and important Christian agency, and an Italian pursuing an MA degree in development who had previously spent a year doing relief work in Palestine.

Most participants arrived the evening before the start of the workshop, and there was some time to socialize. I had mentioned I was a researcher, but over the course of the next day it became clear that because we were such a small group, it was not really an option to "just observe." The instructor wanted to create an interactive atmosphere. I had no relevant experience, but I wanted to "fit in" and contribute at least in terms of energy and commitment.

I had been reading up on humanitarianism for a number of months and had been to a series of seminars and work-

	Narrative description	Objectively verifiable indicator	Sources of information	Risks and assumptions
Principal objective				
Specific objective				
Result				
Activities				

3.1   The logframe

shops, listening to some of the leading academics in the field discuss humanitarian crises and humanitarian policy. Initially, the themes of the discussion during the training seemed familiar, and I felt I could participate in the discussions and in group work. But my attempts to pass came to an end when the trainer referred in passing to the "logframe," and everyone else in the room seemed to know what it was. The logframe was not part of the curriculum of this course—it appeared to have been part of a previous unit, which I had missed. For everyone else in the room, the term "logframe" seemed an accepted part of everyday vocabulary. As for me, not only did I not know what it was; when I first listened to the conversations that included references to the logframe, I could not come up with any idea as to what *kind* of thing it might be.

I have had it explained to me gradually since this first encounter. As an empty form the logframe appears as shown in figure 3.1.

As a completed form, a logframe might look like the document in table 3.1. This is an example of a logical framework matrix, with details about a specific project filled in, that was developed by Oxfam and provided by the European Union's Office for Humanitarian Affairs in order to guide NGOs that are considering applying for funding for relief work.[1] It

1. "Humanitarian Actors—Framework Partnership Agreement: Annex 1—Single Form—Logical Framework Matrix," on the European Commission's European Community Humanitarian Office (ECHO) website, accessed November 9, 2008, http://ec.europa.eu/echo/about/actors/archives _fpa2003_en.htm (site discontinued).

Table 3.1 Logical framework matrix from ECHO (2004)

	Narrative descriptions	Objectively verifiable indicators	Sources of information	Risks and assumptions
Principal objective	The health status of refugees and local villagers is improved.			
Specific objective	The target population have increased access to and make optimal use of water and sanitation facilities, and take action to protect themselves against threats to public health.	Target group uses facilities and resources appropriately, and safely. Water and sanitation facilities are effectively managed by the target community.	Information from other NGOs, focus group discussions. Surveys.	Conflict in the neighbouring country does not spill over and destabilize the host country. The health centres set up by the other INGO remain operational. UNHCR continue to provide sufficient food rations, shelter, and blankets.
Results	1. 8000 refugees have adequate, appropriate and safe sanitary facilities within six months.	Temporary defecation areas set up and used appropriately. 400 latrines constructed and used appropriately. Female refugees use sanitation facilities in safety. Latrines < 50 m from shelters.	Monitoring visits to camp. Latrine monitoring forms. Reports by latrine assistants. Focus group discussions with women and girls.	Government border guards are able to improve security to reduce/prevent rebel raids. Refugees stay in camp.
	2. 8000 refugees and 20000 villagers have access to a water supply of sufficient quantity and quality within six months.	Target group accesses at least 15 litres water/day per person. Maximum distance from shelter/ home to water points is 500m. Water meets international quality standards. Female refugees can access adequate water in safety. Queuing time at water sources no more than 15 minutes.	Engineers monitoring and output records. Records from water point attendants. Weekly water testing records.	

3. 8000 refugees have improved understanding of basic public health and hygiene issues and the means to practice methods of improving hygiene in the camp.	People use drinking water from safe sources. Men, women, and children use latrines appropriately. Men, women, and children wash hands at key times. Latrines and sanitation facilities are kept clean and hygienic. Refugees express increased understanding of health and hygiene.	Observation. Monitoring visits Reports from latrine attendants and water point attendants. Focus group discussions, surveys and interviews.	
Activities	**Means**		Construction materials remain available in adequate amounts. National government gives NGO registration to work in the country.
Result 1: Adequate sanitary facilities in the camp Set up temporary defecation areas. 400 gender-segregated latrines constructed in line with international standards. 40 latrine attendants trained and equipped. Construction of 200 gender-segregated washing facilities. Construction of 80 community washing facilities (laundry). Consultation with female refugees to identify suitable sites for sanitation facilities. Provision of potties for under-fives.	Defecation field kit. Latrine digging kit. Latrine squat plates. Latrine superstructure construction. Training workshops. Construction materials/labour. Maintenance equipment. Potties. Personnel. Direct support costs.		

continued

Table 3.1 continued

Narrative descriptions	Objectively verifiable indicators	Sources of information	Risks and assumptions
Result 2: Adequate clean water Trucking of water (first phase only). Installation of 32 water points in the refugee camp. Training of four water point attendants in camp. Construction of 20 hand pumps in local village. Training of four hand pump attendants in village. Establishment of a stick of community spares for water pumps in village. Establishment of water management committee in local village.	Pipes. Pump kit. Onion tank. Well construction materials and labor. Hand pump and spares. Water treatment chemicals. Water testing kit. Training workshops. Personnel. Direct support costs.		
Result 3: Improved hygiene practices in camp Training of 16 community hygiene promoters in camp. Provision of 3200 water containers. Provision of 160 community hygiene packs. Provision of 1600 household hygiene packs every month for six months (soap, disinfectant, laundry, soap, etc., for one family for one month).	Training workshops. Water containers. Community hygiene packs. Household hygiene packs. Personnel. Direct support costs.	**Costs** Breakdown per result: Result 1: €191,896 Result 2: €277,239 Result 3: €109,839 Total Direct Costs = €578,974	

describes a project providing water and sanitation for refugees in a refugee camp. It covers three aspects central to this sector of relief work: the organization is proposing to dig latrines for the refugees, to build wells, and to teach people about personal hygiene.

This matrix of four rows and four columns is the core of a planning approach that aims to make interventions coherent and rational. The logframe states the overall goal of the project in the top left corner—in this case, the aim is to improve "the health status of refugees and local villagers." The matrix then seeks to establish a link between higher-level goals, such as improved health, and more concrete, lower-level goals or projected results, such as that "refugees have adequate, appropriate and safe sanitary facilities." Finally the matrix links higher-level goals to concrete activities, such as building "temporary defecation areas" or latrines and training latrine attendants.

In column 2 goals, results, and activities are linked to measurable indicators. If 400 latrines are constructed and used appropriately, this indicates that 8,000 refugees have access to appropriate and safe sanitary facilities. The figure "15 liters of water per day and per person" specifies the "sufficient quantity and quality" the agency seeks to provide. This is in line with internationally agreed minimum standards for relief interventions, which I will discuss in more detail in chapter 5.

In column 3, the form specifies the sources of data for comparing actual results to set targets. In this example, the agency will conduct monitoring visits to the refugee camp and will rely on reports by latrine assistants in order to find out whether latrines have been constructed and are being used appropriately. To make sure women have adequate access to latrines, staff will conduct focus group discussions with women and girls. Engineers' output records and testing records will be used to verify whether enough water is provided.

Logframe planning invites managers to clearly state the conditions on which a project's progress depends. Managers should make the assumptions they are relying on in their planning explicit. They should state the external factors that need to be in place so that the goals of the project can be met. In this example, the agency relies on other agencies to provide services and on government border guards to improve security. If the government denies access to NGO staff, the NGO will not be able to deliver. If refugees leave the camp, the NGO's latrines will not contribute to reaching the health goals for them.

These kinds of documents are now widely used in development and humanitarian relief, and institutional donors often ask for them as part of a funding application.[2] Under the name "logic model," they are also used in the planning and delivery of social policy in domestic contexts—organizations use them to plan, for example, HIV prevention programs, domestic violence projects, and programs for young people deemed "at risk" of poverty.[3]

This chapter will examine the history and the role of the logframe in order to bring out more clearly some of the presuppositions of humanitarian relief as it is practiced today. In order to understand how projects have become the unit of accounting and measurement, how populations in need have become an essential part of projects, and how projects have become measured so as to be potentially comparable in a market for products, it is important to examine the history of management practices in humanitarian relief.

Work in the social studies of science and technology,[4] and in the anthropology of policy,[5] as well as critical studies of accounting,[6] have drawn our attention to the implications of the tools and technologies used in different fields of practice. Management tools like the logframe do not determine what people do, but they shape it: they shape what people get to see and know about the world, and people's ideas about what the task before them is.

The logframe has had its critics in development and humanitarian

2. INTRAC and South Research, "Recent Developments in GTZ's Use of the ZOPP," in *A Tool for Project Management and People-Driven Development: Proceedings of the INTRAC and South Research Workshop on LFA and OOIP, Leuven, Belgium, 16-18 May 1994*, pt. 1, *Main Report* (Oxford: INTRAC, 1994), 28–29; and Saeko Nakabayashi, "The Japanese Version of Project Cycle Management: Adoption, Adaptation, and Application of Zopp—A Comparative Analysis of Methods and Methodologies," ISS Working Paper Series/General Series, Working Paper 319 (The Hague: Institute of Social Studies, 2000).

3. Joseph S. Wholey, *Evaluation: Promise and Performance* (Washington, DC: Urban Institute, 1979); Janet Collins et al., "Evaluating a National Program of School-Based HIV Prevention," *Evaluation and Program Planning* 19, no. 3 (1996): 209–18; Constance C. Schmitz, *Leaders against Family Violence: A Fictionalized Account of a W. K. Kellogg Foundation-Sponsored Cluster Evaluation* (Battle Creek, MI: W. K. Kellogg Foundation, 1998).

4. Bruno Latour, *Science in Action: How to Follow Scientists and Engineers through Society* (Cambridge, MA: Harvard University Press, 1987).

5. See, for example, Marilyn Strathern, ed., *Audit Cultures: Anthropological Studies in Accountability, Ethics, and the Academy* (London: Routledge, 2000).

6. Alistair M. Preston, David J. Cooper, and Rod W. Coombs, "Fabricating Budgets: A Study of the Production of Management Budgeting in the National Health Service," *Accounting, Organizations and Society* 17, no. 6 (1992): 561–93; Michael Power, *The Audit Society: Rituals of Verification* (Oxford: Oxford University Press, 1997); Anthony G. Hopwood and Peter Miller, eds., *Accounting as Social and Institutional Practice*, Cambridge Studies in Management 24 (Cambridge: Cambridge University Press, 1994); Peter Miller, "Governing by Numbers: Why Calculative Practices Matter," *Social Research* 68, no. 2 (2001): 379–96; Peter Miller and Ted O'Leary, "Mediating Instruments and Making Markets: Capital Budgeting, Science, and the Economy," *Accounting, Organizations and Society* 32, no. 7/8 (2007): 701–34; and Michele Chwastiak, "Taming the Untamable: Planning, Programming, and Budgeting and the Normalization of War," *Accounting, Organizations and Society* 26, no. 6 (2001): 501–19.

relief, and not all aid agencies use it today.[7] But the logframe has changed the environment for all aid agencies, whether they use the logframe or not. This tool has created the project as a unit of planning and production, the implications of which I discussed in chapter 1. It has also laid the basis for the market for projects examined in chapter 2. It has focused on results but by inserting them in these sets of boxes it has separated evidence of results from broader questions of coverage of people's needs and broader consideration of possible effects. It has linked results to costs, and it has thus made it possible, in principle, to compare projects. The logframe also has created the "beneficiary" as the specific part of a population in need that is selected to be served. It has also created the "beneficiary" as the part of the population in need that can be produced as having been helped, and sold to higher levels in the bureaucracy and external funders.

Tracing the history of the logframe will take us inside state bureaucracies as well as business consultancies. This history is driven by politics with a capital *P*, by high hopes for progressive reform, and by distrust of government. It is also driven by politics with a small *p*, regarding issues of power and control within organizations. It also has a specific history in shifting development doctrines and in discussions about how staff could be managed within development organizations.

The History of the Market for Relief and the Transformation of the State

NGOs are usually conceived of as being separate from the state, and the history of particular NGOs is often written separately from that of the state. From this perspective, NGOs are construed as objects, which exist initially in an autonomous fashion but which are then lamented to have been colonized by the state from the outside.[8] But it is important not to

---

7. Tina Wallace, Sarah Crowther, and Andrew Shepherd, *Standardising Development: Influences on UK NGOs' Policies and Procedures* (Oxford: WorldView Publications, 1997); Des Gasper, "Evaluating the 'Logical Framework Approach' towards Learning-Oriented Development Evaluation," *Public Administration and Development* 20, no. 1 (2000): 17–28; Jens B. Aune, "Logical Framework Approach and PRA—Mutually Exclusive or Complementary Tools for Project Planning?," *Development in Practice* 10, no. 5 (2000): 687–90; Robert Chambers, *Whose Reality Counts? Putting the First Last* (London: Intermediate Technology, 1997); David Hulme and Michael Edwards, *NGOs, States, and Donors: Too Close for Comfort?* (New York: St. Martin's Press, 1997); and Hulme, "Projects, Politics, and Professionals: Alternative Approaches for Project Identification and Project Planning," *Agricultural Systems* 47, no. 2 (1995): 211–33.

8. See the discussion in Wallace, Crowther, and Shepherd, *Standardising Development*, which recognizes also NGOs' own desire for growth as an important factor; see also Hulme and Edwards, *NGOs, States, and Donors*.

forget that NGOs have long been constituted and shaped by state policy.[9] In their present form, relief and development NGOs are partly a product of the expansion of contracting out state services to nonprofit and for-profit private actors, which was made possible through administrative reforms. Relief as we know it today exists partly as a result of the broader transformation of the Western state, and it still forms part of that transformation.[10]

It would be tempting to portray this transformation as a story about "neoliberalism." Indeed, much current writing, both celebratory and critical, on the administrative reforms that I am concerned with here date the origins of these reforms to the early 1980s. Scholars attribute these reforms to the power of "New Right" ideologies in the Reagan and Thatcher era. The reforms are sometimes portrayed as an incursion of the market into the state, and scholars will sometimes emphasize the influence of private-sector actors, such as the lobbying efforts of management consultants.[11]

But for a fuller understanding of these reforms and their implications, they need to be situated in a longer and more complicated history. While of course the early 1980s mark a significant point in this history, the origins of these reforms date back to a much earlier period. As Christopher Hood has pointed out, patterns in arguments about the good state recur across historical contexts, dating back to antiquity.[12] In the twentieth century in the United States, results-based reforms date back at least to the progressive era. Progressives in the early twentieth century targeted corrupt and inefficient city governments; on the federal level, progressive efforts led, for example, to the Budget and Accounting Act of 1921.[13]

While the political right has generally been supportive of these reforms, huge impetus was added by progressives, who had high hopes and noble intentions to make government more rational and effective.

9. Peter D. Hall, *Inventing the Nonprofit Sector and Other Essays on Philanthropy, Voluntarism, and Nonprofit Organizations* (Baltimore: Johns Hopkins University Press, 1992).

10. Ulrich Brand et al., *Global Governance: Alternative zur Neoliberalen Globalisierung? Eine Studie von Heinrich-Böll-Stiftung und WEED* (Münster: Westfälisches Dampfboot, 2000); Brand et al., eds., *Nicht-regierungsorganisationen in der Transformation des Staates* (Münster: Westfälisches Dampfboot, 2001); see also Janice Gross Stein, "Humanitarian Organizations: Accountable—Why, to Whom, for What, and How?," in *Humanitarianism in Question: Politics, Power, Ethics*, ed. Michael Barnett and Thomas G. Weiss (Ithaca, NY: Cornell University Press, 2008), 124–42.

11. Jonathan Boston et al., *Reshaping the State: New Zealand's Bureaucratic Revolution* (Auckland: Oxford University Press, 1991).

12. Christopher Hood, *The Art of the State: Culture, Rhetoric, and Public Management* (Oxford: Clarendon Press, 1998).

13. Robert H. Wiebe, *The Search for Order, 1877–1920* (New York: Hill and Wang, 1967); Michael McGerr, *A Fierce Discontent: The Rise and Fall of the Progressive Movement in America, 1870–1920* (Oxford: Oxford University Press, 2003); on municipal research bureaus see also in Thomas Medvetz, *Think Tanks in America* (Chicago: University of Chicago Press, 2012), 58–60.

In the period after the Second World War, it was administrations on the left in the United Kingdom and the United States that pushed the agenda of results-based management. In the United Kingdom, Labor prime minister Harold Wilson initiated a review of the civil service when the Left came to power in 1964 after thirteen years.[14] In the United States as well, administrative reform was pushed forward in the early 1960s by the left-of-center administration of John F. Kennedy with the help of Robert McNamara.[15] In both cases, progressive administrations were mistrustful of state bureaucracies, which they perceived as having served elites and which they wanted to make accountable on behalf of a broader coalition of voters whom they claimed they represented. In both cases, these administrations had high hopes for what rational government could achieve in terms of social reform. In both cases, these governments had limited resources to pursue their visions.

Business did provide important models for these reformers to draw on, but these management tools are hybrids in their origins, and in their careers often traveled across the boundary between the state and market and back. The biography of a reformer like Robert McNamara illustrates this point. McNamara was trained in economics, mathematics, and business administration, served in the Office of Statistical Control of the United States Army Air Forces during World War II, and became the first nonfamily member to serve as president of the Ford Motor Company. McNamara came into the Department of Defense as a businessman, bringing with him experts in business management. But, perhaps more significantly, he was a modernizer in both worlds—business and the military—putting to work technical expertise independently of tradition, the history of specific organizations, upbringing, or life experience. He later became the first president of the World Bank who was not a banker.

Administrative reforms are not only imposed on state organizations from the outside or from above, they are also fueled by the concerns of some professionals inside the state, as, Christopher Humphrey, Peter Miller, and Robert Scapens,[16] for example, have pointed out, and as we will also see below.

14. Denis Saint-Martin, "Management Consultants, the State, and the Politics of Administrative Reform in Britain and Canada," *Administration & Society* 30, no. 5 (1998): 533–68.

15. Bertram M. Gross, "McNamaran Management," *Public Administration Review* 25, no. 3 (1965): 259–61; Gross, "The New Systems Budgeting," *Public Administration Review* 29, no. 2 (1969): 113–37; Allen Schick, "The Road to PPB: The Stages of Budget Reform," *Public Administration Review* 26, no. 4 (1966): 243–58; and Chwastiak, "Taming the Untamable."

16. Christopher Humphrey, Peter Miller, and Robert W. Scapens, "Accountability and Accountable Management in the UK Public Sector," *Accounting, Auditing & Accountability Journal* 6, no. 3 (1993): 7–29.

From Citizens to Beneficiaries

Results-based management has changed the way the state imagines its own success and how it imagines "the people," the human targets of its policies. Western states have shifted from policies with broad goals and expansive yet nonspecific responsibilities toward people to a regime of accountability for specific results on the level of the intervention.

When scholars have discussed the state's vision or imagination, they have often critically examined how the state constructs aggregates of the population as a whole. Michel Foucault provides a classic account of how the modern state created the "population" as an aggregate object of concern in the context of public health and biopolitics.[17] James Scott has examined various large-scale projects of "development" with regard to the abstractions it engenders.[18] Arjun Appadurai has examined the use of aggregates in the colonial state.[19]

But the state's use of aggregates has changed its meaning in the context of more recent developments. The vision of the 1960s was of a state with a broad set of services available for all citizens, if they chose to claim them, and hopes for development for all based on economic growth. Today, aggregate measures, on the one hand, also operate on a global level, as evidenced by the Millennium Development Goals. On the other hand, with the rise of results-based management, a different set of numbers, which has been neglected by the critical literature on quantification and aggregation, also begins to matter.

Today, any unit of government is under pressure to not only set goals for any unit but to aim for measurable results. As a result of this pressure, policies focus not on aggregate information about populations but on data on specific groups of people who have been selected and intervened upon—a shift in emphasis that has both sociological and political implications. It is not just that citizens have become objects of bureaucratic apparatuses in various ways, a process examined in some detail by both

17. Michel Foucault, *The History of Sexuality*, vol. 1, *An Introduction*, trans. Robert Hurley (New York: Pantheon Books, 1978); and Ian Hacking, *The Taming of Chance*, Ideas in Context 17 (Cambridge: Cambridge University Press, 1990).

18. James C. Scott, *Seeing Like a State: How Certain Schemes to Improve the Human Condition Have Failed* (New Haven, CT: Yale University Press, 1998).

19. Arjun Appadurai, *Modernity at Large: Cultural Dimensions of Globalization* (Minneapolis: University of Minnesota Press, 1996); see also Umamaheswaran Kalpagam, "Colonial Governmentality and the 'Economy,'" *Economy and Society* 29, no. 3 (2000): 418–38.

classic and contemporary work on state bureaucracies.[20] If we consider the populations encountered in the context of those *not* encountered, we see how citizens are now selected and how some of them become part of a result to be maximized. These results become evidence of success, independently of the size of the population in need. Citizens become the beneficiaries of an intervention, arguably no longer an end of policies, but a means of the appearance of politics.

PPB and Repertoires of Rationalization

The reform of government budgeting during the Kennedy and Johnson administrations marked an important step forward for the project of linking planning with results for a single organization. Planning, Programming, and Budgeting (PPB) introduced key themes of all later versions of results-based management, and these themes were to be important for later developments, such as the logframe. In PPB, as in later reforms, government bureaucracy was treated as if it were a business organization, and officials drew on the knowledge of business management experts. Budgeting was to be done by results rather than input; and the focus was to be on measurable outcomes. Managers were freed from commitment to any particular part of the organization. PPB sought to make bureaucracies more accountable and more efficient, but it did so in ways that began to undermine the apparatuses by which citizens could be served broadly.

The Kennedy and Johnson administrations took place at a time of vibrant critique of social inequalities and high hopes for social reform. There was renewed interest in channeling resources toward addressing social problems in the South and in the cities.[21]

---

20. Susan Wright, ed., *Anthropology of Organizations* (London: Routledge, 1994); Wright, *Parish to Whitehall: Administrative Structure and Perceptions of Community in Rural Areas*, Gloucestershire Papers in Local and Rural Planning 16 (Gloucester: Gloucestershire College of Arts and Technology, 1982); Jeff Collmann, "Clients, Cooptation, and Bureaucratic Discipline," in *Administrative Frameworks and Clients*, ed. Jeff Collmann and Don Hadelman, Social Analysis 9 (Adelaide: University of Adelaide, 1981), 48–62; John Clarke et al., *Creating Citizen-Consumers: Changing Publics and Changing Public Services* (London: Sage Publications, 2007); and Elizabeth Vidler and John Clarke, "Creating Citizen-Consumers: New Labour and the Remaking of Public Services," *Public Policy and Administration* 20, no. 2 (2005): 19–37.

21. As a contemporary observed, "There was confidence in the ability of government to eradicate hard-core social and human problems and in its ability to specify and reach long-range objectives. A few years earlier President Kennedy had predicted a moon landing in this decade. Why not set concrete targets for a wide range of social endeavors?" Schick, "Systems Politics and Systems Budgeting," *Public Administration Review* 29, no. 2 (1969): 144.

Democrats had seen huge electoral gains, but incoming progressives were mistrustful of the hierarchies they had inherited from the previous government. Johnson assumed the presidency at a moment when both the Right and the Left were critical of government bureaucracies. The antiauthoritarian left questioned the state apparatus as oppressive and unaccountable. Policy makers began to anticipate the end of the postwar expansion of the economy, and the balance of payment deficit was beginning to impose constraints. Kennedy and Johnson aimed to rein in public spending.[22]

With PPB, Robert McNamara revolutionized the way the Defense Department drew up its budget in the years following 1961.[23] In the 1940s and 1950s, officials reported their budget line by line according to the type of expense, such as personnel, stationery, operations, maintenance, and construction. This was done separately for each military division, be it army, navy, or air force. PPB linked budgeting with planning. Each budget was now done according to the goal and measurable outcome the resources were designated for—according to output rather than input. According to the Department of Defense, PPB "instilled a process that essentially defines a procedure for distributing available resources equitably among the many competing or possible programs."[24]

Michele Chwastiak has analyzed the advantages that PPB offered Kennedy and McNamara in confronting the military bureaucracy that they had inherited.[25] Traditionally, the leaders of each division of the military would say what and how much was needed based on "security needs," which was difficult to challenge for a civilian secretary of defense. The new budgeting device allowed McNamara to pass over the military expertise of staff with battleground experience and privilege his own expertise and training as well as the expertise of his team of systems analysts. It put him and his experts in a unique position to compare and scrutinize existing programs.[26] PPB enables a systematic comparison of programs based on an analysis that relates the achievement of certain goals to cost. This comparison conceives of any particular program as expendable, and it

22. Aaron Major, "Hanging in the Balance: Global Capitalism and the American Welfare State" (PhD diss., New York University, 2008).

23. Schick, "Systems Politics," 138.

24. "Planning, Programming, Budgeting, and Execution: The Historical Context," on US Department of Defense's official website, accessed November 19, 2009, http://www.defenselink.mil/comptroller/icenter/budget/histcontext.htm (site discontinued); quoted in Chwastiak, "Taming the Untamable," 507.

25. Chwastiak, "Taming the Untamable"; see also Paul Y. Hammond, "A Functional Analysis of Defense Department Decision-Making in the McNamara Administration," American Political Science Review 62, no. 1 (1968): 57–69.

26. Chwastiak, "Taming the Untamable," 510.

was the program managers who were providing data used to justify cuts in expenditures.

In the Defense Department, most decisions involved how to best secure safety for all Americans based on hypothetical conflict scenarios, so the comparison among projects in general did not involve comparisons among specific people to be served. But the tools of system analysis could be used to compare programs that directly related to different populations, and, in some cases, decisions that implied a choice between different populations to be protected were considered. Some of the analyses invited by the Department of Defense's Office for Systems Analysis concerning US priorities regarding its extended commitments during the Cold War fall into that category.[27] Some of the planning of civil protection within the United States also involved the comparison of costs for protecting specific parts of the territory, and thus specific parts of the population.[28]

In hindsight, PPB was just one chapter in the long history of administrative reform.[29] The impact of PPB itself in the government of the United States varied among government agencies, and the concrete tools it proposed never fully took hold.[30] Results-based management has since taken various forms and has been implemented with uneven results. Richard Nixon followed up on the agenda of results-based management when, in his second term, he introduced management by objectives inspired by the business management ideas of Peter Drucker.[31] Jimmy Carter introduced zero-base budgeting.[32] During the 1980s and 1990s, so-called new public management ideas gained influence in varied ways in a number of Western countries.[33] The 1993 Government Performance and Results Act

27. See, for example, Draft Presidential Memo on NATO Strategy and Force Structure, January 7, 1969, and Draft Presidential Memo on Asia Strategy and Force Structure, February 1, 1969, Box 4, Tabs A-F, Draft Presidential Memos, 1968–1969, Papers of Alain Enthoven, LBJ Presidential Library, Austin, TX.

28. See, for example, Memorandum for the President, "Civil Defense" First Draft, October 28, 1963, Box 1, Vol. 1, Strategic Offensive and Defensive Forces, Part 1, Papers of Alain Enthoven, LBJ Presidential Library, Austin, TX.

29. Hood, Art of the State.

30. Allen Schick, "A Death in the Bureaucracy: The Demise of Federal PPB," Public Administration Review 33, no. 2 (1973); 146–56; Edwin L. Harper, Fred A. Kramer, and Andrew M. Rouse, "Implementation and Use of PPB in Sixteen Federal Agencies," Public Administration Review 29, no. 6 (1969): 623–32; and Steven E. Jablonsky and Mark W. Dirsmith, "The Pattern of PPB Rejection: Something about Organizations, Something about PPB," Accounting, Organizations and Society 3, no. 3/4 (1978): 215–25.

31. Peter F. Drucker, The Practice of Management (New York: Harper and Brothers, 1954).

32. Allen Schick, "The Budget as an Instrument of Presidential Policy," in The Reagan Presidency and the Governing of America, ed. Lester H. Salamon and Michael S. Lund (Washington, DC: Urban Institute Press, 1985), 91–125.

33. Christopher Hood, "Exploring Variations in Public Management Reform of the 1980s," in Civil Service Systems in Comparative Perspective, ed. Hans A. G. M. Bekke, James L. Perry, and Theo A. J. Toonen (Bloomington: Indiana University Press, 1996), 268–87.

renewed efforts in the United States. Today, results-based management is at the top of the agenda for international organizations as well as international efforts toward government reform.

Administrative reforms have come in spurts and have nowhere fully achieved their vision. But whenever reformers attempted to improve public bureaucracies—regardless of their specific ideological orientation or motivation—they drew on one version or other of results-based management.

In an atmosphere where both the Left and the Right have been critical of bureaucracies, the repertoire of results-based management has set the framework within which politicians and administrators respond to critics on the left and on the right. It has also been the framework within which ministers and civil servants defend expenses in response to external audiences.

The Logframe's Histories

The logframe itself was conceived for the American development agency USAID by a management consultant firm in the late 1960s. A version of results-based management for frontline activity, the rise of logical framework analysis also has to be understood in the context of a broader shift within the ideological orientation of development aid and its conceptual tools, as well as in the context of a shift in the structure of USAID as an organization.

From Growth to a Focus on the Poor

In the 1950s and 1960s, the focus of international aid was on economic development and, more particularly, on economic growth as measured in Gross National Product (GNP). As Martha Finnemore notes in her study of the World Bank, "Development during these years was understood to be increasing GNP, or perhaps GNP per capita."[34] The hope was that growth in turn would lead to a higher standard of living and to less inequality in developing nations.

The role of international aid was seen principally as an initial source of capital. Investments in modern, industrial sectors were thought to trigger growth and more investment and thus help developing nations "catch

---

34. Martha Finnemore, "Redefining Development at the World Bank," in *International Development and the Social Sciences: Essays on the History and Politics of Knowledge*, ed. Frederick Cooper and Randall Packard (Berkeley: University of California Press, 1997), 207.

up" with industrialized nations. It is interesting to reflect on the category "modern, industrial sector." According to Erik Thorbecke, "Clearly the adoption of GNP growth as both the objective and the yardstick of development was directly related to the conceptual state of the art in the 1950s. The major theoretical contributions which guided the development community during that decade were conceived within a one-sector, aggregate framework and emphasized the role of investment in modern activities."[35] USAID at this time put an emphasis on large infrastructural projects, such as dams, power stations, and highways.[36]

The aim of development and the measure of its success in the 1950s and 1960s was growth on a national level, and later, to some extent, national unemployment figures. Macroeconomic indicators have an interesting social history. Timothy Mitchell has described how "the economy" as an aggregate concept on the national level was created by Keynesian economists.[37] Daniel Speich has traced the history of GDP with a special emphasis on debates around its use in comparing developing countries.[38] More differentiated economic data was not necessarily readily available. As Thorbecke explains, "The reliance on aggregate models was not only predetermined by the . . . conceptual state of the art but also by the available data system which in the 1950s consisted almost exclusively of national income accounts."[39]

By the mid-1960s, the optimism of the first years following independence for the new African and Asian states had been dampened; growth— if and when it happened—did not have the desired results. Growth generally failed to trickle down, and there was now more inequality than there was before. In one response to this, dependency theorists pointed at the structural heritage of colonialism, arguing that biased terms of trade prevented former colonies from catching up. Within conventional development economics, experts sought a better understanding of the role of different sectors and subsectors and began to rethink their earlier celebration of all modern sectors and their dismissal of agriculture. Development aid during the 1970s began to have a stronger focus on basic needs

35. Erik Thorbecke, "The Evolution of the Development Doctrine and the Role of Foreign Aid, 1950–2000," in Foreign Aid and Development: Lessons Learnt and Directions for the Future, ed. Finn Tarp and Peter Hjertholm (London: Routledge, 2000), 20.

36. Finnemore, "Redefining Development," 207.

37. Timothy Mitchell, "Fixing the Economy," Cultural Studies 12, no. 1 (1998): 82–101.

38. Daniel Speich, "Der Blick von Lake Success: Das Entwicklungsdenken der frühen UNO als 'lokales Wissen,'" in Entwicklungswelten: Globalgeschichte der Entwicklungszusammenarbeit, ed. Hubertus Büschel and Daniel Speich (Frankfurt: Campus, 2009), 143–74; and Speich, "The Use of Global Abstractions: National Income Accounting in the Period of Imperial Decline," Journal of Global History 6, no. 1 (2011): 7–28.

39. Thorbecke, "Development Doctrine," 22.

and on helping the poor directly. Also in response to these critiques, more aid was delivered to rural areas.

Linking Effort and Outcome

Both critical audiences at home and US Congress have always demanded that expenses for foreign aid be justified. When doubts grew about the overly optimistic assumptions of an aid policy based on modernization theory, pressure for justification rose. Both GDP growth and unemployment figures operate at some distance from any concrete activities by agents of development. USAID was admonished to spend more time evaluating and assessing its own efforts.

A report by the management consulting firm Booz Allen Hamilton concluded in 1965: "It has often been said that AID has an inadequate memory. Evaluation reports on projects in process or completed are rare. . . . In spite of substantial evaluation efforts, frequently on an ad-hoc basis it is still true that AID has not yet developed a systematic process to appraise the consequences and results of its program operations and to exploit the rich accumulated experience by the agency."[40]

Certain features of USAID made it harder to consistently evaluate its efforts. According to the report, one issue was "vague planning": "In general there was no clear picture of what a project would look like if it were successful—the objectives were multiple and not clearly related to project activities." The paper bemoans "unclear management responsibilities": "There were many important factors outside the control of project managers not stated as such (external factors) which made it difficult on the part of the project managers to accept responsibilities for outcomes."[41]

These two factors also meant staff could not, reasonably, be held responsible for the results of an intervention; they could not with their own efforts guarantee good evaluations for their own projects. According to the business management doctrines of the time, this presented a problem for staff as well as for management trying to motivate staff.[42] Evaluation appeared "as an adversary process: in the absence of clear project targets evaluators tended to use their own judgment as to what they thought

---

40. Quoted in Allen Schick, *USAID Program and Operations Assessment Report No. 4: A Performance-Based Budgeting System for the Agency for International Development* (Arlington, VA: USAID Development Information Services Clearinghouse, 1993), 27.

41. Quoted in PARTICIP GmbH, *Introduction to the Logical Framework Approach (LFE) for GEF-Financed Projects—Reader* (Berlin: Deutsche Stiftung für Internationale Entwicklung, 2004), 4.

42. Luc Boltanski and Eve Chiapello, *The New Spirit of Capitalism* (London: Verso, 2007).

was 'good' and 'bad.'"[43] Evaluation results would become the basis for arguments about what was desirable and undesirable in general instead of fostering constructive actions for project improvement.

In response to these concerns, Leon Rosenberg, first with Fry Associates, then with Practical Concepts Incorporated, developed Logical Framework Analysis (LFA)—the logframe—under contract to USAID in late 1969.[44] USAID adopted LFA in 1971, and it radically changed, first, the way projects were evaluated and, later, the way they were planned.

The logframe responded to the management concerns discussed above. It clarifies goals and responsibilities. The logframe invites managers to be clear about what their assumptions are. It allows them to make uncertainty explicit and externalize it. Once assumptions and risks are listed in a separate column, it is possible to separate one's planning from them. Managers can focus on what is really in their control and need no longer worry about column 4. They can turn their focus to column 2 and work toward concrete measurable results for selected people.

As the logframe's initial manual puts it, "It is within the ability of the responsible manager to ensure that inputs result in outputs; we hold him accountable. . . . On the other hand, the hypothesis—if outputs then purpose—is problematic. There is enough uncertainty in this hypothesis that the project manager is held accountable to the reasonable man rule—he must do what a reasonable man would do to realize the purpose, but he is not held accountable for that result."[45]

This approach also rhymed well with the shift toward a focus on the poor and basic needs, and rural areas. Today, some critics suggest that the logframe creates an undue focus on countable outputs and leaves out what might be considered "soft" indicators. But it is worth comparing the evidence encouraged by logframes to the national economic indicators used earlier: the logframe might privilege single goals and counting of outputs, but in ways that are quite different from the "economic" concerns at the time. The logframe actually made it possible to highlight results in non-economic areas, such as food aid, medical assistance, and training.

The logframe, which is also accused of standardizing development and corrupting NGOs, in fact played a central role in facilitating the move to bring in NGOs to implement state policy in the first place. Logical Framework Analysis links broad policy goals with discrete projects; this makes

43. PARTICIP GmbH, *Introduction to the Logical Framework Approach*, 4

44. Leon J. Rosenberg and Larry D. Posner, *The Logical Framework: A Manager's Guide to a Scientific Approach to Design and Evaluation* (Washington, DC: Practical Concepts Incorporated, 1979). I am indebted to Matthew Hall for his help in locating this document.

45. Rosenberg and Posner, *Logical Framework*, II-2.

it easier for governments to cut pieces out of large programs and hire an NGO to do the work; it can be the basis of a contract and creates a fiction of comparability across projects. Indeed, the donors can leave the initiative to NGOs to some extent and invite them to identify and propose projects.

Susan Watkins, Ann Swidler, and Thomas Hannan have diagnosed a shift in development practice toward lofty aims as concrete goals turn out to be unachievable. They note: "In essence, failure to achieve more limited goals led to ever more ambitious goals as success seemed to require radical transformation of the basic human and social materials required for development."[46] This is certainly part of what has been going on in the development world to the extent that there has been a new emphasis on participation and empowerment, but I would suggest that the reverse has also happened, and the logframe is both a symptom and a driver of this. Disillusioned regarding their ability to fulfill the ambitions of development, managers focused on very concrete outcomes, such as, literally, the number of tents and pots and pans distributed. This in turn has facilitated the rise of humanitarian relief NGOs—in the midst of and differing from development NGOs—since the 1990s.

The Logframe and Humanitarian Relief Today

The logframe today has many critics. NGO staff tend to see it as an imposition by donor agencies,[47] and even among officials in donor agencies, it has its detractors. In the terms of the cultural binaries that structure office talk in formal organizations across different fields, it is associated with numbers, paperwork, and managerialism and opposed to values, service to those in need, and practical experience. In other words, it is associated with formal rationality and critiqued in the name of substantive rationality. There are alternative approaches to planning and delivering relief and development work. However, it is important to realize that these alternative approaches have come to meet the logframe on its own terrain today.

The logframe has created the project as the unit of humanitarian and development work. It has encouraged a focus on single goals.[48] The logframe focuses attention on measurable results for a specified target popu-

46. Susan Cotts Watkins, Ann Swidler, and Thomas Hannan, "Outsourcing Social Transformation: Development NGOs as Organizations," *Annual Review of Sociology* 38 (2012): 296.

47. See, for example, Wallace, Crowther, and Shepherd, *Standardising Development*.

48. See Hulme's critique. He argues that this practice is questionable for public projects, where goals are necessarily multiple and contested. Hulme, "Projects, Politics, and Professionals."

lation in a specific time frame. In this way, the logframe separates evidence of results from questions of coverage, and it separates evidence of one specific project result from all other effects NGO work might be having.[49]

The logframe specifies costs for the project and relates these costs to very narrow outcomes. In a memo accompanying the example that I discussed above, ECHO advises agency staff to be as specific as possible in this procedure: "It is also useful to split costs by result if this is possible so that the actual costs of each result can be determined from the logical framework with personnel and direct support costs apportioned on an appropriate basis."[50] In the example provided (see table 3.1), costs for sanitation, water, and hygiene are thus listed separately.

In these ways, the logframe helps to make this project comparable to other projects, and it can rationalize the exchange between donor agencies and NGOs. The proposed project helps specific people, who, one assumes, would otherwise be without the water and sanitation facilities they need. It also provides a water and sanitation package for 8,000 people for €578,974, which can be compared to a similar package for another group of people.

The logframe has made its way into the assumptions that structure relief work in humanitarian organizations even if they do not use the logframe itself. The project, with specific outcomes, definite start and end dates, and established budgets is today the unit of relief work. The attempt to set specific goals is built into project planning. The emphasis on specific results is reflected in the development of specific sectors for humanitarian relief, which now form the basis of emergency response planning, goal setting for projects, and humanitarian coordination meetings.

Alternative planning tools often draw on rich philosophical traditions, such as ideas about participation and empowerment, but they are often used as an alternative approach to planning a project, not as alternatives to project planning.[51] Participatory Rural Appraisal, for example, draws on the ideas of educator Paulo Freire and on the anthropological tradition. The tradition provides a variety of tools to facilitate knowledge sharing: a relief worker might, for example, facilitate a social mapping exercise where locals share information about the layout of the village, different social

49. As David Mosse puts it, "Success and failure are policy-related judgements that obscure project effects." Mosse, *Cultivating Development: An Ethnography of Aid Policy and Practice* (London: Pluto Press, 2005), 19.

50. "Humanitarian Actors—Framework Partnership Agreement."

51. Mosse, "The Making and Marketing of Participatory Development," in *A Moral Critique of Development: In Search of Global Responsibilities*, ed. Philip Quarles van Ufford and Ananta Kuma Giri (London: Routledge, 2003), 43–75.

groups, or available services. Seasonal diagrams can be used to analyze the major changes that affect a household or a community over the year. Preference rankings can be used to clarify stakes and interests. Wealth ranking generates information about vulnerability and social hierarchies.[52] These techniques may lead to better projects, and many experienced development and relief workers will say that the more participatory the planning, the better the results. But these approaches do not in themselves change the time frame or budget range of projects. Even if they are not just used to fill in a logframe, they do not in themselves change the type of commitment that is mediated by the market for projects. The questions to be asked of interventions that aim to bypass the market for projects are not about commitment in terms of ideas or attitudes, but commitment in terms of resources and the time frames of planning and follow-up.

Conclusion

Humanitarian relief, as it is organized today, depends on a number of conditions of possibility. Listing them can help us explain how we arrived at the present moment, and, at the same time, helps to circumscribe in a precise way the form that relief takes. When we ask what needs to be in place for humanitarian relief to exist the way it exists today, it may seem obvious to think of the triggers of crisis first: natural disasters, say, and civil wars. But it is important to also mention a more fundamental lack of access to basic provision for populations across the world and to think through all the social conditions of possibility of this condition of possibility. This includes the incapacity or unwillingness of the state to respond to peoples' needs, the broader history of structural adjustment, dependency, and ultimately, perhaps, the shortcomings of the capitalist system. If these are the conditions of need, we need to add the conditions of response, such as the apparent interest of Western governments and the Western public in the relief of suffering, as well as in influence and stability. As Thomas Haskell has pointed out, the *means* for learning about suffering and the means for providing relief for distant publics have a very specific history.[53]

52. Robert Chambers, *Rural Development: Putting the Last First* (London: Longman, 1983); and Chambers, *Whose Reality Counts? Putting the First Last* (London: Intermediate Technology, 1997); see also the account in chapter 5 of Erica Bornstein, *The Spirit of Development: Protestant NGOs, Morality, and Economics in Zimbabwe* (Stanford, CA: Stanford University Press, 2005).

53. Thomas L. Haskell, "Capitalism and the Origins of the Humanitarian Sensibility, Part 1," *American Historical Review* 90, no. 2 (1985): 339–61; and Haskell, "Capitalism and the Origins of the Humanitarian Sensibility, Part 2," *American Historical Review* 90, no. 3 (1985): 547–66.

This chapter has focused specifically on the transformation of the state, which created the conditions for contracting to NGOs and for-profit private actors, the loss of hope in development, and the emergence of a global scale for the comparison of products. The logframe has been an essential element in this last aspect of the history of humanitarianism and it has profoundly influenced the assumptions and management practices that shape the way humanitarian NGOs do their work. The next chapter will consider the history of a specific form of humanitarian authority as another important condition of possibility of humanitarian relief in its present form.

From the early attempts at results-based management in government, government bureaucracy was treated as if it were a business organization, and officials drew on the knowledge of business management experts. Budgeting was to be done by results rather than inputs, and the focus was to be on measurable outcomes. Managers were freed from commitment to any particular part of the organization and any particular group of clients. Populations in need then became opportunities for organizations to produce results, and entered into competition with each other.

Government reform has sought to make bureaucracies more account-able and more efficient, but it did so in ways that began to undermine the apparatuses with which citizens could be served broadly. The logframe came out of a later version of results-based management within USAID. In this case, efforts to make development aid more responsible resulted in the abdication of responsibility beyond very specific project aims.

A logframe invites managers to state explicitly the assumptions on which the success of the proposed intervention depends. The rational-ization of bureaucracy as a whole has also included some important assumptions, and I would suggest these assumptions lie at the heart of the tragedy of the history of planning in aid and relief, in particular, but in public-sector provision more generally. We have rationalized parts of organizations to make them more effective and efficient, and we have put much thought and effort into this project. In pursuing this, we have assumed that these improved parts would also add up to a better whole. It is this assumption that is proving problematic in the fragmented system of humanitarian relief, and it is in that sense that earlier ambitions of "de-velopment" have been shortchanged.

FOUR

The History of Humanitarian Authority and the Divisions of the Humanitarian Field

There is no "yes," to which there would not be a "no" attached. You can do whatever you want, and you can find twenty beautiful ideas that are for it and twenty that are against it. One might think it is like in love or hate or hunger, where taste has to be different so that everyone gets that, which is his due. ROBERT MUSIL, *THE MAN WITHOUT QUALITIES*

Chapters 1, 2, and 3 have focused on the ways in which the shared space of humanitarian relief agencies produces common practices. This chapter explores how that same shared space also produces differentiation among relief agencies.

Humanitarian staff today disagree with each other about some fundamental questions of policy and practice and engage in intense debates about the very essence of what it means to be a humanitarian actor.[1] Relief workers confront dilemmas in which many lives are at stake—both in their immediate context and in their larger implications. Should humanitarian agencies accept funding from a belligerent Western country to deliver aid alongside its army? What conditions from recipient countries should agencies be will-

---

1. See also Volker Heins, *How to Meet the First Public Obligation: Contending Discourses in Humanitarian Organizations*, KSG Carr Center Working Paper (Cambridge, MA: KSG Carr Center, n.d.).

ing to accept in order to be allowed to operate? Humanitarian agencies develop very different answers to these questions.

I argue that in developing their distinctive positions, agencies do not just draw on different principles or different intellectual or national histories, though those matter too.[2] I will show that agencies are also oriented by each other and actively seek to differentiate themselves from other agencies within the global field of humanitarian relief NGOs.

Today, when we, as a donating public, confront distant suffering, our response is mediated by both aspects of the logic of practice of the humanitarian field: by the shared practices and routines of the field of humanitarian relief and also by the reflexive position-taking and symbolic positioning within it.

In what follows, I first sketch some of the differences among humanitarian organizations as described by relief workers and observers. I then show how humanitarianism has become a field in which symbolic position-taking makes sense. The shared space of humanitarian relief agencies has its origins in a move that combined the authority of the suffering produced by war with the authority of the states responsible for that suffering, and the authority of the medical profession. This humanitarian authority contributes to the specific role relief agencies play today, and the history of this authority is the last element that I will add to my analysis of the conditions of possibility of relief in its current form.

The analysis of the shared space of humanitarian relief agencies as a space of symbolic distinctions with reference to humanitarian authority will help us make sense of the diversity of humanitarian agencies. It can also help us explain recurring patterns in the debates about the relationship of humanitarian action to politics, religion, and human rights. These debates are often framed in terms of stark choices between purity and pollution or between naiveté and realism. Contributions from observing academics tend to restate these dilemmas or develop an analysis that travels back and forth between the poles of these debates. From a sociological perspective, we can take these oppositions as an object of analysis and explain the rhetorical positions with reference to the social space that makes them possible. While some field approaches posit a division between economic and cultural capital, I suggest we can map organiza-

2. Michael Barnett, "Humanitarianism Transformed," *Perspectives on Politics* 3, no. 4 (2005): 723–40; for an in-depth exploration of how national differences do matter, see Sarah S. Stroup, *Borders among Activists: International NGOs in the United States, Britain, and France* (Ithaca, NY: Cornell University Press, 2012). Stephen Hopgood and Leslie Vinjamuri, "Faith in Markets," in *Sacred Aid: Faith and Humanitarianism,* ed. Michael Barnett and Janice Stein (Oxford: Oxford University Press, 2012), 37–54, also situate their argument about the market for donations in opposition to intrinsic differences.

tions along the dimensions of field-specific capital, on the one hand, and different kinds of capital dependent on other fields, such as the political field or the religious field, on the other hand.

Differences

To understand how distinctions among humanitarian actors are drawn by humanitarian actors themselves, I asked the desk officers and directors of operations I spoke to what made their agency different from other agencies. Distinctions were drawn first between NGOs, on the one hand, and UN agencies and states, on the other hand—but many officers also drew distinctions within the NGO community.

Respondents often began by mentioning their own area of expertise or mandates: "We are a medical relief agency," a desk officer with MSF France told me. "We are obviously distinctive because of our focus on children," a desk officer with Save the Children UK said. One desk officer at a Christian agency explained his own organization's lack of technical focus by making a distinction between department store agencies and boutique agencies. His organization, he explained, was a department store agency. A boutique agency, he said, specializes rather narrowly and then picks and chooses projects that fit that narrow identity; a department store agency, on the other hand, offers projects in a variety of geographical areas and technical fields of expertise.

Some desk officers distinguished between organizations of different specializations and different sizes, but respondents also brought up more evaluative distinctions. Some agencies, they said, are "professional" agencies, whereas others are "less professional." Another distinction concerns whether an agency is delivering assistance directly in the field or whether it works with partners. For many agencies with a background in development, working through partners is not just a technical decision but an important ethical or political choice. Many Christian agencies, for example, work exclusively through local partners and are proud of how well they work with them.

Officers distinguished between financially independent and government-dependent agencies, and between religious and secular agencies. There is also a dividing line between national camps of agencies. That line is drawn in different ways. It is sometimes drawn between French organizations and all other organizations, sometimes between Continental-European organizations and Anglo-Saxon organizations; it is sometimes drawn between European and American organizations, and sometimes between American organizations and all other organizations.

Many relief workers recognized the special position of the ICRC and of MSF and other groups of "French doctors." The ICRC stands out because of the special role accorded to it by international humanitarian law, and because of its independence. MSF is famous for going to difficult places first, for its outspoken stances, and also for its criticism of other agencies. MSF is also uniquely successful in raising funds from the general public. Professionals working inside MSF are fiercely proud of the open climate of discussion and criticism in the organization. Médecins du Monde (MDM) grew out of a split within MSF and remains close to MSF's version of humanitarianism.[3] Action Contre la Faim also sees itself in an independent, French tradition; it was founded in 1979 by a group of intellectuals around anti-Communist intellectual Bernard-Henri Lévy in response to the conflict in Afghanistan and works on hunger in crises and emergencies.

The distinction between religious and secular organizations matters in the field of humanitarian relief, but the boundary between religious and secular is perhaps most sharply drawn by some in the secular camp. A desk officer with an agency without any explicit religious affiliation told me: "We are very far from some NGOs such as World Vision, Christian Aid, and Samaritan Purse, which are big NGOs but Christian NGOs with a different mandate compared to our mandate, [they are] not only working for the benefit of the population in my mind but also for political issues. . . . People in the streets—they don't see any difference. For them it's all NGOs at the end; among ourselves we really see a line between those NGOs and us."[4]

Within organizations associated in some way with religion, I have talked to people for whom their agency's religious affiliation did not matter much. One desk officer explained that she was hired despite having a different Christian denomination than the one her employer was associated with, and that the agency's link to faith was just like any other commitment to values in an organization. A head of operations in a different agency explained that the religious affiliation was useful mainly because of the advantages it brings to the organization's fundraising.

For others who work for humanitarian organizations, however, faith

3. See Pascal Dauvin and Joanna Siméant, *Le travail humanitaire: Les acteurs des ONG, du siège au terrain* (Paris: Presses de Sciences Po, 2002).

4. I report this here, of course, not so much as evidence of any objective difference between "secular" and "religious" agencies with regard to integrity, but rather as evidence of a symbolic boundary drawn by some within secular agencies.

is inseparable from everything they do. A desk officer at an evangelical agency in the United Kingdom, mentioned faith as the distinguishing mark of his organization:

I think we're very different from other agencies. I think we have a fundamentally different belief that Christ came into this world, lived and died and left behind not a building society or a bank or any other institution. He left the church. And the church is responsible not just for making a Hindu into a Christian or a Muslim into a Christian in a sort of very limited spiritual sense. Actually Christ left behind the church for all people in every way to engage with all of humanity, and therefore the idea of working through the church to engage with human beings, not just in a spiritual sense, but physically, mentally, emotionally, economically, and politically. . . . What is distinctive is the idea of working with the church, working through the local church and challenging the church to go beyond its narrow views of vision.

In this account, being a Christian humanitarian does not only mean taking a position within humanitarian relief. It also involves a distinctive move within the faith community. What drives this man's professional work is not so much a desire to see humanitarian agencies more engaged with faith and values, but a desire to see more activist and more socially engaged churches.[5]

Fields and Difference

I have discussed humanitarianism as a field in the most general sense of a shared environment. But to understand the role of differences among organizations, it is necessary to go back just a little into the history of organizational sociology. The scholars who initially talked about fields in the English-speaking social sciences—a group now known as the neoinstitutionalists—used the concept to emphasize the role of culture. While others at the time stressed rationality, technical demands, and efficiency, the neoinstitutionalists drew attention to culture and norms as relatively independent factors in organizational life.[6] In an important shift, scholars emphasized that organizations are oriented toward legitimacy as well

5. For an engaging account of these kinds of symbolic struggles inside churches in the US context, see Penny Edgell Becker, *Congregations in Conflict: Cultural Models of Religious Local Life* (Cambridge: Cambridge University Press, 2000).

6. John W. Meyer and Brian Rowan, "Institutionalized Organizations: Formal Structure as Myth and Ceremony," *American Journal of Sociology* 83, no. 2 (1977): 340–63.

as output or income maximization. They also pointed out that organizations, as they contend with political pressure, uncertainty, and professional ideologies, mimic each other's practices rather than responding in a rational way—if indeed there is one rational way.[7]

In emphasizing culture and norms, these scholars chose to emphasize *shared* culture and *shared* norms. Scholars in this tradition thus emphasize and explain homogeneity among actors. But how do we understand heterogeneity within a field? And, as we are talking about legitimacy as well as about profit or income, what are the sources of legitimacy and the origins of that legitimacy?

We might look to population ecology approaches, which have taken up the question of diversity much more explicitly: scholars have asked why there are so many different kinds of organizations. In this, they follow biologists who had asked: Why are there so many different kinds of animals?[8] These approaches usefully examine specialization and diversification as the result of populations of organizations competing for a finite set of heterogeneous resources. But they have not offered a theory of the boundaries of ecologies and of the kind of stakes that actors compete over specifically in the social world or in specific social worlds.

The work of Pierre Bourdieu and colleagues offers tools that can help inquire into shared understandings as well as symbolic differentiation among actors.[9] It also offers a starting point from which to formulate

7. Walter Powell and Paul DiMaggio, *The New Institutionalism in Organizational Analysis* (Chicago: University of Chicago Press, 1991).

8. Michael T. Hannan and John Freeman, "The Population Ecology of Organizations," *American Journal of Sociology* 82, no. 5 (1977): 929–64; Glenn R. Carroll and Anand Swaminathan, "Why the Microbrewery Movement? Organizational Dynamics of Resource Partitioning in the US Brewing Industry," *American Journal of Sociology* 106, no. 3 (2000): 715–62.

9. A group of scholars within the neoinstitutional tradition also ask the question about diversity within fields of organization. Drawing on Friedland and Alford's contribution to Powell and DiMaggio's 1991 volume, they ask how institutional logics intersect within a field, producing diversity. It is one of the strengths of this position, also in contrast to the tendencies of Bourdieu's work, to connect organizational sociology to a certain version of macrosociology; but in contrast to the position adopted here, the logics are thought to be constituted externally to the field, and the approach does not develop a theory of the relative autonomy of a field with a consideration of internal sources of symbolic divisions within a field; see Roger Friedland and Robert R. Alford, "Bringing Society Back In: Symbols, Practices, and Institutional Contradictions," in *The New Institutionalism in Organizational Analysis*, ed. Walter W. Powell and Paul J. DiMaggio (Chicago: University of Chicago Press, 1991), 232–63; Michael Loundsbury, "Institutional Sources of Practice Variation: Staffing College and University Recycling Programs," *Administrative Science Quarterly* 46, no. 1 (2001): 29–56; Patricia H. Thornton and William Ocasio, "Institutional Logics and the Historical Contingency of Power in Organizations: Executive Succession in the Higher Education Publishing Industry," *American Journal of Sociology* 105, no. 3 (1999): 801–43; and Loundsbury, "Institutional Rationality and Practice Variation: New Directions in the Institutional Analysis of Practice," *Accounting, Organizations and Society* 33, nos. 4–5 (2008): 349–61.

more specific empirical questions. Bourdieu's theory of cultural production starts with a sociologist's interest in questions about truth, beauty, and religion. In the tradition of a theory of differentiation, following Weber among others, Bourdieu asks how these concerns have become organized into separate spheres of life. He advances a specific set of claims about fields such as art, religion, and law that are organized around versions of the sacred, around supposed transcendental sources of authority.[10]

These fields, Bourdieu argues, are organized around a field-specific form of symbolic capital. Actors in a field compete for field-specific capital; positions in the field are differentiated according to the type of capital they draw on—that is, whether they draw on capital specific to the field or on forms of capital external to the field. A field is relatively autonomous from other areas of practice and mediates the impact of other resources, such as economic capital or state power. This approach can help us to understand the specific role humanitarian authority plays in the relationship among these agencies but also with regard to their role in international politics.

I have argued that humanitarian managers have to produce "good" projects, and I have described the patterns of exchange in this field as a market in projects. A market, according to Harrison White, is not defined by a product or territory but by producers, who look to what other producers are doing; producers look to each other rather than, say, to "the market" in the abstract or to consumers.[11]

This is precisely what we see also when humanitarian agencies orient themselves toward each other. But it is important to note that in contrast to markets for simpler commodities, humanitarian relief is not so much directly shaped by competition for funding or other economic resources as by competition for a specific type of symbolic capital, humanitarian authority.[12] This is what makes symbolic differentiation between producers and their products so important, and this is what makes the space these agencies share not only a market but also a field in Bourdieusian terms.

10. Pierre Bourdieu, "The Force of Law," *Hastings Law Journal* 38 (1987): 805–53; Bourdieu, "Genesis and Structure of the Religious Field," *Comparative Social Research* 13 (1991): 1–44; Bourdieu, *The Rules of Art: Genesis and Structure of the Literary Field* (Stanford, CA: Stanford University Press, 1995).

11. Harrison C. White, *Markets from Networks: Socio-Economic Models of Production* (Princeton, NJ: Princeton University Press, 2002).

12. Stephen Hopgood and Leslie Vinjamuri analyze differences among agencies as a form of branding; Hopgood and Vinjamuri, "Faith in Markets." The advantage of a specifically Bourdieusian approach is to link an account of competition more strongly with the relative autonomy of the authority of humanitarian relief.

Humanitarian Ideas, Humanitarian Practice, and the Genesis of the Field of Humanitarian Relief

Some scholars in the Bourdieusian tradition have a tendency to assume that there are fields and to think of fields and their symbolic dimensions in static terms, but field theory provides only a starting point for further inquiry. Each field has a specific history. A given area of social life might or might not be bounded by shared assumptions, and it might or might not be shaped by competition for symbolic capital. Fields can be more or less autonomous or lose the character of "fieldedness" altogether.[13]

Of any given area of practice, we might thus ask: Is it fielded? Are actors oriented by each other? How is symbolic capital defined? What are the distinctions that matter among actors? What exchanges do we see with actors from other fields? In the case of humanitarian action, we might ask: How does this field relate to politics, the market, religion, or human rights? This approach allows us to bracket the question of what humanitarianism is. The task is not to adopt one definition or another but to observe the universe of all claims that are made in the name of humanitarianism and to try to discern patterns in the ways these claims are distributed historically, geographically, and across social and symbolic space, and to try to discern patterns in the authority these claims command.

It is important to distinguish between the history of humanitarian ideas, the history of humanitarian practice, and the history of the field of humanitarian organizations. Humanitarian ideas have a long history, dating back at least to the founding texts of the major religions,[14] but they are institutionalized in very different ways. Humanitarian practices—the universe of practices that at one point claimed or were claimed to be humanitarian, that is, claimed to be responding to human suffering out of a concern for human dignity alone—are diverse and have a long history.

We can find humanitarian practice in the long history of charity toward the poor and the sick.[15] In the history of humanitarian prac-

---

13. Craig Calhoun, "Habitus, Field, and Capital: The Question of Historical Specificity," in *Bourdieu: Critical Perspectives*, ed. Craig Calhoun, Edward Lipuma, and Moishe Postone (Chicago: University of Chicago Press, 1993), 61–88.

14. Philippe Ryfman, *Une histoire de l'humanitaire* (Paris: La Découverte, 2008).

15. We can find it in responses to famines or natural disasters. Local authorities responded to famines in the Elizabethan era in England; see Alexander de Waal, *Famine Crimes: Politics and the Disaster Relief Industry* (London: James Currey, 1997). The earthquake of Lisbon features prominently in the modern imagination because of its impact on philosophers and writers and the wide-ranging response by the government and the military; see Susan Neiman, *Evil in Modern Thought: An Alterna-*

tice, the history of the medical profession, and in particular the history of public health, are important.[16] Services for wounded soldiers are an important forerunner of current humanitarian practice; they have always been part of warfare, though of course not every leader accorded the same weight to such services, and not every wounded soldier would be tended to.[17] Even during the eighteenth century, commanders debated how to adjust care for wounded soldiers to changing conditions of warfare and discussed the status of doctors on the battlefield.[18]

The important point here is that in much of its history, humanitarian practice has been part of religious practice, medical practice, or political practice, and practices claiming to be humanitarian continue in those fields today. The history of the humanitarian field asks how the field has emerged as a field of practice distinct from other realms of practice, and how people and organizations have started to identify as humanitarian such that competing claims to be humanitarian have became intelligible and important.[19]

In order to answer these questions and to write this history, we have to accord a special place to the history of the International Committee of the Red Cross (ICRC).[20] It is this history that makes current debates about humanitarianism possible. The most controversial debates concerning humanitarianism today are not about the relative weight of humanitarian as opposed to other considerations; they are about who or what is legitimately humanitarian.

I will distinguish three phases in the history of the humanitarian field. The first phase is marked by the invention of modern humanitarianism as

tive History of Philosophy (Princeton, NJ: Princeton University Press, 2002). Philippe Ryfman's short account in Une histoire de l'humanitaire is also very good on the multiple prehistories of humanitarian relief.

16. Doctors responded to the plague in Athens; see Dorothy Porter, Health, Civilization, and the State: A History of Public Health from Ancient to Modern Times (London: Routledge, 1999); see also George Rosen, A History of Public Health (Baltimore: Johns Hopkins University Press, 1993); Stephen Greenberg, "Plague, the Printing Press, and Public Health in Seventeenth-Century London," Huntington Library Quarterly 67, no. 4 (2004): 508–27.

17. De Waal, Famine Crimes; Pierre Boissier, Histoire du Comité international de la Croix-Rouge: De Solférino à Tsoushima (Paris: Plon, 1963). Historians date the beginning of medical care for wounded soldiers to the early professional armies of urban empires in Mesopotamia; in Roman times, medical staff traveled with the imperial army; see Richard Gabriel and Karen Metz, A History of Military Medicine (New York: Greenwood Press, 1992). See also Michael Barnett, Empire of Humanity: A History of Humanitarianism (Ithaca, NY: Cornell University Press, 2011), 76–97.

18. John Hutchinson, Champions of Charity: War and the Rise of the Red Cross (Boulder, CO: Westview Press, 1996).

19. Compare here to Barnett, Empire of Humanity, who, with a different analytical agenda, offers unique insights about the history of humanitarianism in insisting that the world (and politics) has always been part of humanitarianism.

20. Barnett, Empire of Humanity; Boissier, Histoire du Comité international de la Croix-Rouge.

a distinctive practice by the ICRC. The second phase begins with the initial challenge to this position by MSF. This challenge opened up a space in which actors could claim humanitarianism from different positions. The third phase is the expansion of the field since the late 1980s.

1. The ICRC and the Invention of Humanitarianism, 1863–1971

The Red Cross was founded in 1863 as the International Committee for Relief to the Wounded, following the initiative of a Swiss businessman, Henri Dunant. On a business trip in 1859, Dunant had witnessed the suffering in the aftermath of the battle of Solferino, an engagement in the Austrian-French War, and had started an international campaign for better care for those wounded in war. He initially assembled a group of men from established Geneva families, the "Committee of the Five," and then worked to facilitate the formation of national Red Cross societies all over Europe in the following decades.

It is important to note that the Red Cross organizations were not the first to service those wounded in war, and that they were not the only ones doing so at the time. Florence Nightingale had achieved international fame for her medical work in the Crimean War a few years earlier, in 1854. When Dunant tended to the wounded in Solferino, he served alongside aristocratic ladies from the surrounding towns who also organized relief.[21] When the Geneva Committee sent the surgeon Louis Appia to the sites of the Schleswig war as a neutral observer in 1864, he was much impressed by the medical work that members of the Order of St. John were already doing on the battlefield. The Protestant branch of the Order of St. John, said to originate from an order serving pilgrims in a hospital in Jerusalem, had been revived in Prussia as a relief organization by aristocrats at the beginning of the nineteenth century. It was prepared to deploy mobile hospitals by 1850.[22] When Dunant first published *A Memory of Solferino* in 1862 and sought support for his initiative to improve health care in war, he was able to join an existing conversation among military surgeons and generals who had already been concerned with the issue.

The efforts of Dunant and the Geneva Committee, and later the ICRC, were unique and pioneering in a number of ways. The Red Cross was not content to quietly do relief work; it became the first organization to ask for public recognition of its role. It publicly claimed a right for nonstate

---

21. Henry Dunant, *The Origin of the Red Cross: Un souvenir de Solferino* (Philadelphia: John C. Winston Co, 1911).
22. Hutchinson, *Champions of Charity*.

actors to treat wounded soldiers; it was the first organization to claim neutrality and the first to initiate a cross-national, nongovernmental effort. It linked humanitarian action to a specific profession, the medical profession, and to crisis and war. Eventually, its founders secured provisions that today form the main body of international humanitarian law. The Geneva Conventions of 1882 and 1906 mandated protections for civilians and wounded and captured soldiers. They also accorded special status to medical personnel wearing the emblem of the Red Cross.

The ICRC chose a very specific position vis-à-vis the system of states, which was to have important consequences for the history of humanitarianism. The "Committee of the Five" was initially brought together by a concern to avoid the suffering described by Dunant. It is significant to note that as their next step they moved to organize a conference and decided to try to invite government delegates. From its very beginnings, the ICRC chose independence from any specific state—but thereby it accepted allegiance to the system of states as a whole.

The reactions to the initiative represented by the Geneva Committee reveal a great deal about the different ways humanitarianism can encounter preexisting state interests. In response to the invitation to join the conference and support the formation of a national Red Cross society in 1864, British leaders stated that they had already drawn the lessons from the Crimean War, and insisted that they could take care of the wounded in war by themselves. The Prussian government was the most energetic sponsor of the project; its leaders recognized the problem regarding the wounded in war but felt that they could not afford the expense of having the military address this problem. The French king let himself be convinced that he could not let this opportunity for leadership pass to the Prussians.[23]

The ICRC has had its critics from the very beginning of its history. Interestingly, Florence Nightingale had little sympathy for Dunant's proposal: "Such a [voluntary relief] society would take upon itself duties which ought to be performed by the government of each country and so would relieve them of responsibilities which really belong to them and which they can properly discharge and being relieved of which would make war more easy."[24] Nightingale spoke as an Englishwoman, whose government had accepted the need to provide for the victims of war as a matter for the state. She objected to the plan for an international Red Cross for the same reason that led the Prussian leadership to support it—

23. Ibid.
24. Ibid., 40.

namely that it would ease the pressure on political actors to look after the victims themselves. As a critique of humanitarianism, this analysis is echoed in some of MSF's positions today: MSF leaders, like Nightingale, are always wary of the temptation for humanitarian actors to be institutionalized in a way that eases pressure on political authorities to address suffering in a more sustainable way.

Yet for many decades there was no organization able to challenge the Red Cross's authority on its own terms—the Red Cross was able to define nongovernmental, transnational, neutral humanitarian relief. There were other relief organizations, such as Save the Children, founded in 1919 as an offshoot of the Fight the Famine Fund, which had been set up to deal with the consequences of the First World War. But these other organizations were no real competition for the ICRC. Either they followed the model of the ICRC very closely and added to its efforts in lobbying for legal protections for more groups of people. Or they lacked the engagement with the system of states altogether or confronted states more in the manner of a political social movement. They also lacked a basis in one of the professions and were thus assimilated into the broader sector of charities and reform groups. In the 1930s, with the rise of isolationist tendencies, and the economic crisis, funds for cross-national philanthropic efforts decreased.

During the Second World War, some of the limitations of the ICRC's mode of operation became clear for all to see. In response to the detention and killing of several million Jews, Sinti, and Roma, as well as handicapped people, the ICRC was largely limited to sending aid packages to the concentration camps. For whatever limited access the German Nazi regime chose to grant them, the ICRC accepted a duty to be silent. Advocacy groups, both internal ones, like the Hungarian Red Cross, and external, such as the Jewish World Congress, urged the organization to do more. But this criticism of the ICRC came from advocacy groups, not from actors who were in a position to offer the public a better response.[25] There were no major alternative claims from within the ICRC paradigm in this case as to how to do this type of work. Critics may have found fault with the ICRC or with humanitarianism in general, but a claim to be a better humanitarian agency than the ICRC would not have been understood until the foundation of Doctors Without Borders in the early 1970s. That development changed the terms of the debate dramatically and established humanitarianism as a field of competing positions.

---

25. Jean-Claude Favez, *The Red Cross and the Holocaust* (Cambridge: Cambridge University Press, 1999).

2. MSF and the Establishment of a Field of Symbolic Differentiation, 1971–1989

Classical humanitarian action as provided for in international law is bound by the principles of neutrality, impartiality, and independence. As I have discussed, the version of humanitarian action established by the ICRC includes a far-reaching respect for state sovereignty. The foundation of MSF as a breakaway from the ICRC in the early 1970s opened up a space for nongovernmental action beyond these narrow confines, while still claiming the heritage of the ICRC.

MSF initially grew out of the experiences of a group of doctors who served with the ICRC during the Nigerian civil war. When the southern Nigerian region of Biafra announced its secession in 1967, the central military government responded with war. Aid workers serving in Biafra witnessed what they thought were war crimes as well as a famine, which they felt was the result of a blockade from the government in the north. The ICRC interpreted the principle of neutrality in a way that committed it to silence, and asked its doctors to sign agreements not to speak about their observations. They were expected to simply serve the wounded on both sides.

Bernard Kouchner and some of his colleagues interpreted this as a gag order. They argued they would be complicit in the atrocities they witnessed if they did not speak out, and denounced the Nigerian government and the ICRC in the French media. In collaboration with a French journal for the medical profession they founded MSF in 1971 and made a commitment to bearing witness and speaking out as well as treating the ill. They also proclaimed the right of humanitarian actors to get involved across borders, independently of the consent of receiving governments.[26]

When Bernard Kouchner and his colleagues broke with Red Cross protocol to denounce the Nigerian government, they created a new practical position for Western actors vis-à-vis crisis and conflicts in the non-Western world. It is significant that these doctors invented this position in the aftermath of decolonization, when a broad range of interested actors were confronting the question of how to relate to the non-Western world in a new way.[27]

26. Anne Vallaeys, *Médecins Sans Frontières: La biographie* (Paris: Fayard, 2004). But see Philippe Biberson and Ronny Brauman, "Le 'droit d'ingérence' est un slogan trompeur," *Le Monde Internationale*, 23 October 1999.

27. Frederick Cooper and Randall Packard diagnose a similar role for "development" in a similar historical moment: development "provided a means by which imperial powers could reconcile them-

MSF's position was unique in many ways. Unlike the ICRC, MSF sought to raise awareness and speak out as well as provide medical assistance. Unlike Western states, it abstained from larger political engagement. Unlike social movements or development NGOs, MSF drew on its professional expertise and focused on suffering alone rather than on rights or empowerment. At a time when religious charities played an important role in aid and development, MSF was fiercely secular.

MSF broke with the ICRC, which at the time embodied humanitarianism. But in doing so, MSF did not simply walk away from humanitarianism; in its rhetoric and practice it claimed to represent humanitarianism in a purer form. In this way, MSF has played a role for the humanitarian field that is similar to the role Gustave Flaubert played for the field of art in the analysis of Pierre Bourdieu.[28] One account of Flaubert's role casts him as the lone genius who invented art for art's sake and as the ideal of the starving artist in the second half of the nineteenth century in France. In Bourdieu's analysis, this account is both true and not true: Flaubert's career did indeed mark in many ways the "invention" of art as an autonomous practice, but this was also overdetermined by his social and historical position. Flaubert rebelled against the art sanctioned by the academies and sponsored by the inheritors of the ancien régime. He embraced art for art's sake and the poverty of the artist, but this position was structurally enabled by the new market for literature provided by the bourgeoisie. This social position enabled him to provide a biting analysis of all the other actors' social dependency. It also led him to establish the art world as a world of inverted values, where artistic value is defined in opposition to all other forms of sponsorship and valuation.

In the same way it would be both true and not true to say contemporary humanitarianism was invented by MSF. MSF in 1971, like Flaubert ca. 1857, denounced the efforts of its predecessors as compromised by the world and its interests. MSF provides a critical and, we might say, sociological analysis of other actors. It insists on radical independence and prioritizes principles and purity, over money certainly, but also over access to vulnerable populations, and at times over practical results. The principled action of Kouchner and associates invented a form of humanitarian action—witnessing as an end in itself—that is similar to the ethos of purists in other fields. Witnessing is not constrained by any considerations

selves to their loss of power while maintaining a connection with their ex colonies and a continued sense of their mission in shaping their future." Cooper and Packard, introduction to *International Development and the Social Sciences: Essays on the History and Politics of Knowledge*, ed. Cooper and Packard (Berkeley: University of California Press, 1997), 7.

28. Bourdieu, *Rules of Art.*

of efficacy, just as art for art's sake is not dependent on political success, market success, or truth value.

An important part of MSF's independence is financial, as it draws a relatively small proportion of funds from donor governments.[29] It is also intellectual and practical. Since its founding, it has continued to make decisions that are controversial among other humanitarian actors. MSF was among the few agencies to provide medical assistance to the muja-hideen in Afghanistan during the 1980s.[30] During the Ethiopian famine in 1984, the Ethiopian government launched a resettlement campaign, which MSF saw as causing tens of thousands avoidable deaths. Many aid agencies chose to participate in the resettlement efforts; MSF spoke out against it.[31]

MSF France ceased operations in the camps of Goma during the Rwanda crisis, when it felt the relief efforts there were doing more harm than good.[32] Following the 2004 tsunami, MSF announced it had received enough donations to satisfy needs in the region—a move that other orga-nizations protested as being irresponsible vis-à-vis the affected popu-lations, as well as vis-à-vis the cause of fund-raising for humanitarian purposes.[33]

MSF's willingness to speak out brings the organization many admirers but makes it at times unpopular within the aid community itself, a fact that MSF staff sometimes joke about with some pride. Officials in other NGOs sometimes express fear that MSF's stance—principled or radical, depending on one's point of view–will make it harder for them to do their job. When MSF adopts an uncompromising stance in negotiating access to a population with local power holders, they say this makes it harder for others to operate in any given territory.

The innovations of MSF's positions are real and have opened up a range of positions; yet they were made possible by a set of social condi-tions and interests that continue to shape but also define the limits of the impact of *sans frontièrisme*. MSF emerged at a moment when colonial ties had sensitized Western publics to the plight of non-Western populations, yet decolonization had limited the ways Western governments could intervene directly; many students and intellectuals found themselves dis-

---

29. Development Initiatives, *Public Support for Humanitarian Crisis through NGOs* (London: De-velopment Initiatives, 2009).

30. Vallaeys, *Médecins Sans Frontières*, 397–461.

31. Ibid., 511–51; see also François Jean, *From Ethiopia to Chechnya: Reflections on Humanitarian Action*. (New York: MSF, 2008)

32. Fiona Terry, *Condemned to Repeat? The Paradox of Humanitarian Action* (Ithaca, NY: Cornell Uni-versity Press, 2002).

33. Reuters, "Stop Sending Us Money, French Aid Group Says," January 4, 2005.

illusioned with the hopes of the old Left, while the Cold War also limited the kinds of issues and causes organizations on the left would take on.[34]

Today, MSF often accuses other humanitarian organizations of "losing the faith." The argument here is that if relief agencies cooperate too closely with donor governments, or if they have too broad an agenda for their own work, they compromise the purity of humanitarian action and undermine the respect humanitarian organizations command in the field—a precondition for safe and effective operations.[35] Somewhat ironically, however, MSF's breakaway from the ICRC can also be seen as the beginning of a deregulation of humanitarian action. This argument is made, for example, by David Chandler.[36] Humanitarian law and the protection it provided for humanitarian actors rested on the idea of an unambiguous humanitarian position. MSF's innovation, though it had "purity" on its flags, clearly formulated an alternative to the ICRC, and so called into question the foundations of the enterprise. There was no longer one clear position with the ICRC as its spokes-organization; thus MSF's move made it easier for a range of other actors to claim the label "humanitarian."

3. Expansion since 1989

Since the mid-1970s the humanitarian field has expanded significantly. This may have been partly a result of changed realities on the ground. Decolonization initially changed the conditions under which conflicts were carried out in the Global South. The erosion of Cold War stability contributed further to "new wars," which were internal rather than between sovereign nation-states, and which made civilians especially vulnerable to being caught up in violence.[37] Ecological problems may have been more severe, and population growth, continuing poverty, and the social and economic consequences of restructuring policies contributed to making people vulnerable. But, as Craig Calhoun has suggested, "it is not clear that the last thirty years have seen more natural disasters, more death from wars, or simply more human suffering than earlier eras. That bad things are happening is not, then, sufficient explanation for

---

34. Samuel Moyn traces a similar trajectory in more detail in the excellent *The Last Utopia: Human Rights in History* (Cambridge, MA: Harvard University Press, 2010).

35. Nicolas de Torrente, "Humanitarianism Sacrificed: Integration's False Promise," *Ethics* 18, no. 2 (2004): 3–12.

36. David Chandler, *From Kosovo to Kabul: Human Rights and International Intervention* (London: Pluto Press, 2002).

37. Mary Kaldor, *New and Old Wars: Organized Violence in a Global Era* (Cambridge: Polity Press, 2006).

the prominence of humanitarian action or thinking in terms of humanitarian emergency."[38] Media attention in the West to crises elsewhere has grown, as Martin Shaw has shown,[39] but the specific form this attention has taken, and its distribution, are part of what needs to be explained.

More and more actors have attached themselves to the authority of humanitarian action, making claims to be humanitarian. And more and more resources have been attached to the cause. Official humanitarian assistance, once a very small item in state budgets, has risen from $2.1 billion in 1990 to $12.9 billion in 2012.[40] A large share of these funds is contributed by a small number of donor governments.[41] Donor governments have come to see a broad variety of issues and stakes through the lens of a humanitarian emergency. This list includes civil wars, famines, earthquakes, HIV/AIDS, the civilian costs of war, refugee camps, sexual violence, and the absence of or failing government.[42] Public donations have also gone up, particularly around a number of high-profile crises with some connection to a specific donating public. The conflict in former Yugoslavia in the 1990s brought the "new wars" close to Western Europe. Conflicts in Afghanistan and Bosnia mobilized an Islamic public.[43] The Indian Ocean tsunami in 2004 saw unprecedented levels of public support, partly because it affected many Westerners on Christmas vacation in Thailand and India.

Existing humanitarian organizations have grown. MSF, for example, has grown into an international network of nineteen semi-independent branches with a combined annual budget of $900 million in 2011.[44] Development organizations have moved into relief—this includes the return of organizations such as Oxfam and Save the Children that were initially founded to respond to sudden-onset disasters and wars, then

38. Craig Calhoun, "The Idea of Emergency: Humanitarian Action and Global (Dis)Order," in *Contemporary States of Emergency: The Politics of Military and Humanitarian Interventions*, ed. Didier Fassin and Mariella Pandolfi (New York: Zone Books, 2011), 1. For an attempt to correlate IDP numbers and expenditure that also acknowledges some of the complexities in how these numbers are produced, see James D. Fearon, "The Rise of Emergency Relief Aid," in *Humanitarianism in Question: Politics, Power, Ethics*, ed. Michael Barnett and Thomas G. Weiss (Ithaca, NY: Cornell University Press, 2008), 49–73.

39. Martin Shaw, *Civil Society and Media in Global Crises: Representing Distant Violence* (New York: Pinter, 1996).

40. Development Initiatives, *Global Humanitarian Assistance Report, 2013* (London: Development Initiatives, 2013).

41. Ibid.

42. Calhoun, "The Idea of Emergency."

43. Ismael Yaylaci, "Communitarian Humanitarianism: The Politics of Islamic Humanitarian Organizations" (paper presented at the Workshop on Humanitarism and Religion, American University, Cairo, 3–5 June 2008); Jonathan Benthall and Jerome Bellion-Jourdan, *The Charitable Crescent: Politics of Aid in the Muslim World* (London: I. B. Tauris, 2003).

44. Médecins Sans Frontières, *International Financial Report 2011* (Geneva: MSF International, 2012).

turned to development work, and now are concerned with emergencies again. Oxfam US opened a department for humanitarian relief. World Vision took up emergency work to complement its development work and access funds in these areas.

Religious organizations have long been involved in serving and governing populations in the Global South. They were involved in the colonial era.[45] They had been doing development work; and they had of course been locally engaged in response to war, disaster, and disease for a long time. The influx of attention and resources under the label "humanitarian action" led many of these organizations—some local, some with extensive international links—to engage more with the traditional humanitarian organizations. New agencies were founded and became established. Each high-profile emergency led to the foundation of new small organizations that have been competing with established agencies, including some for-profit organizations.

This expansion has brought agencies closer together around a set of common symbolic and material stakes and has led to two trends. One is a pattern of institutionalization and standardization, as noted by Michael Barnett.[46] The other is an intensified symbolic competition around the label "humanitarianism." Regarding the first trend, humanitarian relief has formalized its knowledge and its training. In this regard, the field is hardly recognizable to those who got involved in the 1970s and 1980s when it was driven by committed volunteers. Since the early 1990s an increasing number of universities have started to offer postgraduate degrees in humanitarian relief. There are more and more continuing education opportunities for aid agency staff. There has been a movement for quality control, triggered by a striving for self-improvement, by competition, and by donor pressure.[47] ALNAP (Active Learning Network for Accountability and Performance), for example, established in 1997, is a network of agencies for learning and increased accountability that encourages sharing of evaluations, publishes practical guidebooks, and facilitates meetings. There have also been various attempts to develop

---

45. John Comaroff and Jean L. Comaroff, *Of Revelation and Revolution: Christianity, Colonialism, and Consciousness in South Africa* (Chicago: University of Chicago Press, 1991); Bertrand Taithe, "Pyrrhic Victories? French Catholic Missionaries, Modern Expertise, and Secularizing Technologies," in Barnett and Stein, *Sacred Aid*; see also Laura C. Thaut, "The Role of Faith in Christian Faith-Based Humanitarian Agencies: Constructing the Taxonomy," *Voluntas: International Journal of Voluntary and Nonprofit Organizations* 20, no. 4 (2009): 319–50; Ryfman, *Histoire de l'humanitaire*.

46. Barnett, *Humanitarianism Transformed*; see also Barnett, *Empires of Humanity*; Peter Walker and Catherine Russ, *Professionalising the Humanitarian Sector* (Cardiff: ELHR, 2010); Peter Walker and Daniel G. Maxwell, *Shaping the Humanitarian World* (London: Taylor and Francis, 2008).

47. Peter Walker, "Cracking the Code: The Genesis, Use, and Future of the Code of Conduct," *Disasters* 29, no. 4 (2005): 323–36.

standards for humanitarian practice, with the Red Cross Code of Conduct as an early list of principles, formulated in 1992. I will examine these efforts and their implications more fully in the next chapter.

The Symbolic Structure of the Field

Common stakes have brought agencies closer together. Within this more integrated space, however, there has also been a lot of debate and disagreement. The expansion of humanitarianism has created a set of common stakes, which create both engagement and competition. How can we make sense of these divisions?

A common response from scholarly observers is to develop typologies. There are three influential typologies of humanitarian relief organizations: that of Abby Stoddard, that of Peter Weiss, and that of Dennis Dijkzeul and Markus Moke. Abby Stoddard compares organizations to determine whether they are Dunantist or Wilsonian, and whether they are in favor of rule-based coordination or not. Dunantist organizations seek to position themselves in a neutral space outside the sphere governed by state interests; Wilsonian organizations are more pragmatic and see their work as compatible with the aims of Western, and in particular as comparable with US, foreign policies. In each of these two camps, some agencies are in favor of working with other agencies to create a community of practitioners, and others insist more on their independence (fig. 4.1).[48] Peter Weiss diagnoses a spectrum of attitudes from classicist to solidaristic (fig. 4.2).[49] Dennis Dijkzeul and Markus Moke draw a map according to whether organizations are independent or subcontractors, impartial or solidaristic (fig. 4.3).[50] With this they take Weiss's representation one step further by recognizing that there are several types of departures from the classicist view.

Each of these typologies points to important differences among humanitarian relief agencies. But they are based on classifying positions rather than classifying the way distinctions between positions are drawn, and the differences discussed do not exhaust the distinctions drawn among agencies. They focus, for example, exclusively on secular agencies

48. Abby Stoddard, "Humanitarian NGOs: Challenges and Trends," in *Humanitarian Action and the "Global War on Terror": A Review of Trends and Issues*, ed. Joanna Macrae and Adele Harmer, Humanitarian Policy Group Report 14 (London: Overseas Development Institute, 2003), 25–36.

49. Ibid.

50. Dennis Dijkzeul and Markus Moke, "Public Communication Strategies of International Humanitarian Organizations," *International Review of the Red Cross*, n.s. 87 (2005): 673–92.

In favor of rule-based coordination	CARE Save the Children US IRC	Oxfam Save the Children UK Concern Worldwide
Independent/ rule-averse	Americares other in-kind donation organizations	Médecins sans Frontières Action contre la Faim Médecins du Monde
	Wilsonian	**Dunantist**
	More dependent on and cooperative with governments Short time horizon Service delivery emphasis	More independent of and oppositional toward government Long time horizon Advocacy emphasis

4.1 Lines of demarcation within the secular NGO traditions. Redrawn from Stoddard, "Humanitarian NGOs," 29.

	Classicists ←→	←→	←→ Solidarists
Engagement with political authorities	Eschew public confrontations	←———————→	Advocate controversial public policy
Neutrality	Avoid taking sides	←———————→	Take the side of selected victims
Impartiality	Deliver aid using proportionality and nondiscrimination	←———————→	Skew the balance of resource allocation
Consent	Pursue as *sine qua non*	←———————→	Override sovereignty as necessary

4.2 The political spectrum of humanitarians and their attitudes toward traditional operating principles. Redrawn from Weiss, "Principles, Politics, and Humanitarian Action," 3.

Independent	ICRC				NPA
		MS			Churches in Biafra
			Oxfam SCF-UK ACF		
				MDM WVI Care CRS IRC	Religious NGOs
Public Service Contractor			SCF-USA		
					US Cold War NGOs
	Impartial				**Solidarity**

4.3 Mental map of large international NGOs. Redrawn from Dijkzeul and Moke, "Public Communication Strategies," 676.

but do not theorize the distinction between religious and secular agencies. They also do not offer an explanation of how these distinctions are produced or an analysis of what this tells us about the relationships with other actors both inside and outside the humanitarian field, in which organizations are embedded. I argue that we can identify the grammar that produces this position-taking in social-theoretical terms. In contrast to those who suggest that these debates are the result of the different orientations and histories that agencies bring to the field,[51] I want to argue they are perhaps more reactions by agencies to each other, and to the opportunities and constraints of the humanitarian field in the present.

I have noted that in Bourdieu's view actors in a field compete for field-specific capital, a specific form of symbolic capital. In order to operate in the real world, actors usually also need some money and links to political power. Actors vary in how they combine different resources. Positions in the field are differentiated according to the combination of types of capital (field-specific or field-external) actors draw on. We expect a field to have an autonomous pole, which is very high in field-specific resources and low on resources from other fields, and an heteronomous pole, which is more dependent on resources from other fields.

This expectation sometimes leads to maps among scholars following Bourdieu that are two-dimensional, with one axis ranging from a predominance of field-specific capital, on the one hand, to a predominance of forms of capital external to the field, on the other hand, and the other axis measuring the total volume of capital. But we can make better sense of the divisions in the humanitarian field if we take into account that the sources of pollution are many and of different kinds. Differences in the humanitarian field can be better understood by positing an underlying dynamic with a double-edged autonomous pole, and various heteronomous poles. Actors within the field treat resources from other fields as sources of pollution.

On the autonomous pole, the ICRC and MSF are independent in slightly different ways, which correspond to different dangers of pollution. The ICRC adheres very strictly to neutrality between warring parties but at the price of a certain dependence on the system of nation-states as a whole; the ICRC accepts state's rights to control access to its territory, for example. MSF insists on speaking out about injustices that staff members observe in the field. With the practice of witnessing, MSF asserts its independence vis-à-vis host countries. At times, this position brings it

51. Barnett, *Humanitarianism Transformed;* Stroup, *Borders among Activists.*

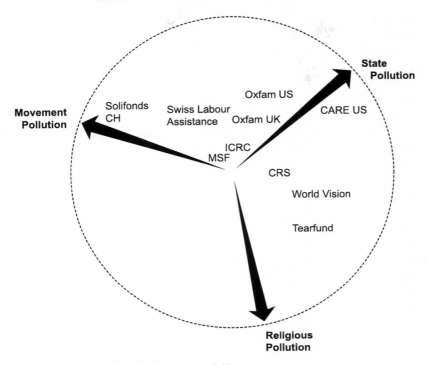

4.4   Purity and pollution in the humanitarian field

somewhat closer to certain nonstate political actors, such as social movements or rebel groups.

The authority of humanitarian relief draws on the suffering of the
people it aims to serve; yet in both of its most distinct forms it prioritizes the purity of humanitarian principles over actual benefits for suffering populations. Both MSF and the ICRC would privilege compliance
with humanitarian principles over serving any particular population. In
its pure form, humanitarianism is humanitarianism for humanitarianism's sake. In contrast to this position of purity, it is possible to identify
other resources as sources of heteronomy or pollution (in the field's own
terms); these could be nonstate political actors or one of many donor governments, they could be religious agendas, money or for-profit activity, or
the media.

Figure 4.4 shows the view of the field in terms of the distribution of
field-specific capital, and some of the key sources of pollution in the field.
The map indicates donor governments, social movements, and religious

organizations as the main sources of pollution—though others could be added; we could imagine it as a space with more dimensions. This is not the only map that can be drawn of relief agencies, but it is one that all organizations have to contend with, insofar as actors draw on claims to be "humanitarian": the classical vision of humanitarianism is the position most distinct from other realms of practice.

I will further explore the symbolic structure of the field by examining how it is expressed in discussions about the relationship between humanitarianism and politics, on the one hand, and that between humanitarianism and religion, on the other hand. Based on an analysis of the field of humanitarian relief organizations and based on a distinction between ideas, fields of organizations, and practice, we can also recast substantive questions about the relationship between humanitarian practice, on the one hand, and politics and religion, on the other.

Humanitarianism and Politics: Ideas, Field, Practices

There has been much debate about the relationship of humanitarianism to politics. Is humanitarianism inherently political? Or are humanitarianism and politics mutually exclusive? ICRC president Claudio Sommaruga gave expression to the second view when he said in front of the UN General Assembly in 1992: "Humanitarianism and political action must go their separate ways if the neutrality and impartiality of humanitarian work are not to be jeopardized."[52] On the other side of the debate, some commentators urge us to accept that humanitarian relief is obviously political—and some advise us to embrace the responsibility that comes with that. Hugo Slim, who has held leadership positions in humanitarian organizations and in the academy, wrote: "Humanitarianism is always politicized somehow. It is a political project in a political world. Its mission is a political one—to restrain and ameliorate the use of organized violence in human relations and to engage with power in order to do so."[53]

52. Quoted in Daniel Warner, "The Politics of the Political/Humanitarian Divide," *International Review of the Red Cross* 833 (1999): 109; it is a topos of debates about humanitarian relief to decry its "politicization." Nicolas de Torrente, president of MSF USA, for example, argued that the use of aid to further political objectives in Iraq violated fundamental humanitarian principles. He sees absolute independence of humanitarian actors as "necessary to ensure that humanitarian action only serves the interests of war victims and not political, religious, or other agendas." De Torrente, "Humanitarianism Sacrificed," 4.

53. Hugo Slim, "Is Humanitarianism Being Politicised? A Reply to David Rieff" (paper presented at the Dutch Red Cross Symposium on Ethics in Aid, The Hague, 8 October 2003), 1. Paul O'Brien, director of CARE in Iraq during the initial phase of the war, responding to De Torrente, concluded: "1) humanitarianism is and should be political 2) humanitarians can and should speak out about the

To make sense of this debate, it is useful to distinguish between different meanings of the term "political," based on a distinction between ideas, fields of organizations, and practice, and then ask how humanitarian organizations relate to those meanings. "Political" at its most general might mean "having implications for the production and distribution of symbolic and material resources," and in that sense humanitarian action in all its versions can be said to be inherently political—indeed almost any social practice is.

"Political" can also mean "associated with organizations in the field of specialized political claim-making, that has the aim of competing for votes, and/or influencing state policies." Humanitarian action might be political in its implication but a humanitarian organization is very different from a political party. The claim to relief suffering situates humanitarian actors in a common terrain with actors like states, human rights organizations, social democratic parties, and feminist movements. Humanitarian NGOs often work closely with states, and many do advocacy in order to influence policies.

But humanitarianism has a center of autonomy of its own. Humanitarian action is identifiable by its distance from politics. Humanitarian action as humanitarian action is not support of a political movement, it is not dependent on party politics in the Western state, and it is not development aid. It is independent of political ideology, it is only conceived for a period of crisis, and it does not have long-term goals. Politics has its own versions of the sacred (the nation, the public sphere, the people, individuals' rights), which in this context are considered a source of pollution.

This independence had been established by the Red Cross and by MSF and is the basis of authority. While it has its roots in cooperation with state actors, its usefulness for politics depends precisely on its relative distance from it. To talk about a military "humanitarian intervention" is to some extent to expresss an oxymoron, as purists will point out. But this is precisely its appeal to those who use it to justify their projects; an odd sort of respect is paid to the autonomy of humanitarian action in exploiting it.

Human suffering may inherently produce a form of authority. This authority has been greatly enhanced as we have come to read more and more issues through the lens of an emergency imaginary, as Craig Calhoun has analyzed it, which demands quick action and solutions based

---

justice or injustice of war and 3) accepting funding from belligerents in war can both make principled and pragmatic good sense." Paul O'Brien, "Politicized Humanitarianism: A Response to Nicolas de Torrente," *Harvard Human Rights Journal* 17, no. 1 (2004): 31.

on what is exceptional about a situation.[54] Various actors—political, familial, or religious—will try to claim the authority produced by the situation. But actors identified as humanitarian have accumulated that type of authority over time and can bring it to any new situation of suffering.

The debate about politics among actors in the field of humanitarian organizations is a staging—explicitly and implicitly—of their relationship to various actors in the political field. One of the dimensions of differentiation in the humanitarian field today can be mapped according to the range of political actors that can pollute the purity of humanitarian relief. The way an agency positions itself vis-à-vis political actors—whether donor states, recipient states, or nonstate actors—will affect its symbolic standing. Humanitarian authority is inversely related to resources accessed through political actors.

The most important actors are donor governments, such as the American USAID and British DfID, and institutional donors, such as the European Union's ECHO. The United States accounts for more than a third of total official humanitarian assistance. The United Kingdom, Germany, the Netherlands, Sweden, and Norway are next on the list of biggest donors. EU countries combined contribute half of the total global official relief budget.[55] The question of the relationship to donor governments has been posed in a new way in the years since Kosovo, and especially during the wars in Afghanistan and Iraq. Major donors could always be suspected of pursuing interests of some kind, but in these cases they were directly involved as parties to the war.[56]

The divisions here are not only between those NGOs that are independently funded and those that are dependent on governments. Donor governments have different positions in relation to the world order and are differently positioned vis-à-vis different crises. The division between French agencies and Anglo-Saxon agencies is related to the distinction between independent and contracting NGOs. French and also Scandinavian agencies seem more independent, not only because of a different ideological content, or a greater independence from their home governments, but also because of the way their home countries are positioned in the global order. The United States has been so important globally in the last couple of decades that "independence" is to some extent measured

54. Craig Calhoun, "A World of Emergencies: Fear, Intervention, and the Limits of Cosmopolitan Order," *Canadian Review of Sociology and Anthropology* 41, no. 4 (2004): 373–95.

55. Development Initiatives, *Global Humanitarian Assistance 2009/2010*.

56. Antonio Donini, Larry Minear, and Peter Walker, "The Future of Humanitarian Action: Mapping the Implications of Iraq and Other Recent Crises," *Disasters* 28, no. 3 (2004): 190–204.

by distance from the US government. The US-led wars against Afghanistan and Iraq produced a polarization within relief—they discredited the United States in the humanitarian community and allowed some other donor agencies to appear in a neutral and peaceful light.

Reputation for independence depends also on which donor an agency is working with, particularly which donor one is working with in which particular crisis. It is a respected strategy, for example, for an agency to seek to match donors to crisis in a way that minimizes interference by strategic interests. A desk officer at a French agency, for example, explained to me that he has made some effort to fund a project in Chad from official sources in the United States rather than work with the French government in an area that used to be under its colonial control.

The lowest field-specific capital is afforded to those who act directly as subcontractors for governments with an obvious political agenda. Military or commercial actors doing so have very little authority in the field. Relationships to other political actors pose related questions about independence. Receiving states are in a position to provide or deny access, and this "resource" can also be a source of pollution. What conditions should an agency be willing to accept for entering a territory, and how might these conditions compromise its independence? The ICRC accepted access in exchange for secrecy in Nazi Germany, in Biafra, and, more recently, in Guantanamo. MSF goes furthest in making an effort not to assent to any compromises when negotiating access to territories—they will speak out against restrictions for humanitarian personnel and will sacrifice access if necessary.

One version of the dilemma regarding compromises for access is addressed in the debate concerning whether or not one should accept armed protection in a territory.[57] The issue arose in Iraq, where it was long virtually impossible to operate independently of the US Army. Does cooperation with the US Army in Iraq on security matters compromise one's status as a humanitarian agency? Agencies may make different choices for various ethical and political reasons, but they would mostly agree that it does, to some extent. Similarly, it is currently necessary to accept protection by the Russian state when operating in Chechnya. How can one be neutral under such conditions? Accepting armed protection has symbolic costs, yet political and economic benefits for any agency.

Nonstate actors can also be a source of pollution. MSF was accused of

---

57. Peter Hoffman, "When Hired Guns Guard Humanitarian Spaces: Norms and Humanitarian Agency-Security Contractor Interactions" (PhD diss., CUNY Graduate Center, 2008). See also James Cockayne and International Peace Institute, *Commercial Security in Humanitarian and Post-conflict Settings: An Exploratory Study* (New York: International Peace Institute, 2006).

getting too close to the Taliban during the Afghan war, when they provided medical aid behind rebel lines. In South Sudan aid workers occasionally became too close to the Sudan People's Liberation Army, which
more than one respondent discussed as a problem for their humanitarian
status. Independence from nonstate actors requires conscious effort and
self-work in everyday interactions in the field, as one relief worker
explained to me regarding the situation in Sudan: "There are a lot of very
charming rebel commanders. And to this day I don't know which of them
were good guys, and which of them were bad guys. But they would come
and talk to me, and we'd have long chats. . . . I don't think there was anything wrong with . . . talking to people, and drinking tea with people.
But you have to make sure that doesn't err over into the side of compro-
mising one's neutrality." He explained that there are many occasions
where it would simply be more convenient to exchange favors with local
actors.

Many people with experience with the left-wing solidarity movement
of the 1980s are active in the sector today. They face a choice as to whether
to associate themselves with the humanitarian field. Solidar, for example,
is a network of agencies with links to the European labor movement that
are increasingly seeking to access humanitarian funds and acquire professional humanitarian skills. Others, such as the Swiss organization
SOLIFONDS, see themselves as supporting struggles of liberation in the
poorest parts of the world. They remain primarily political organizations,
and their humanitarian authority is relatively low.

The Meaning of "Religious": Belief, Field, Practices

The distinction between religious and secular agencies plays an important
role in this field. But what do humanitarians mean by this distinction? It
is worth noting that the distinction is not drawn in terms of ideology,
personal belief, or practices. Secular agencies do not insist that their staff
be atheists, and not all so-called religious agencies care about the personal
faith of their employees. The decisive question for drawing the boundary
between secular and religious agencies is how faith relates to one's work—
more specifically, how adherence to organized religion relates to one's
work, and how the organization as a whole relates to organized religion.[58]

58. For a distinction between mission, donor base, employment policies, and ties, see Thaut, "Role
of Faith"; for a distinction between individual and organizational identity, see Hopgood and Vinjamuri "Faith in Markets."

Religious agencies are those that as organizations evoke beliefs associated with organized religion and target a set of donors identified by their association with organized religion. They may or may not have a formal relationship with organized religion in Western countries and may or may not work through church partners abroad.

Those in secular agencies make a strong distinction between secular and religious agencies. When secular agencies try to distance themselves from religious agencies, they worry about pollution by stakes from outside the humanitarian field.[59] The fear regarding pollution by organizations' interests in the religious field is not in principle different from the fear of political co-optation. Religious pollution is only one of many possible forms of "unpredictability." To the established agencies, celebrity-led efforts also seem determined by outside forces in ways that make them unpredictable and unreliable; newer agencies are often suspected of opportunism.

This worry about pollution finds its expression in a distinction between professional and reliable agencies, on the one hand, and "crazy" or unpredictable agencies, on the other hand. This distinction is also drawn within and among religious agencies. Some religious organizations—such as the Lutheran World Federation, World Vision, and Caritas—played an important part in efforts to develop shared standards and in regulating the sector, most notably in the drafting of the Sphere standards. These organizations are keen to emphasize that their primary engagements are in the field of humanitarian NGOs, not the religious field.

It is worth noting that professionalism in the sense of a commitment to technical quality is not only an adaptation by religious agencies to a secular world; it is itself an ideology with religious origins. Some of the people who are most passionate about the idea of professionalism in humanitarian relief work for religious agencies. Evangelical relief workers have evoked the idea of being good stewards of the money entrusted to them.[60] When I asked a senior member of the Lutheran World Federation and a leading early proponent of the Sphere standards about the role of faith in relief, she replied by quoting Martin Luther: "The Christian shoemaker does his Christian duty not by putting little crosses on the shoes, but by making good shoes, because God is interested in good craftsmanship."

59. For a critique, see Alastair Ager and Joey Ager, "Faith and the Discourse of Secular Humanitarianism," *Journal of Refugee Studies* 24, no. 3 (2011): 456–72. Andrea Paras and Janice Gross Stein, "Bridging the Sacred and the Profane in Humanitarian Life," in Barnett and Stein, *Sacred Aid*, 211–40, also discuss the sacred dimension of ostensibly secular organisations.

60. On this point, see especially Erica Bornstein, *The Spirit of Development: Protestant NGOs, Morality, and Economics in Zimbabwe* (Stanford, CA: Stanford University Press, 2005).

Catholic Relief Services would be one example of an organization consistently recognized as a professional religious agency by relief workers. Samaritan Purse, and much more so Scientology, which was very active in the 2004 tsunami aftermath, are perceived to be on the "unpredictable" end by outsiders. In Christopher Hitchens's analysis, the orphanages associated with Mother Theresa are a clear case of a diversion of humanitarianism toward a conservative Catholic agenda of opposing abortion.[61]

Islamic relief agencies may face the suspicion of pollution in a specific way; in a Western world that still treats Christianity as the unmarked category, ties to Islamic religious organizations and suspected ties to Islamic political organizations may seem more notable, more political, and more impure than their Christian equivalent. Bruno De Cordier notes that Islamic agencies have been suspected of being agents of jihad since the war in former Yugoslavia.[62] Officials with Islamic Relief, an NGO founded in Britain in the 1980s, note that this situation is reversed in some Muslim areas, where the organization is more readily accepted as humanitarian by the population on the ground.[63]

Religion is not an important axis of differentiation between actors in the field of art or law in the same way. Nor does it seem to play such an important dividing role in human rights work or environmental activism, two areas in which activists have also been inspired by faith.[64] There might be several reasons for this. Humanitarianism might be more central to Christianity for theological reasons than to environmentalism or human rights—which might lead Christians to set up their own organizations rather than work with others in purely issue-based campaigns. Human rights doctrine may come into conflict with church doctrine or with church institutional interests in a way relief does not; but to understand why religion matters so prominently as a line of explicit differentiation, we have to also consider that humanitarian relief is a very resource-intensive process.

Large relief programs require much larger budgets than human rights

61. Christopher Hitchens, *The Missionary Position: Mother Teresa in Theory and Practice* (London: Verso, 1995).

62. Bruno De Cordier, "Faith-Based Aid, Globalisation, and the Humanitarian Frontline: An Analysis of Western-Based Muslim Aid Organisations," *Disasters* 33, no. 4 (2009): 608–28.

63. See Nida Kirmani, Ajaz Khan, and Victoria Palmer, *Does Faith Matter? An Examination of Islamic Relief's Work with Refugees and Internally Displaced Persons* (London: Islamic Relief, 2008); De Cordier, "Faith-Based Aid."

64. Michael Guggenheim, "Organisierte Umwelt: Umweltdienstleistungsfirmen zwischen Wissenschaft, Wirtschaft und Politik" (Bielefeld: Transcript, 2005); Chris Rootes, ed., *Environmental Movements: Local, National, and Global* (London: Frank Cass, 1999); Rootes, ed. *Environmental Protest in Western Europe* (Oxford: Oxford University Press, 2003); Rootes, "Global Civil Society and the Lessons of European Environmentalism," in *Creating a Better World*, ed. Rupert Taylor (Bloomfield, CT: Kumarian Press, 2004), 147–69.

programs, for example, and most relief organizations rely on government contracts to fund most of their work. Very few agencies can support large programs purely on donations from individuals, and in this context, faith-based organizations have a distinctive advantage.[65] While public interest in distant disasters and emergencies has grown, the public for humanitarian appeals does not just exist as an abstract entity. Faith-based organizations can rely on additional ties to a specific base of donors. They may use faith in their public communication strategy, and many have specific organizational ties to churches.[66]

Diversity and the Branding of Projects

I should revisit the question of how organizations decide on where and how to do a project. All agencies assume that there should be projects, and that there should be projects that "add value" and "make a difference." But the symbolic differentiation among agencies shapes the conditions that need to be fulfilled for an agency to consider working in an area, and shapes the content and the criteria for what an agency thinks makes a project good.

There are several voices in the field that claim to do better than "normal" good projects, but there is not one choice between "purity" and "selling out," as is sometimes implied. Different agencies emphasize different aspects of what makes their projects special. MSF is very prominent as an organization that positions itself at the same time against humanitarianism, in its present form, and as the embodiment of humanitarianism. MSF is very critical of the self-interests of humanitarian organizations, very reflexive and honest, and it emphasizes the role of humanitarian principles in setting limits on what kind of work it will or will not undertake. Other agencies have a different claim to not just do "good projects" but to do "really good projects." Agencies coming from the development tradition, for example, emphasize the importance of beneficiary participation in project design and implemention—a discourse that is foreign to MSF, partly because it is a medical organization. Other agencies emphasize a relationship to beneficiaries specifically based on religious values.

MSF is very consistent in performing its unique position. It consistently insists on its independence and distances itself from the pollution of political capital and economic capital. This means, for example,

65. See De Cordier, "Faith-Based Aid"; see also Hopgood and Vinjamuri, "Faith in Markets."
66. Development Initiatives, *Public Support for Humanitarian Crisis.*

that MSF refuses to be driven by donors' agendas in its choice of projects. It means MSF would not accept US money in Iraq; and after the Indian Ocean tsunami in 2004, it announced at a certain point that it had received enough funds. It also means that MSF is very cautious about undertaking projects in contexts where it would rely on local power holders for physical protection.

MSF does sometimes go to places where nobody else goes, and it often goes to places first, and others then follow. But while MSF defends needs-based humanitarianism, it refuses the role of an organization that is asked to simply step in, and it refuses the role of filling the gaps left by others. The MSF line tends to emphasize that governments are ultimately responsible for caring for populations and that relief is an ethical duty, but that relief workers should not accept the role as a Band-Aid, and relief work, while providing short-term relief, should never stop to also be a call for others to provide long-term solutions.

MSF is guided by medical needs and uses quite formal medical indicators. But, among the relief managers I spoke to, some of MSF staff were clearest about the fact that needs alone cannot determine the allocation of resources. "That there is need is not enough for us to justify a project," one desk officer at one MSF section told me.

This clarity is the result of a high level of reflexivity, and it certainly makes more reflective choices possible. This clarity can also lead to the embracing of a certain symbolic dimension of choosing projects. One desk officer told me: "Most of the time I discuss with some teams who are coming back from an assessment. Yes, for sure the needs are there, but we need what we call right now in internal language a political angle [axis]." This political angle is not a political dimension as it is conventionally understood, in the sense of obeying outside political interests.

Rather, MSF sometimes looks for projects that allow it to make certain points. As one desk officer explained to me,

If I go to the north and I say, "OK, we have a huge amount of malnourished children," it can be interesting for us to demonstrate that even in a big desert with populations who are moving all the time, [the treatment] is working very well. It will be a political angle, for example, in launching a campaign for a new product of nutrition. . . . So we need something, that is difficult to explain; it is a feeling, that comes by experience, not experience for ten years, but a couple of months—sometimes a couple of years for people who are a bit reluctant—that enables you to say what is the MSF fit.

MSF has very good reasons for doing this, and there are important benefits of this aspect of MSF's work. For example, MSF has done important work showing that HIV-AIDS can be treated in Africa. There had been a widespread assumption that it is impossible to deliver HIV treatment in Africa because it is impossible to get people to take the medicine regularly over a long period of time.[67] This assumption was of course also convenient for an international system struggling with inertia—and worse—in responding to the crisis of HIV/AIDS in poor settings.

A desk officer with one MSF section has explained to me how it had chosen suitable sites in Africa to demonstrate the efficacy of treatment in this context. This enabled MSF to make the point forcefully that it was possible to treat HIV-AIDS in Africa and that the challenge was on the side of response—not the side of Africans—and that this challenge could be overcome with political will.[68]

Some critics say that MSF adopts stances that are controversial within the field in order to attract media attention and to raise funds. MSF is right to insist that money is not its goal. I believe the managers who have explained to me that MSF tends to have more money than qualified staff.

MSF has done important work for the people it has treated. It defends humanitarian principles and shows what health care can do in the Global South. It has opened up space for political demands, where previously populations were often blamed for their own lack of access to medical care. But because MSF refuses to fill gaps for other agencies and sometimes chooses projects as demonstration projects, its work does not correct the limitations of the allocation of resources via projects and we cannot expect it to single-handedly restore humanitarian action "according to need."

Conclusion

Agencies develop their policy positions not only directly in response to practical dilemmas but from within a field, in which they react to other agencies' views. They actively differentiate themselves from each other.

67. E.g., A. D. Harries et al., "Preventing Antiretroviral Anarchy in Sub-Saharan Africa," *The Lancet* 358, no. 9279 (August 2001): 410–14.

68. E.g., Jean-Michel Tassie et al. "Highly Active Antiretroviral Therapy in Resource Poor Settings: The Experience of Médecins Sans Frontières," *AIDS* 17, no. 13 (2003): 1995–97. The work of Paul Farmer and Partners in Health was also important in this struggle to prove that an effective response is possible and that victims should not be blamed for the failures of the response; see Paul Farmer et al., "Community-Based Approaches to HIV Treatment in Resource-Poor Settings," *The Lancet* 358 (2001): 404–9, as well as the contributions collected in Haun Saussy, ed., *Partner to the Poor: A Paul Farmer Reader* (Berkeley: University of California Press, 2010). See also Kathy Attawell and Jackie Mundy, *Provision of Antiretroviral Therapy in Resource-Limited Settings: A Review of Experience up to August 2003* (London: DFID Health Systems Resource Centre in Collaboration with the World Health Organisation, 2003).

This space has its origins in a move that combined the authority of the suffering produced by war with the authority of the states responsible for that suffering, and the authority of the medical profession. When the ICRC's position was challenged on its own terms by MSF in 1971, a field of positions opened up. Ironically, MSF's intervention, though purist in spirit, opened up a range of positions for other actors to adopt and triggered a certain deregulation of humanitarian principles. Humanitarianism, as we know it today, is partly the result of that move. In the decades since then, a variety of actors have attached a variety of resources and causes to the humanitarian label.

The humanitarian field has a twofold center of authority, with the ICRC and MSF occupying key positions that are pure in slightly different ways. A variety of positions draw on a combination of humanitarian as well as other symbolic and material resources. Various political actors' resources are considered sources of pollution. In its current structure, the field is also shaped by a division between religious and secular agencies.

The field-theoretical account of the symbolic structure of this space has different implications than a typology of organizations. A typology is based on classifying organizations; a field-theoretical account is based on classifying classifications. The former implies a mediation by a single organization and its values; the latter implies a mediation by a set of relations that shape positions in a field, which the agencies on the autonomous pole of the field are also a part of. A typology of organizations implies a choice between different organizations and their values; a field-theoretical approach calls for a response to the whole set of relations that constitute the field. Based on a typology, one might judge proclaimed values; based on a field-theoretical mapping one might rather judge performances that make better or worse use of an agency's specific position.

I have now discussed the principal elements of the logic of practice of the field of humanitarian relief organizations. We have seen that humanitarian relief agencies produce projects and strive to deliver good projects. There is a shared logic as to how agencies differentiate themselves from each other as well, which is part of the market for projects. Our efforts to assist through NGOs are mediated by these practical constraints and by the symbolic logic of the field.

I have also analyzed some of the elements of the history of that logic of the field of humanitarian relief: I have analyzed the genealogy of the project as a unit of planning through the history of the logframe, and I have traced the evolution of humanitarian authority.

The final two chapters will discuss two cases in order to to reexamine the logic of the field of humanitarian relief NGOs. First, I will examine efforts to improve and reform humanitarian relief, and we will see how the impact of these efforts has been mediated by that logic of practice; different reform projects, against their intentions, have ended up contributing to the infrastructure of the market for projects. I will then look at what an analysis of the logic of fields of practice means for our understanding of the role human rights play in mediating distant suffering, and of the role the concept has played in humanitarian relief.

FIVE
___

The Reform of Humanitarianism

> If a significant man gives the world an idea, it is taken over by a process of dis-tribution that consists of sympathy and antipathy; . . . soon nothing remains of the big achievement, other than a reservoir of aphorisms, to which friend and enemy help themselves as it suits them. ROBERT MUSIL, *THE MAN WITHOUT QUALITIES*

The first four chapters have analyzed the elements of the logic of practice of the field of humanitarian relief agencies. I have discussed both shared practices of project management and the ways agencies position themselves vis-à-vis each other to produce symbolic differentiation. I have also discussed the way projects are produced for exchange. These elements, I have suggested, together constitute a relatively autonomous logic that mediates between interests and values, on the one hand, and what humanitarian agencies do or not do, on the other hand. To put it simply, this logic mediates between what is put into humanitarian relief and what it puts out.

This chapter adds to this analysis by including the forms of self-observation and reflexivity within the humanitarian field in its object of analysis:[1] it addresses attempts to reform humanitarian relief from within. As many observers have noted, humanitarian relief is a very reflective and a very

---

1. This is loosely inspired by the questions raised, from a systems-theoretical perspective, in André Kieserling, *Selbstbeschreibung und Fremdbeschreibung* (Frankfurt: Suhrkamp, 2004).

126

self-critical field. Some have also pointed out that the self-criticism can seem ritualistic; Alex de Waal commented, for example, that "the humanitarian international appears to have an extra-ordinary capacity to absorb criticism, not reform itself, and yet emerge strengthened."[2] Not all self-criticism is merely rhetorical, however. Since the late 1980s and early 1990s, a number of initiatives have set out to change relief, help it learn from past mistakes, and make it better. I will discuss two of the most important and most successful initiatives to reform humanitarianism, and some of their effects. The first is the Sphere Project, which aims to establish standards for how relief work is done and what affected populations ought to receive as part of a humanitarian response. The second reform initiative, the Humanitarian Accountability Project (HAP), aims to make aid agencies more accountable to the recipients, rather than the donors, of relief work.

Sphere and HAP are interesting cases to examine because they combine the idealism of humanitarian relief with managerial know-how and resources. These initiatives appeal to the highest values of the sector—the dignity of every human being, the voice of beneficiaries—and they are based on a serious analysis of some of the limitations of real-existing humanitarian relief. They have been led by some of the most experienced managers in the sector and have been accompanied by thoughtful efforts to maximize impact and buy-in among practitioners.

In the context of this book, considering these reforms has three main purposes. First, it allows me to include the latest and, according to some, the best versions of humanitarianism in my examination. Second, looking at these reforms gives me an opportunity to return to the questions about the role of ideas in improving the world raised in chapter 1. In its limitations, the reform of humanitarianism since the 1990s has mirrored the broader project of humanitarian reform since the late eighteenth century in important ways. Both start with the highest ambitions and best intentions. Facing undefined evil—and drawing legitimization from an undefined evil—actors then focus on a limited aspect of reality that they feel they can do something about. The impact of reforms is then, in a second step, mediated by existing institutions and power relations.

Third, studying these reforms allows me to take another look at the logic of the field of humanitarian relief organizations. We will see how resilient this logic is in the face of attempts at reform and how it shapes the impact these reform projects are able to have. The impact of these

2. Alexander de Waal, *Famine Crimes: Politics and the Disaster Relief Industry* (London: James Currey, 1997), xvi.

reforms has come to be mediated by the focus of agencies on producing projects and by the symbolic divisions among actors in the field. Reform projects have become incorporated into the logic of the humanitarian field. Among other effects, these initiatives also contribute to building a thicker infrastructure for the market for projects.

I will begin the chapter by situating these reforms in a specific moment in the history of the field of humanitarian relief organizations. I will then discuss how each project encounters the organizational dynamics of the field as it seeks to translate its ideas into practical impact. Each project finds its own way of approaching the logic of the humanitarian field in this process and, explicitly or implicitly, draws on different equivalents in other markets as metaphors for its own role. Sphere connects with the practicalities of relief by becoming a standard for the *products* of relief; in some tension with the intentions of the project, it begins to work in analogy to a technical, and not a professional, standard.

HAP is based on the analysis that beneficiaries do not have the power that consumers have in other sectors, and that external pressures are necessary to change the incentive structures for relief agencies. But it does not give consumer power to beneficiaries; rather, it has come to operate like a fair trade or voluntary labor standard, seeking to encourage ethical consumption among donors and seeking to empower those producers who are willing to avoid the forms of competition that are most exploitative toward people involved in the process of production.

Reform Initiatives in Humanitarian Relief since 1992

Sphere and HAP are part of a group of reform initiatives that date back to the early 1990s.[3] These initiatives not only formalized reflexive conversations about humanitarian relief; they also brought different agencies together around a range of issues—from rethinking humanitarian principles under new conditions to sharing expertise in personnel management (see table 5.1).

The emergence of these initiatives came at a particular moment in the history of the humanitarian field. The time immediately preceding and following the end of the Cold War in 1989 was a moment of growth and new opportunities for humanitarian action. It was also a moment

3. André Griekspoor and Egbert Sondorp, "Enhancing the Quality of Humanitarian Assistance: Taking Stock and Future Initiatives," *Prehospital and Disaster Medicine* 16, no. 4 (2001): 209–15; Dorothea Hilhorst, "Being Good at Doing Good? Quality and Accountability of Humanitarian NGOs," *Disasters* 26, no. 3 (2002): 193–212.

Table 5.1 Reform initiatives in humanitarian relief since 1990

	Initiative	Actors	Aims
1993	Mohonk Principles[1]	World Conference on Religion and Peace, supported by large religious relief agencies and UN agencies	Reassert the traditional ICRC principles of neutrality and impartiality for complex emergencies
1993	Providence Principles[2]	Humanitarianism and War Project, Brown University	Establish the Providence Principles and a code of conduct for practitioners operating in war zones
1997	ALNAP	Sector-wide initiative, 65 members among NGO, donor, and UN agencies	Provide a network for sharing performance-enhancing activities
1997	People in Aid[3]	NGOs as members organizations	Improve human-resources skills of agencies
1997	The Sphere Project	IFRC, Oxfam, Steering Committee for Humanitarian Response	Create Humanitarian Charter and Sphere standards
2003	Good Humanitarian Donorship initiative[4]	UN, NGOs, Red Cross movement, donor governments	Establish the Principles and Good Practice of Good Humanitarian Donorship
2003	Humanitarian Accountability Project (HAP)	60 members, including NGOs and institutional donors	Establish Code and Accreditation Programme concerning accountability to beneficiaries
2005	Emergency Capacity Building Project (ECB)	7 large NGOs, IRC, with support from the Bill and Melinda Gates Foundation, Microsoft, and ECHO	Improve accountability and impact measurement, risk reduction, and information and technology requirements
2007	Compas Tool[5]	URD (emergency, rehabilitation, development)	Shift from ex-post quality control to quality assurance during the process

1. Jon M. Ebersole, "Mohonk Criteria for Humanitarian Assistance in Complex Emergencies," *Disaster Prevention and Management* 4, no. 3 (1993): 192–208.
2. Larry Minear and Thomas G. Weiss, *The Humanitarianism and War Project* (Boulder, CO: Lynne Rienner Publishers, 1993).
3. Sara Davidson, *People in Aid Code of Best Practice in the Management and Support of Aid Personnel* (London: Overseas Development Institute, 1997).
4. Johan Schaar, "The Birth of the Good Humanitarian Donorship Initiative," in *The Humanitarian Response Index 2007: Measuring Commitment to Best Practice*, ed. Silvia Hidalgo and Augusto Lopez-Claros (London: Macmillan, 2008), 37–45.
5. Hugues Maury and Rémi Russbach, "The Quality Compass—A New Tool to Manage and Evaluate Humanitarian Assistance," *International Journal of Disaster Medicine* 2, no. 3 (2004): 106–10.

of new challenges and dilemmas. The way humanitarian relief agencies responded to this moment was shaped by a specific generational constellation, in terms of both the biographies of relief agencies and the biographies of staff.

I have dated the emergence of the humanitarian field as a field of shared practices and symbolic contestation to the years following MSF's breakaway from the ICRC in 1971. There were a number of prominent crises in the 1970s and 1980s, and relief agencies grew in visibility, size, and number during that time. Also during that time, the field developed a significant workforce for the first time. But in those years there was no structured path for joining these agencies. The first generation of relief workers entered the field as young development workers, doctors, engineers, or simply adventurers—some joined up while they were traveling—and they often had had very little formal training.

By the early 1990s, humanitarian agencies, and the emergency departments of development agencies, were led, for the first time, by people who had a whole career in humanitarian relief to look back on. These leaders had accompanied relief agencies as these had become engaged in new and challenging environments and had lived through some of the defining crises of the 1980s—and then later the 1990s—such as the famine in Ethiopia in 1984 and 1985 and the wars accompanying the breakup of former Yugoslawia in the early 1990s, which were defining also in the sense that they raised new questions about the limits and unintended consequences of relief.[4]

During that same time, funding to humanitarian relief increased dramatically, and the sector was growing, as I discussed in chapter 4. Established agencies opened new field sites and hired new staff. Newer, smaller agencies came into the field. From the perspective of the older generation, some of the new staff lacked experience and training. The smaller agencies were seen as competition, and potentially as incompetent competition. The large and established NGOs also feared competition from commercial actors attracted by the increase in funding for humanitarian causes.

With the new investment in the field on the part of institutional donors came new demands for accountability from above, demands that were heightened by perceived failures of the response to specific crises, such as Rwanda.[5] When asked for improvements and accountability, those in senior positions in established agencies felt they were in a position to respond and contribute in a way that both leveraged and contributed to their position of leadership in the field.

4. See, e.g., Fiona Terry, *Condemned to Repeat? The Paradox of Humanitarian Action* (Ithaca, NY: Cornell University Press, 2002).

5. David Millwood, ed., *The International Response to Conflict and Genocide: Lessons from the Rwanda Experience* (Geneva: Steering Committee of the Joint Evaluation of Emergency Assistance to Rwanda, 2006).

The Case of Sphere: Principles, Standards, and Indicators

The Sphere Project began in 1996 as an effort to ground humanitarian relief in human rights and to develop standards for humanitarian work—standards that would provide some guidance to staff in the field on what to do, and would ensure adequate provision for those affected by disaster and wars across agencies and across different settings. Building on earlier initiatives by an NGO umbrella organization, Peter Walker, then with the International Federation of the Red Cross, and Nick Stockton, then with Oxfam, assembled technical experts from a number of agencies to reflect on good practice in the sector and draft guidelines for humanitarian work.[6]

Sphere is best known today for its handbook, a white-orange book that circulates widely in the humanitarian world. The Sphere Handbook has three main elements: the Humanitarian Charter, the Sphere standards, and a set of indicators. The Humanitarian Charter is about principles and commitments; it affirms, alongside humanitarian principles such as independence and neutrality, "the right to life to an adequate standard of living and to freedom from cruel, inhuman or degrading treatment or punishment." In standards and indicators, Sphere then brings the sector's technical experience to these rather abstract human rights norms and tries to specify very concretely what every person should have in order for us to say that he or she has an adequate standard of living.

According to Sphere trainers, it is very important to distinguish between standards and indicators. Standards are formulated quite generally. The standard for water, for example, states: "People have adequate facilities and supplies to collect, store and use sufficient quantities of water for drinking, cooking, and personal hygiene, and to ensure that drinking water remains safe until it is consumed." The indicator is much more concrete and suggests a quantitative measure.[7] According to the Sphere Handbook, 15 liters of water per person per day within a maximum distance from the house of 500 meters is an indicator that the right to water is fulfilled.

Sphere standards and indicators come in different technical sectors,

6. Margie Buchanan-Smith, *How the Sphere Project Came into Being: A Case Study of Policy-Making in the Humanitarian Aid Sector and the Relative Influence of Research* (London: Overseas Development Institute, 2003); Peter Walker and Susan Purdin, "Birthing Sphere," *Disasters* 28, no. 2 (2004): 100–111.

7. Sphere Project, *The Sphere Project Training Package: Humanitarian Charter and Minimum Standards in Disaster Response* (Geneva: The Sphere Project, 2003), 69.

such as nutrition, water and sanitation, health, and shelter. What does the right to food mean? One of the relevant Sphere indicators suggests that if each person has access to 2100 kilocalories per day with 17 percent of energy provided by fat and 10–12 percent of energy provided by proteins, we can be hopeful that the right to food is realized in that setting. What does the right to shelter mean? One of the relevant Sphere indicators suggests that if all affected individuals have an initial minimum covered floor area of 3.5 square meters per person, we can be hopeful that the right to shelter is realized in that setting.

The Spirit of Sphere

It is important to bear in mind the idealist side of the Sphere Project. Sphere sees itself as translating between the highest values of the humanitarian profession and the mundane technical details of building a latrine, between the sacred core of what it means to be human and the material requirements of staying alive. The Sphere Project is understood by some as an attempt to ground humanitarian work in the concept of human rights. For Hugo Slim, for example, "the humanitarian charter," which is the first section of the Sphere Handbook, "marks the passing of key sections of the international NGO community–on paper at least—from philanthropy to rights."[8]

In this tradition, humanitarians argue that people not only *need* food, water, health care, and shelter, but that they have a *right* to food, water, health care, and shelter. The concept of human rights, in this view, could be the basis for a new relationship to the populations agencies work with, shaping an encounter with beneficiaries as rights holders rather than primarily as people in need. The Sphere standards are meant to be understood as a concretization of the Universal Declaration of Human Rights. "Sphere can be seen as an attempt by a wide spectrum of agencies to articulate what the minimum content of a right to life without dignity must be. Perhaps more accurately it is an attempt to define the related parameters for adequate and appropriate humanitarian assistance."[9]

What is designed to be universally valid—that people have access to adequate water supplies—is the standard. The indicator—15 liters a day—the trainers insist, is only an indicator and may be applied flexibly. When

8. Hugo Slim, "Not Philanthropy but Rights: The Proper Politicisation of Humanitarian Philosophy," *International Journal of Human Rights* 6, no. 2 (2002): 14.

9. James Darcy, "Locating Responsibility: The Sphere Humanitarian Charter and Its Rationale," *Disasters* 28, no. 2 (2004): 113.

critics thus ask how universal standards can be reconciled with local needs—what if, for example, for cultural reasons people need more, or less? Or what if the Sphere indicator asks for much more than what local people in surrounding areas are used to? Sphere trainers would argue that this misunderstands the role Sphere has envisioned for indicators: the intervention of Sphere is to ask agencies to explain why a specific indicator was chosen or not chosen, thus fostering a reflexive and reasoned conversation about what people need and what can be delivered.

Sphere and the Market for Projects

Sphere has in many ways been very successful. It has been translated into twenty-five different languages. It is used in several training events a month at headquarters in the Global North and on the ground across the world.[10] It has shaped agencies' internal training, and it is also used by local partners. Sphere has thus become one important means for passing down basic knowledge to those who are new to the field, and for fostering reflexivity in practitioners. But its impact as a reform of humanitarianism as a whole has also been mediated by the focus of agencies on producing projects and by the symbolic divisions of the humanitarian field. It became incorporated into the market for projects as a tool for standardizing products.

Sphere is sometimes used in lobbying efforts and advocacy work. After the 2006 earthquake in Pakistan, for example, aid workers referred to the Sphere standards to argue for better provisions for affected populations in the camps run by the Pakistani military.[11] But the most obvious way for a relief agency to use Sphere is as part of producing a project. The Humanitarian Charter speaks of people's right to an adequate standard of living, and the Sphere standards give aid workers an indication as to what an adequate standard of living might mean concretely. But by declaring these as rights that everyone holds in theory, Sphere provides no answer as to who should get what, given that not everyone gets everything they need. Sphere will then be used to determine what a given group of select beneficiaries receive. Sphere standards and indicators become criteria for how a good project in a given area of expertise can be recognized.

This issue of coverage—of different parts of populations, and of dif-

10. The Sphere website has regular updates on current developments and dissemination activities; http://www.Sphereproject.org.
11. Andrew Wilder, *Perceptions of the Pakistan Earthquake Response: Humanitarian Agenda 2015 Pakistan Country Study* (Medford, MA: Feinstein International Center, Tufts University, 2008).

ferent kinds of needs—rather than the issue of universalism and cultural specificity seems to me to be the aporia of the Sphere standards. During the planning of a water and sanitation project for five hundred people, the Sphere standards can be used to determine how much water to provide relatively independently of how much people need water there, compared to, say, other things or who else needs water.[12]

If and when Sphere is used as part of producing projects, Sphere standards become standards for products, taking on the meaning of "standards" in fields like engineering rather than the meaning of "standards" in human rights, against some of the intentions of the project. This is true even if the handbook is used wisely, in a way that respects the distinction Sphere draws between standards and indicators. If projects are products and Sphere is used to plan and assess projects, it is also not surprising that standards and indicators are conflated.

Sphere seems to provide a way to compare results, not just against initial goals but to an external set of criteria. It is one of the declared intentions of the Sphere Project to eliminate differences in quality delivered by different agencies in different areas. In a field where "serving need" is the product, Sphere helps to address the problem of qualitative differences in different peoples' needs. By suggesting, for example, an indicator of a minimum of 15 liters per day per person, those 15 liters can take the place of the individuals' need in planning and accounting. Sphere makes the qualitative differences of need regarding people manageable. While of course the amount of work necessary to get peoples' provisions up to the standards demanded by Sphere varies, the tendency in planning to assume that people have nothing to some extent eliminates also the quantitative difference regarding needs. This means Sphere can be read to make prices for provision per person across very different areas of practice and very different regions and problems more comparable. Together with the logframe it could be used as a pricing tool. In an extreme reading, Sphere could be used to reduce all qualitative differences to the number of people serviced in a given sector.

12. One version of this problem is reflected in the common criticism of Sphere, which alleges that it focuses only on the technical details of relief, at the expense of protection issues; see, for example, Charlotte Dufour et al., "Rights, Standards, and Quality in a Complex Humanitarian Space: Is Sphere the Right Tool?," *Disasters* 28, no. 2 (2004): 124–41. The water standard can indeed be used quite independently of whether people are being killed while wells and waters are being provided. It could in principle be used also to assess an agency's practice in retrospect, independently of whether people were being killed while wells and water were being provided. It is quite difficult to relate the Sphere standards to the possibility of that violence in practice. The evaluation of the Sphere standards has noted that "some donors seem to choose to concentrate on and to acknowledge the technical portion of the project while 'opting out' of the rights-based approach"; see Marci Van Dyke and Ronald Waldman, *The Sphere Project Evaluation Report* (New York: Mailman School of Public Health, 2004), 33.

As an external and agreed-on set of numbers, Sphere indicators have certain effects purely by being there. Of course not every donor believes that projects are comparable purely based on price per people helped in a given sector; and certainly agency staff largely do not believe this if it is put to them as a proposition. But the possibility of interpreting it that way remains, and the possibility that other actors interpret it that way remains. There is some evidence that agencies feel under pressure to provide services up to the Sphere indicators, then sometimes called "standards," and will go where they can most easily fulfill them. A report on relief to Darfur notes that "the strategy among some international groups interviewed was to expand only when minimum standards had been achieved in their current program. . . . Agencies may play safe and keep their programs small, manageable, and risk-free in order to ensure that they will have the best possible evaluation."[13] One of my respondents recalled, for example: "We were discussing possible sites for a project, and my project managers said of a location: 'We won't go there. It is impossible to deliver up to our professional standards there, and the donors won't like it.'"

Sphere and the Deprofessionalization of the Humanitarian Field

The Sphere Project and its standards were quite heavily contested in the beginning, and some organizations still do not subscribe to them. Considering these contestations allows me to examine the way Sphere has been mediated by the symbolic differentiation within the field of humanitarian relief organization. These contestations also allow me to analyze the relationship and possible tensions between fields and processes of professionalization for the case of humanitarian relief.[14]

It has become commonplace to associate the most recent transformation of humanitarian relief—the expansion, the cooperation between agencies, the rise of formal training—with processes of professionalization.[15] Some voices in the debate consider this a bad thing; others wel-

---

13. Helen Young et al., *Darfur—Livelihoods under Siege* (Medford, MA: Feinstein International Center, Tufts University, 2005), 117.

14. These types of questions have been raised by Rudolf Stichweh, *Wissenschaft, Universität, Professionen* (Frankfurt a. M.: Suhrkamp, 1994); and Andrew Abbott, "Linked Ecologies: States and Universities as Environments for Professions," *Sociological Theory* 23, no. 3 (2005): 245–74.

15. See Michael Barnett, "Humanitarianism Transformed," *Perspectives on Politics* 3, no. 4 (2005): 723–40; Barnett, "Faith in the Machine? Humanitarianism in an Age of Bureaucratization," in *Sacred Aid: Faith and Humanitarianism*, ed. Michael Barnett and Janice Gross Stein (New York: Oxford University Press 2011), 188–211; Philippe Ryfman, *Une histoire de l'humanitaire* (Paris: Le Decouverte, 2008),

come the trend and say humanitarian relief should be professionalizing. Sphere is often discussed as part of the professionalization in humanitarian relief. Indeed, Sphere is often called a "professional standard," and we might think of it as a professional standard similar to the norms of the classical professions, such as law and medicine. But it is important to remember that these classical professions precisely resist the standardization of output.

In the classical professions, standardization is in tension with professional autonomy. It is one of the justifications of the closure associated with professionalization in medicine and law that some aspects of their work cannot be standardized and thus require the regulation not of a *service* or *output* but of the kind of *person* who provides it.[16] To guard against external interference, professionals have to balance a claim to abstract knowledge with a claim that only they personally can apply it.[17]

The innovation of Sphere is not in the standard for conduct—here the project was able to incorporate earlier lists of principles—but in the standard for products. In the humanitarian context, what is sold to donors is coverage for specific groups of people in specific sectors. In its standards, Sphere subsumes both doctors and engineers under the same form of technical accountability. While product standards are also contested among engineers,[18] they are much more common there than in medicine. For doctors, oriented in their self-understanding toward a one-on-one relationships with patients, this is a form of meta-accountability that they resist as managerialism in domestic contexts—what sociologists call "deprofessionalization"[19]—and that they newly confront in emergency settings as part of subcontracting from donor governments.

89–90; Peter Walker and Catherine Russ, *Professionalising the Humanitarian Sector* (Cardiff: ELHR, 2010).

16. Talcott Parsons, "The Professions and Social Structure," *Social Forces* 17, no. 4 (1939): 457–67; Parsons, "A Sociologist Looks at the Legal Profession," in *Essays in Sociological Theory*, by Parsons (New York: Simon and Schuster, 1954), 370–85; Rudolf Stichweh, *Wissenschaft, Universität, Professionen* (Frankfurt a. M.: Suhrkamp, 1994); Stichweh, "Professions in Modern Society," *International Review of Sociology* 7, no. 1 (1997): 95–102.

17. Andrew Abbott, *The System of Professions: An Essay on the Division of Expert Labor* (Chicago: University of Chicago Press, 1988), 51; Owen Whooley, "Diagnostic Ambivalence: Psychiatric Workarounds and the Diagnostic and Statistical Manual of Mental Disorders," *Sociology of Health & Illness* 32, no. 3 (2010): 452–69.

18. Stuart Shapiro, "Degrees of Freedom: The Interaction of Standards of Practice and Engineering Judgment," *Science, Technology & Human Values* 22, no. 3 (1997): 286–316; Mark Coeckelbergh, "Regulation or Responsibility? Autonomy, Moral Imagination, and Engineering," *Science, Technology & Human Values* 31, no. 3 (2006): 237–60.

19. W. Richard Scott, "Professionals in Bureaucracies—Areas of Conflict," in *Professionalization*, ed. Howard M. Vollmer and Donald L. Mills (Englewood Cliffs, NJ: Prentice Hall, 1966), 265–75; Gloria V. Engel, "The Effect of Bureaucracy on the Professional Autonomy of the Physician," *Journal of Health and Social Behavior* 10, no. 1 (1969): 30–41; Engel, "Professional Autonomy and Bureaucratic Organiza-

Some fields in the Bourdieusian sense coincide with a profession, such as the field of law. The field of humanitarian relief organizations is a field that incorporates different kinds of roles and different kinds of expert knowledge, including some classical professions. This creates some tensions within the field. At the same time that Sphere is associated with processes of professionalization, it has also been criticized because it reduces professional autonomy. Indeed, it is the medical organizations that have resisted standardization most strongly; the most outspoken critics of the Sphere standards have been associated with MSF.[20]

The critique of the Sphere standards has often taken the form of an opposition of the sacred and the profane, of value rationality and instrumental rationality: Sphere is said to be reducing the noble humanitarian mission to mere technicalities and formal criteria. This opposition between the sacred and the profane is attributed by some writers to cultures as a whole, and it is also attributed more specifically to the dynamic within fields of cultural production in general by writers following Bourdieu.[21] But in this case it is not just any form of contestation about the sacred and the profane; rather, it is part of the resistance by doctors to a deprofessionalization they newly encounter in the context of the transformation of the field of humanitarian relief.

In their criticism of the Sphere standards, MSF representatives have emphasized that Sphere blurs the question as to whose responsibility it is to make sure that the standards for a life with dignity are fulfilled.[22] MSF insists that agencies should never assume a task that should be the government's. This would not only ease the responsibility of governments to care for their populations; it would also reduce the noble vocation of relief to a cog in a bureaucratic machine. Resistance against Sphere here emphasizes the independence and autonomy of the humanitarian project as a whole as MSF envisions it. MSF here voices the authority of the autonomous pole of the humanitarian field in analogy to doctors' professional identity. Humanitarianism is a case of a field, whose autonomous pole happens to be enacted by a profession.

The antistandardization movement gains some additional impetus in the humanitarian field from the biography of those who moved into

tion," *Administrative Science Quarterly* 15, no. 1 (1970): 12–21; George Ritzer and David Walczak, "Rationalization and the Deprofessionalization of Physicians," *Social Forces* 67, no. 1 (1988): 1–22.

20. Peter Giesen, "Sphere and Accountability: A View from MSF," accessed September 8, 2011, http://www.Sphereproject.org; Jacqui Tong, "Questionable Accountability: MSF and Sphere in 2003," *Disasters* 28, no. 2 (2004): 176–89; Dufour et al., "Rights, Standards, and Quality."

21. Pierre Bourdieu, *The Rules of Art: Genesis and Structure of the Literary Field* (Stanford, CA: Stanford University Press, 1996).

22. Giesen, "Sphere and Accountability"; Tong, "Questionable Accountability."

this field to avoid the boredom and meaninglessness work can sometimes assume in domestic settings. This is true of managers who join humanitarian relief from the corporate world. It is also true of doctors. A number of doctors I have spoken to quite explicitly stated a desire to leave the boredom of domestic hospital work behind and recover their original excitement for serving people within humanitarian relief.[23]

The Indeterminacy of Evil, Humanitarian Reform, and the Reform of Humanitarianism

There is a long tradition in the social sciences of studying projects of reform, and many of these projects are humanitarian in some broad sense. This is true of the prison reformers who became the subject of Michel Foucault's *Discipline and Punish*,[24] the campaign against slavery,[25] and the missionaries described by Jean and John Comaroff in *Of Revelation and Revolution*.[26] This kind of humanitarian reform is a relatively new phenomenon, and it is an ironic consequence of the emergence of humanitarianism as a field that it now has itself become the subject of self-conscious reform.

The classic work on humanitarian reform in the social sciences has shown that the humanitarian reform of society starts with the highest ambitions and best intentions. To the extent that this work also shows unintended consequences, I would suggest, these are not just explained by problems with the content of the ideas of humanitarian actors or underlying interests, but also by the indeterminacy of the evil that they face and their relative lack of power. Facing indeterminate evil, actors focus on a very limited aspect of reality that they can control. The impact of reforms is then mediated by existing institutions.

Consider the example of the evangelical missionaries, active in South Africa since the early 1800s, described by Jean and John Comaroff.[27] The missionaries arrived with the aim to spread God's word for the benefit of

23. For related research on the intersection between the medical profession and humanitarian research, see Matthew R. Hunt, "Moral Experience of Canadian Health Care Professionals in Humanitarian Work," *Prehospital and Disaster Medicine* 24, no. 6 (2009): 518–24.

24. Michel Foucault, *Discipline and Punish: The Birth of the Prison* (New York: Pantheon Books, 1977).

25. David Davis, *The Problem of Slavery in the Age of Revolution, 1770–1823* (Ithaca, NY: Cornell University Press, 1975).

26. Jean Comaroff and John L. Comaroff, *Of Revelation and Revolution: Christianity, Colonialism, and Consciousness in South Africa* (Chicago: University of Chicago Press, 1991).

27. Ibid.

local people; they developed some kind of conception of what was wrong in what they encountered in the living conditions of villagers, which were already shaped by colonialism. The missionaries had a genuine vision of a different and humane society, but they had no power to actually implement that vision.

Consider now one version of the story of the origins of Sphere. To the extent that the story of Sphere is told today as the story of the response to the genocide in Rwanda, it is worth looking at that narrative in a larger frame and examining the pattern that is suggested here: Rwanda was an event of violence on a massive scale; it unfolded rapidly, but it was also shaped by long-standing colonial dynamics. Foreign governments and foreign publics watched from afar. UN troops as well as aid agencies found themselves powerless bystanders to the genocide itself. Agencies found themselves responding to the ensuing refugee crisis, and that response too had its unintended consequences.[28]

We should note that the world did not confront the genocide in Rwanda as a whole but rather delegated "Rwanda" to a set of specific organizations that could perhaps do something about it. Somehow in the donor evaluation,[29] "Rwanda" became a story not of the world leading to Rwanda happening, the world failing to intervene in the genocide itself, or the world failing to respond to the aftermath in a meaningful way. Rather, it became a story of the failure of relief agencies to provide a pure and effective Band-Aid. Agencies accepted that verdict to some extent. To the extent that Sphere is the result of Rwanda, it responds to some questions about Rwanda but in very specific ways. The Rwandan genocide had shown how powerless humanitarian action is. Yet out of the ashes came the response to commit, against the odds, to a better, more necessary humanitarianism, which, it was hoped, would deliver even more.

Humanitarian reform of the first order may have higher, unintended consequences. One of the unintended consequences of the missionaries' work in South Africa was to make Africans more compliant, and to prepare them for jobs in the mining industry that were exploitative and, in too many cases, killed them. The reform of humanitarianism, because of its second-order nature, on the other hand, is further removed from any meaningful claim to respond to the original evil.

28. Terry, *Condemned to Repeat?*; Michael Barnett, *Eyewitness to a Genocide: The United Nations and Rwanda* (Ithaca, NY: Cornell University Press, 2002).

29. John Eriksson et al., *The International Response to Conflict and Genocide: Lessons from the Rwanda Experience* (Copenhagen: Steering Committee of the Joint Evaluation of Emergency Assistance to Rwanda, 1996).

The Case of the Humanitarian Accountability Project

If Sphere is the reform project that has reached the widest number of people working in the humanitarian world, the Humanitarian Accountability Partnership (HAP) is the most far-reaching and radical in terms of impact on the organizations that embrace it. It is also the project that most explicitly tries to change the role beneficiaries play in relief.

Initially the project came out of the Humanitarian Ombudsman Project, a research project triggered by the donor evaluation of the humanitarian response to Rwanda. Unlike other projects, this initiative provides a process of formal certification for agencies that comply with a set of agreed-upon standards.[30] Agencies participating in this initiative are ready to accept the criticism that agencies tend to cater to the preferences of those with resources, or as they would put it, they are "more accountable to donors rather than beneficiaries," and are now implementing procedures that are meant to address this imbalance.

HAP first established a list of principles. This list included a commitment to established humanitarian standards and principles, but it uniquely emphasized the need for agencies to communicate with all stakeholders about programs to be undertaken, to involve beneficiaries in planning, and to provide complaints procedures. [31] The HAP standard, which was developed in a second step, then shifts attention to the policies and processes that should enable an agency to work in accordance with these principles and to monitor and report its own compliance.[32] Eight agencies have been fully certified (CAFOD, Christian Aid, DanChurchAid, Danish Refugee Council, MERCY Malaysia, Office Africain pour le Développement et la Coopération [OFADEC], Tearfund, and Concern Worldwide); fifteen other agencies have undertaken baseline analysis; overall sixty-one organizations support the project by being full members.

30. HAP: Humanitarian Accountability Partnership, *HAP 2007 Standard in Humanitarian Accountability and Quality Management* (Geneva: HAP International, 2007).

31. HAP: Humanitarian Accountability Partnership, "Principles of Accountability," accessed September 8, 2011, http://www.hapinternational.org/projects/standard/development/principles-of-accountability.aspx.

32. HAP, *HAP 2007 Standard*; HAP: Humanitarian Accountability Partnership, *The 2010 HAP Standard in Accountability and Quality Management* (Geneva: HAP International, 2010).

Defining Accountability

But what does accountability to beneficiaries mean? One of the founders and chairman of the HAP project—a former sociology lecturer and relief veteran—explained to me that the motivation for the project was beneficiaries' relative lack of power. Beneficiaries lack effective means to hold aid agencies accountable—be they political means by way of elections or economic means by way of purchasing power. The beneficiaries' lack is unspecific and indeterminate. Beneficiaries lack many things, and this lack could be addressed in many different ways. But HAP chose a specific version of accountability among the different kinds of accountability mechanisms one might imagine. It emerged out of discussions about an ombudsman in the tradition of the Scandinavian welfare state—which was thought not to be workable in the absence of a strong overarching authority. HAP is inspired, instead, by a quality management model borrowed from the private sector, which has also been influential in the public sector in association with so-called new public management.[33]

HAP asks its certified members to have effective feedback mechanisms to improve products and services for beneficiaries as one would for customers. Agencies become accountable by providing information to people about who they are and what they are doing, by involving them in decision making, and by providing them with means to give feedback and submit complaints.

That is, however, not necessarily the notion of accountability held by aid recipients. One agency's experience with complaint boxes illustrates some of the tensions in the current efforts to reform humanitarian relief. I will recount the experiences of the manager of a Christian agency that participates in HAP. He is very committed to the project and has put much work into its implementation. He also spoke to me of some of the problems that arose with the complaint box for beneficiaries suggested by the project: "Well, sometimes you don't get much—nothing, really," he explained. "Or we'll get complaints about, say, the government, and then the government got extremely upset because they wanted [to see the comments]. . . . The communities were not aware that it was specifically

33. See Ben Ramalingam et al., *Counting What Counts: Performance and Effectiveness in the Humanitarian Sector* (London: ALNAP 2009). As the authors of this study note, there is a tension between results-based management and Total Quality Management—in humanitarian relief they come together in the sense that results-based management has established the product, and Total Quality Management is now used to tinker with processes.

about our programming, and so they would practically—it was nothing to do with the government—they would complain about UN issues which we can represent to the UN. But whether or not anything happens is another issue."

Populations need to be prepared for giving the kind of feedback that counts as constructive within the constraints of the practices of humanitarian relief agencies:

Where it has been problematic, we have introduced it too quickly. So we haven't done enough to help our own staff or particularly the community to understand its purpose and how it works. So simply sticking a box outside your gate doesn't do anything. You do actually need to explain to people the whole principle and help them understand, you know, why we would want your complaints and why is it good for you to be critical against this—but actually, there are limits to your criticism.

Agencies are genuinely interested in beneficiaries' feedback, but only a specific kind of feedback speaks to their work—feedback that works within the existing mandate and specifically the existing program design. Recipients have to be socialized into a specific role. They have to bridge the gap between their own needs and wishes, on the one hand, and agency reality, on the other hand:

So you can't complain to us about stuff that's wholly outside our control or if you do, that's lovely, but actually we're not going to do anything about it. And so, explaining and doing more preparatory work in helping communities to understand the complex process, I think, is quite important. You know, I think here in the West where we're quite used to train operators' complaints processes or airlines' complaints processes, we kind of think it is a no-brainer, but if you're in a community which has traditionally been extremely hierarchical, in which you accept your place in society and just get on with life, the whole concept of complaints and complaining upwards . . . is new.

HAP as a Fair Trade Standard

Toyota is often cited as a model with regard to quality management, and the founder of HAP has cited Toyota as an inspiration for how relief agencies could improve. He explained to me:

[Toyota has] produced a model with the lowest possible ecological impact of any mass-produced car that you can get hold of at the lowest possible fuel consumption, and the highest degree of basic reliability and a very low level of servicing—in terms of its return period that you need for taking it back to the garage. Now these are all characteristics that I want. And you know, Toyota got there by talking to people like me and listening and doing something about it. Now, you know, that to my mind is very similar to what the aid agencies need to do.

As HAP is inspired by the role that Total Quality Management (TQM) has played in the car industry, it is worth revisiting how TQM has reshaped production in the car industry, to better understand its role. The problem that TQM was supposed to respond to in the car industry was faulty parts. While earlier forms of quality assurance accepted statistical errors and responded through processes of inspection external to production itself, TQM was designed to build in quality at all stages, so that each recipient—from those at later stages in the assembly line to firms involved in later stages of production to the end consumer—could count on there not being a technical defect. TQM, in its systemic approach, allows every receiving agent at every step of the production chain to hold those delivering products responsible for faults. In the car industry this has allowed for greater control of the supply companies by final assemblers.[34]

TQM does bring in the consumer, not in the mode of market research or consumer consultation, however, but through systemic thinking.[35] The consumer is the last step in the chain, and he or she can benefit from process norms aimed to maximize reliability. While TQM focuses on faulty parts and the safety of the car, it remains for the consumer to decide whether or not they want a Toyota, or any car for that matter.

TQM is a process standard that communicates reassurance to those up the chain, who can choose between different suppliers. HAP is also a process standards, and it has taken great pains to reinforce this standard by external accreditation. It is a process standard that specifically focuses on how beneficiaries are treated as part of the production of relief projects. But it is still a process standard that communicates up the chain, a chain that in this case stops with the donors, who are the end consumers.

HAP has not introduced power for beneficiaries as consumers; rather, HAP most closely resembles a standard for fair trade certification, which allows consumers, in this case donors, to know themselves and to be known as consuming products that fulfill higher process standards of

34. Ramalingam et al., *Counting What Counts*; Steven Casper and Bob Hanckj, "Global Quality Norms within National Production Regimes: ISO 9000 Standards in the French and German Car Industries," *Organization Studies* 20, no. 6 (1999): 961–85.

35. Alan Tuckman, "The Yellow Brick Road: Total Quality Management and the Restructuring of Organizational Culture," *Organization Studies* 15, no. 5 (1994): 727–51.

an ethical kind.[36] As the ethical standards here concern the treatment of beneficiaries, and I have discussed the fact that beneficiaries labor as part of the process of producing relief products, one could also compare HAP standards to labor standards, albeit of the voluntary, privatized kind associated with ethical consumerism rather than with state protection. If labor standards are traditionally won by workers and backed up by the state, and the audience is the courts, labor standards akin to fair trade standards serve to discipline consumers who would otherwise succumb to price-only competition.

The Un(der)served Beneficiary as a Wound to Humanitarian Relief

If Sphere responds in a very specific way to the failures of a pure form of relief, which disregards all formal criteria and external effects in the face of extreme violence, HAP responds to the constant symbolic wound that is the "beneficiary." Beneficiaries are the legitimizing end point of humanitarian action, be it directly in reference to suffering or needs or indirectly via the celebration of humanitarian principles. Yet there is some awareness that beneficiaries as a symbolic referent remain always absent and out of reach.

Aid workers of course serve concrete beneficiaries, but in the awareness that so much more needs to be done, it is hard to make the concrete beneficiaries approximate the symbolic beneficiary—let alone populations in need in general. There also seems to be some awareness that beneficiaries, as concrete people, are not driving the business. This means that the symbolic beneficiary remains available for a symbolic countermobilization, against which it is difficult to defend oneself as an agency. It is in this context that we can understand HAP's question to those considering signing up: "Can you afford not to?"

In the case of HAP too, as we have seen, the response is to a very specific version of what might be the problem of the beneficiary in humanitarian relief—the way the beneficiary is incorporated is regulated, but he

36. Tim Bartley, "Certifying Forests and Factories: States, Social Movements, and the Rise of Private Regulation in the Apparel and Forest Products Fields," *Politics & Society* 31, no. 3 (2003): 433–64; Bartley, "Corporate Accountability and the Privatization of Labor Standards: Struggles over Codes of Conduct in the Apparel Industry," *Research in Political Sociology* 14 (2005): 211–44; Bartley, "Institutional Emergence in an Era of Globalization: The Rise of Transnational Private Regulation of Labor and Environmental Conditions," *American Journal of Sociology* 113, no. 2 (2007): 297–351.

or she is incorporated as someone who comments on very specific project aims, using very specific feedback forms.

There has not been the same kind of symbolic struggle around HAP as we have seen around Sphere, though not every organization is part of HAP, and it is not surprising that MSF has not applied for accreditation, given its emphasis on independence. HAP came later in the history of the humanitarian project, and it might be that the struggle around managerialism, here called professionalization, had been more or less settled when HAP began, with those striving to be part of shared initiatives less ambivalent and more committed, and the others resigned to the others doing it. But it also seems that because HAP makes beneficiaries so central to how it defines its work, and the beneficiary has such symbolic importance in relief, those who did not join the initiative did not feel it appropriate to contest it very loudly.

Conclusion

The reform of humanitarianism, like humanitarian reform of society, starts with the highest ambitions and best intentions. Facing undefined evil—and drawing legitimization from undefined evil—actors then focus on a limited aspect of reality that they feel they can do something about. The impact of the reforms of humanitarianism is mediated by existing practices and institutions. The logic of the field of humanitarian relief organizations is not only resilient in the face of these reforms; it reasserts itself. Both Sphere and HAP have become incorporated into the processes of producing projects, and with their respective standards shape specific products and add to the infrastructure of the market for projects.

Sphere standards, though they are based on universal human rights and include principles about process, begin to operate in analogy to a standard for products, helping to determine what a good project in a given technical area for a select group of beneficiaries should look like. Though Sphere is often associated with the "professionalization" of humanitarian relief, it represents a deprofessionalization for the doctors in the field and is resisted as a form of managerialism. The case raises the question of the relationship between fields and professions in the sociological sense. The field of humanitarian relief is one that does not coincide with a profession, like the field of law; rather, it incorporates one of the professions among different kinds of roles and forms of knowledge, leading to disagreements about which forms of accountability are appropriate.

HAP is based on the insight that beneficiaries do not have consumer or voting power vis-à-vis aid agencies. But by implementing process standards inspired by quality management, it does not give beneficiaries the role of consumers; rather, it comes to operate like a fair trade standard that allows donors to signal that they consume ethically higher-value products, and allows agencies to avoid destructive competition at the expense of beneficiaries involved in the process.

In the final chapter, I turn to one of the important alternative lenses for confronting global suffering. I will discuss the concept of human rights and the activities it inspires to consider its implications both for humanitarian relief and for the account of global order I have presented here based on the sociology of specialized fields of practice.

SIX

What about Human Rights?

I swear that neither I nor anybody else knows what the true anything is, but I can reassure you that it is about to be put into practice. ROBERT MUSIL, *THE MAN WITHOUT QUALITIES*

Humanitarianism is not the only discourse that plays a role in framing how Western audiences read social problems in faraway places. "Development" has been an important concept since the end of colonialism, but it has lost some of its power, partly because of the rise of humanitarian relief. "Human rights," on the other hand, emerged as a concept that organizes practice at roughly the same time as humanitarian relief and now stands alongside it in shaping our relationship to distant suffering. To return for a moment to the example of the crisis in Darfur, which I cited at the beginning of the introduction to this book, the conflict in Western Sudan and the suffering of the people there has been seen in the West both as a "humanitarian emergency" and as an issue of "human rights." It has sometimes also been discussed as an issue of "conflict resolution" and "peacekeeping," but rarely has it been framed in terms of development, even though Sudan has long been host to development agencies.

In this final chapter, I examine the role of human rights in mediating distant suffering from the particular perspective of a sociology of specialized fields of practice and from the perspective of a focus on the practices of humanitarian relief organizations. This allows me, on the one hand, to revisit the role that ideas do and do not play in responding to human suffering. It also allows me to discuss what many hail as the major alternative to humanitarian relief as a way of relating to distant suffering. Broadening the range of forms of mediation considered with the conceptual tools on which this book is based in this way also allows me to start carving out the choices that I think do and do not matter when we consider the different forms of politics we might adopt toward distant suffering, which I will take up again in the conclusion.

I have analyzed the field of humanitarian relief, and in discussing human rights I will start by noting that human rights has itself become the center of a field of organizations, with its own shared routines and its own symbolic divisions.[1] In its shared routines and practices the organizations that form part of the field of human rights select from the range of meanings that the concept of human rights might have in terms of action. In their symbolic contestations human rights organizations debate what it means to be a "legitimate" human rights organization, just as humanitarian organizations debate what it means to be a humanitarian organization.

Second, I will analyze how relief workers have used the concept of human rights.[2] Humanitarian relief NGOs have used the language of rights and human rights more and more since the late 1990s. Relief workers have drawn on human rights claims in a variety of different contexts, and with different practical implications. As I will show, the way relief workers have taken up the concept has been rather selective. This selectivity has been shaped by the shared practices of the humanitarian field and the symbolic contestations within the humanitarian field.

I will discuss three ways in which relief workers use the concept of human rights. First, relief workers often equate the concept of human rights with a concern for violence against people in crisis situations, and associate action in the name of human rights with the agenda of "protection." But protection becomes an agency's practical concern mostly as a project for specific beneficiaries and a product for specific donors. Second, aid agencies take up the concept of human rights in the context of "rights-based relief." The impact of this attempt to give relief a foundation

1. For two leading accounts of this, see Yves Dezalay and Bryant Garth, "From the Cold War to Kosovo: The Rise and Renewal of the Field of International Human Rights," *Annual Review of Law and Social Science* 2 (2006): 231–55; and Nicolas Guilhot, "Limiting Sovereignty or Producing Governmentality? Two Human Rights Regimes in U.S. Political Discourse," *Constellations* 15, no. 4 (2008): 502–16.

2. James Darcy, "Locating Responsibility: The Sphere Humanitarian Charter and Its Rationale," *Disasters* 28, no. 2 (2004): 112–23; David Chandler, "The Road to Military Humanitarianism: How the Human Rights NGOs Shaped a New Humanitarian Agenda," *Human Rights Quarterly* 23, no. 3 (2001): 678–700; International Council of Voluntary Agencies, "Proceedings: Workshop on the Development of Human Rights Training for Humanitarian Actors, Geneva, 29–30 November 2001," http://www.icva.ch/doc00000748.html.

in human rights is limited by standards being implemented in projects for specific beneficiaries chosen by the relief organization; people's right to relief can become the right of those who are served by relief agencies to the services the relief agency has to offer. Third, relief workers also express concerns and desires about long-term consequences of relief work using the language of human rights.

Before I discuss the ways the use of rights language is practiced and contested in these fields, I need to discuss the ways "human rights" and "humanitarianism" or "humanitarian relief" are constructed as objects of inquiry in discussions of global civil society. I will suggest that a focus on human rights or humanitarianism as (unitary) bodies of ideas obscures rather than illuminates the phenomena involved, and I introduce a number of distinctions that I suggest are more helpful in examining practices and institutions (and, as I will suggest, political choices) in this area.

The International Community: Ideas, Practices, Fields of Organizations

When we hear about hopes associated with the "international community" or "global civil society," human rights work and humanitarian relief are sometimes implied to be pulling in the same direction. The Canadian intellectual and politician, Michael Ignatieff, for example, has hailed a "revolution of moral concern," a revolution of which he thinks both human rights and humanitarian assistance form a part.[3] This unity is sometimes also assumed by critics who dismiss *both* human rights work and humanitarian relief as tools of imperialism.[4]

Others see the two as fundamentally different modes of engagement drawing on an old opposition between "charity" and "politics" or "rights." On one side of the debate, commentators draw on a long tradition of dismissing charity in the name of rights (Immanuel Kant), real change (Karl Marx and Friedrich Engels), or political action (Hannah Arendt), arguing that humanitarian work is short-term and only palliative. For some human rights activists, human rights is meant to address the "real" suffering—associated with state violence, and forcible death, rather than the "soft" issues such as health care or nutrition—and the real politics—long-term in orientation, addressing the causes of suffer-

3. Michael Ignatieff, *The Lesser Evil: Political Ethics in an Age of Terror* (Princeton, NJ: Princeton University Press, 2004).

4. E.g., Costas Douzinas, "Humanity, Military Humanism, and the New Moral Order," *Economy and Society* 32, no. 2 (2003): 159–83.

ing and based on respect of people as holding rights, not just as having needs.[5] Some associated with humanitarian relief and charity value the merits of their tradition over and above human rights work, which they consider unduly political.[6]

Whether scholars and commentators assume an essential unity or an essential difference between these approaches, whether they prefer one over the other, subscribe to both or reject both, they often share a focus on the *content* of ideas. I have argued in chapter 1 that ideas are not just contested, or contradictory, but are, on a very basic level, in their relationship to practice, indeterminate. I will now argue that in order to understand the role of human rights and the relationship between human rights and humanitarian relief, we need to distinguish first between human rights and humanitarian relief as sets of ideas, second between the universe of practices that are or could be claimed to be human rights or humanitarian practices, and third between the field of human rights organizations and the field of humanitarian relief organizations.

I have argued that the practices that could be claimed to be humanitarian practices are diverse and are not confined to specific organizations or actors. Similarly, the practices that could be claimed to be human rights practices are not confined to human rights organizations. Practices by local social movement actors, and state officials, for example, are or could be claimed as human rights practices according to one definition or another.[7]

If we consider the universe of practices that have been or could be claimed to be human rights and humanitarian practices with some reason, we find it to be diverse along axes of variation that crosscut a division into

<hr />

5. Immanuel Kant, *Perpetual Peace, and Other Essays on Politics, History, and Morals*, trans. Ted Humphrey (Indianapolis: Hackett, 1983); Karl Marx and Friedrich Engels, *The Communist Manifesto* (London: Penguin, 1967); Hannah Arendt, *The Human Condition* (Chicago: University of Chicago Press, 1958); Hannah Arendt to Wystan Auden, February 14, 1960, General Correspondence, 1938–1976, Hannah Arendt Papers, Manuscripts Division, Library of Congress; for a digitized version, see http://memory.loc.gov/ammem/index.html.

6. David Rieff, *A Bed for the Night: Humanitarianism in Crisis* (New York: Simon & Schuster, 2003); Chandler, "Road to Military Humanitarianism."

7. See the following for accounts of a broader set of human rights practices from a sociological and anthropological perspective: Richard Wilson, *Human Rights, Culture and Context: Anthropological Perspectives* (London: Pluto, 1997); Kate Nash, *The Cultural Politics of Human Rights: Comparing the US and UK* (Cambridge: Cambridge University Press, 2009); Kate Nash, "Human Rights, Movements, and Law: On Not Researching Legitimacy," *Sociology* 46, no. 5 (2012): 797–812; Fuyuki Kurasawa, *The Work of Global Justice: Human Rights as Practices* (New York: Cambridge University Press, 2007); Sally Merry and Mark Goodale, *The Practice of Human Rights: Tracking Law between the Global and the Local* (Cambridge: Cambridge University Press, 2007); Sally Engle Merry, "Rights Talk and the Experience of Law: Implementing Women's Human Rights to Protection from Violence," *Human Rights Quarterly* 25, no. 2 (2003): 243–381; Merry, "Transnational Human Rights and Local Activism: Mapping the Middle," *American Anthropologist* 108, no. 1 (2006): 38–51.

short-term goals/ long-term goals

short-term funding/ long-term funding

short-term needs/ long-term needs

local/ within national borders/ across national borders/ within the borders of an empire

respect/ patronising attitude

state-sponsored/not state-sponsored

volunteers/ full-time paid staff

self-organized/ on behalf of others

managerial concerns/ grassroots struggle

targeting groups/ targeting issues/ targeting individuals

political rights/ economic and social rights/ no distinction

6.1   Distinctions among practices in human rights and humanitarian relief

"relief" and "rights." We cannot assume that human rights and humanitarianism stand up as relatively stable groupings based on the content of
ideology, associating human rights with respectful practices and long-
term orientation, for example, and relief with short-term commitments
by nonstate actors. Practices can be sponsored by a state or be independent
of government funding. They can be implemented in a managerial way or
be closely connected to grassroots struggle. They can involve a long-term
commitment of resources or a short-term commitment of resources. All
the distinctions in figure 6.1 are potentially independent of each other.
That means that if we care about one or another of these attributes, we
have to examine it independently of the others, and independently of the
groupings of "human rights" and "humanitarianism."

The Field of Human Rights Organizations

In previous chapters, I have analyzed the field of humanitarian relief
organizations, its history, its shared practices, and its symbolic structure.

During the course of the 1970s, the concept of human rights also became the center of an organized field of practice, with its own shared routines and its own symbolic divisions. There is a set of organizations that understand themselves as humanitarian organizations and see humanitarian organizations as their peers, and a set of organizations that understand themselves as human rights organizations and see human rights organizations as their peers. I focus here on what Alex de Waal has termed secondary—as opposed to primary—human rights organizations.[8] The practices in the field of human rights organizations are only a subset of all human rights practices—but the organizations that strive to be part of the global field of human rights organizations have been influential in the way the concept of human rights is imagined in the international arena.[9] In its shared routines and practices, the organizations that form part of the field of human rights select from the range of meanings that the concept of human rights might have in terms of action.

This field has a specific history as well, starting with specific organizations and more recently consolidating to fully show the kind of dynamics we associate with fields in the Bourdieusian tradition. Specialized human rights organizations already played a role in the interwar years: the International Federation of Human Rights Leagues, for example, was founded in 1922. Symbolic divisions appeared relatively early: in the early years of the Cold War, the US government supported the International Commission of Jurists in opposition to the liberal Association Internationale des Juristes Democrates.[10] Amnesty International was founded in 1961 and remains perhaps the most prestigious human rights organization.

But only since the 1970s have human rights NGOs begun to play the prominent role we are accustomed to today.[11] Samuel Moyn has argued that it was during this time that references to human rights really became part of general political discussion, and that the concept took on the particular meaning associated with it today. The project of human rights became an utopian project framed in opposition to politics; human rights became framed in opposition to states.[12] The number of human

8. Alex de Waal, "Human Rights, Institutional Wrongs," in *Rethinking International Organizations: Pathology and Promise*, ed. Dennis Dijkzeul and Yves Beigbeder (New York: Berghahn, 2003), 234–60.

9. De Waal, "Human Rights, Institutional Wrongs."

10. Dezalay and Garth, "From the Cold War to Kosovo."

11. De Waal, "Human Rights, Institutional Wrongs"; de Waal, *Famine Crimes: Politics and the Disaster Relief Industry* (London: James Currey, 1997); Guilhot, "Limiting Sovereignty or Producing Governmentality?"

12. Samuel Moyn, *The Last Utopia: Human Rights in History* (Cambridge, MA: Harvard University Press, 2012). For a history that emphasizes continuity across a longer period, see Lynn Hunt, *Inventing Human Rights: A History* (New York: Norton, 2007).

rights organizations multiplied during the 1980s and 1990s, and funding increased significantly.[13] As Yves Dezalay and Bryant Garth have argued, it was in this period that the symbolic divisions between human rights organizations ceased to be simple reflections of opposing Cold War strategies and developed their own relative autonomy.[14]

It is important to note that the most prominent specialized human rights organizations interpret the concept of human rights in a specific way. As part of its consolidation as a field, human rights has taken a legal turn, a development that does not by necessity follow from the ideas handed down as human rights, for example, in the antislavery movement.[15] Human rights organizations of this type call for very specific practices. Human rights organizations focus on collecting evidence in specific ways, and on writing reports. They engage in advocacy work, conduct campaigns, and educate people about rights. As Alex de Waal has pointed out, these organizations combine a focus on research, documentation, and publication with the skilled use of the media and lobbying of politicians to make their concerns known. The basic premise of these activities is that if people or the public know about an abuse, they will be moved to want to stop it.[16] Clifford Bob identifies the product in what he analyzes as "the market for human rights" as "information."[17]

Specialized human rights NGOs have also chosen a specific substantive focus. Amnesty International has built its authority partly through its focus on a single type of victim and an especially pure one, the nonviolent prisoner of conscience. Most organizations still focus attention on the most direct violations of fundamental rights, such as torture, arbitrary detention, and execution, combined with some concern for civil and political rights more broadly. Social and economic rights have traditionally been less prominent.[18]

This field of human rights organizations is in itself divided. Nicolas

---

13. Jackie Smith, Ron Pagnucco, and George A. Lopez, "Globalizing Human Rights: The Work of Transnational Human Rights NGOs in the 1990s," *Human Rights Quarterly* 20, no. 2 (1998): 379–412.

14. Dezalay and Garth, "From the Cold War to Kosovo."

15. Ibid.

16. De Waal, "Human Rights, Institutional Wrongs," 243; see also Claire Moon, "What One Sees and How One Files Seeing: Human Rights Reporting, Representation and Action," *Sociology* 46, no. 5 (2012): 876–90; and Ron Dudai, "'Can You Describe This?' Human Rights Reports and What They Tell Us about the Human Rights Movement," in *Humanitarianism and Suffering*, ed Richard Ashby Wilson and Richard D Brown (Cambridge: Cambridge University Press), 245–65.

17. Bob, Clifford, "The Market in Human Rights," in *Advocacy Organizations and Collective Action*, ed. Aseem Prakash and Mary Kay Guggerty (Cambridge: Cambridge University Press, 2010), 133–55.

18. De Waal, "Human Rights, Institutional Wrongs." However, after much internal discussion, Amnesty International has taken on social and economic rights since 2001, and both Amnesty and Human Rights Watch now produce reports on labor issues.

Guilhot diagnoses a division between activists who use international law to limit state sovereignty, on the one hand, and others, associated with neoconservative agendas, who see the principal aim of human rights work as democracy promotion.[19] A division between purity and pollution also structures the field of human rights. To take up some of the distinctions discussed above, some organizations pursue state-sponsored projects, and others rely on private donations. Amnesty International preserves its status as a membership-driven organization and resists professionalization and managerial concerns to some extent, whereas Human Rights Watch fully embraces professional fund-raising and public relations strategies.[20]

The Use of Human Rights in the Field of Humanitarian Relief

Humanitarian relief organizations have increasingly engaged with the concept of human rights in recent years.[21] This trend has been prompted and shaped by the rising profile of human rights organizations, the rising power of the concept in development aid, [22] and, most importantly, the rise of the "complex emergency" and the "emergency imaginary."[23]

19. Nicolas Guilhot, *The Democracy Makers* (New York: Columbia University Press, 2005); Guilhot, "Limiting Sovereignty or Producing Governmentality?"

20. Steven Hopgood, *Keepers of the Flame: Understanding Amnesty International* (Ithaca, NY: Cornell University Press, 2006). See also Wendy Wong, *Internal Affairs: How the Structure of NGOs Transforms Human Rights* (Ithaca, NY: Cornell University Press, 2012) for an excellent analysis of how organizational structures affect the outcomes of human rights work, including an excellent account of Amnesty International.

21. See Darcy, "Locating Responsibility"; Chandler, "Road to Military Humanitarianism." In 1998, the Inter-Agency Standing Committee for UN and NGO actors created a task force for human rights and humanitarian action and brought humanitarians together for discussions about training humanitarian staff in human rights law (see International Council of Voluntary Agencies, "Proceedings: Workshop on the Development of Human Rights Training for Humanitarian Actors"). Many agencies have developed their own handbooks regarding rights-based relief; see CARE Human Rights Initiative, "Basic Introduction to Human Rights and Rights-Based Programming" (N.p.: CARE Human Rights Initiative, n.d.); Maureen O'Flynn and International Save the Children Alliance. *Child Rights Programming: How to Apply Rights-Based Approaches in Programming; A Handbook for International Save the Children Alliance Members* (Stockholm: Save the Children Sweden, 2002). Many mission statements use the language of human rights: Save the Children refers to children's rights; Oxfam's goal is "a just and safer world in which people take control over their own lives and enjoy basic rights"; see Darcy, "Locating Responsibility."

22. Kate Manzo, "Africa in the Rise of Rights-Based Development," *Geoforum* 34, no. 4 (2003): 437–56; see also Hannah Miller, "From 'Rights-Based' to 'Rights-Framed' Approaches: A Social Constructionist View of Human Rights Practice," *International Journal of Human Rights* 14, no. 6 (November 2010): 915–31.

23. Craig Calhoun, "A World of Emergencies: Fear, Intervention, and the Limits of Cosmopolitan Order," *Canadian Review of Sociology and Anthropology* 41, no. 4 (2004): 373–95; Calhoun, "The Idea of Emergency: Humanitarian Action and Global (Dis)Order," in *Contemporary States of Emergency: The*

Both humanitarian and human rights organizations have been concerned with some of the same high-profile crises—Rwanda and Darfur, for example; and both have been associated with these crises by the public. These settings have pushed both sets of organizations beyond their traditional concerns. Human rights organizations developed an interest in working with the United Nations and with humanitarian agencies in crises like those in Mozambique, Rwanda, and Sierra Leone. As de Waal observed, "Many of the places where human rights violations are most acute are no longer authoritarian states but so-called complex emergencies—otherwise known as civil wars—that have unleashed mass human displacement and hunger. . . . Where there are no effective governments (e.g. Somalia) conventional human rights activism cannot work."[24] Relief agencies, in turn, today work not only in natural disasters but also in refugee camps and drawn-out civil wars. Agencies' experiences in these settings have led them to question the limitations of classic conceptions of relief as urgent and short-term. Agencies found themselves working in relief camps for years, and this led them to doubt the focus on material basic needs and has raised questions about the role of education, for example.[25] Long-term work also prompted reflections on how exactly to conceptualize the relationship between the agency and the people being helped.

Some associated with the sector have high hopes for the role the concept of human rights can play within humanitarian relief. Hugo Slim, for example, wrote in 2000 that "the development of universal human rights whose fundamental value is a human dignity founded in individual equality, personal freedom and social and economic justice, easily encompasses humanitarian and development activity and shows them to have common ends."[26]

I shall argue here, however, that the concept of human rights cannot provide unity for humanitarian relief in practice. It cannot even fulfill that role for human rights work. As I will show in the remainder of this chapter, the impact of the concept of human rights on humanitarian relief has been mediated by what agencies have been doing already as well as by the symbolic divisions of the humanitarian field.

Politics of Military and Humanitarian Interventions, ed. Didier Fassin and Mariella Pandolfi (New York: Zone Books, 2011).

24. De Waal, "Human Rights, Institutional Wrongs," 244.

25. On the relationship between humanitarianism and education, see Aurora Fredrikson, "Making Humanitarian Spaces Global: Coordinating Crisis Response through the Cluster Approach" (PhD diss., Columbia University, 2012).

26. Hugo Slim, "*Dissolving the Difference between Relief and Development: The Making of a Rights-Based Solution,*" *Development in Practice* 10, no. 3 (2000): 493.

There are three main ways in which humanitarian relief agencies have assimilated the term "human rights" into their work, which I will discuss in turn. First, relief workers have translated a concern with human rights into an agenda of *protection*. Second, humanitarian relief agencies have formulated the program of *rights-based relief*. Third, relief agencies have used the language of human rights as a way to reflect on the *long-term consequences* of humanitarian work.

It is also worth noting what humanitarian relief organizations have *not* done as a response to human rights discourses. They have largely not taken on the practices of human rights organizations, such as monitoring and reporting, though they have discussed how they relate to these practices, because specialized human rights organizations such as Amnesty International and Human Rights Watch have had such an influence on how human rights are understood. But unlike human rights organizations, humanitarian relief agencies need access and a substantial presence in the field in order to deliver relief, and they have voiced fears that reporting abuse might damage their relationship to host governments. Humanitarian relief agencies have also not aimed to provide coverage for needs, and they have not institutionalized any legitimate expectations toward themselves, as states have been forced to do in the past.

Human Rights as the Danger of Violent Death: The Agenda of Protection

Relief workers talk about "protection" to express a concern about violence against civilians and the wish to do something about it. Protection has roots in international humanitarian law reaching back to the nineteenth century, but it has become a more prominent issue in discussions about global affairs since the 1990s. The crises of Rwanda (1994) and Bosnia (1995) in particular put the question of protection on the international agenda; both these crises represent not only atrocities but atrocities that a humanitarian presence in situ failed to deter. Humanitarians who write about protection tend to assume that the agenda of protection and the question of the role of human rights in humanitarian relief are one and the same.[27]

Violence directed at civilians is not a new phenomenon. Civilians have long become victims of warfare between states. The distinction between

---

27. Richard J. Brennan and Gerald Martone, "The Evolving Role of Relief Organizations in Human Rights and Protection," in *Fear of Persecution: Global Human Rights, International Law, and Human Well-Being*, ed. James D. White and Anthony J. Marsella (Lanham, MD: Lexington Books, 2007); Mark Frohardt, Diane Paul, and Larry Minear, *Protecting Human Rights: The Challenge to Humanitarian Organizations*, Occasional Paper 35 (Providence, RI: Thomas J. Watson Jr. Institute for International Studies, 1999).

combatants and noncombatants has not been obvious to warring parties in the past—as historians of warfare confirm for the warriors described in the Hebrew Bible and the Viking raiders and as is clear for the Germans in Namibia, the United States in Vietnam, and the parties in the conflict in former Yugoslavia.[28] Internal conflicts and civil wars have a long and painful history. Physical violence against subjects or citizens has also always had a role to play in maintaining power. There has also long been concern on the part of outsiders about violence against civilians, especially when it coincided with cultural ties or national interest.[29]

As an area of extensive practical activity for nongovernmental organizations, however, protection is a relatively recent phenomenon. The ICRC's original focus was on treating those wounded in war, not on preventing violence. Following the First World War and in response to the refugee crisis of the 1920s and 1930s, the ICRC expanded its range of activities. It organized visits to prisoners of war and relief operations for refugees outside Russia in the early 1920s, during the Italo-Ethiopian War in 1935–36, and during the Spanish Civil War. The ICRC tried to enhance the legal protection of civilians caught up in armed conflict during the interwar years and secured protections for prisoners of war in 1929.[30] The Holocaust prompted new discussions among states about legal protections for civilians targeted inside a state, and these discussions have had a significant impact on international law. Today, legally speaking, refugees are protected under refugee law. International humanitarian law is applicable during times of international and internal armed conflict and extends to refugees as long as they flee to an occupied or belligerent or internally conflicted country. Internally displaced people are protected by international human rights law.[31]

There was concern about violence against civilians, and there were legal protections, but practically speaking, during the Cold War, protection of civilians was limited to the ICRC and the United Nations' refugee agency, UNHCR. Human rights organizations were focused on writ-

28. Susan Niditch, *War in the Hebrew Bible: A Study in the Ethics of Violence* (Oxford: Oxford University Press, 1993); Christopher T. Allmand, "War and the Non-Combatant in the Middle Ages," in *Medieval Warfare*, ed. Maurice Keen (Oxford: Oxford University Press, 1999), 253–72; Hugo Slim, "Why Protect Civilians? Innocence, Immunity and Enmity in War," *International Affairs* 79, no. 3 (2003): 481–501; Geoffrey Francis Andrew Best, *Humanity in Warfare* (London: Weidenfeld and Nicolson, 1980).

29. Gary Bass, *Freedom's Battle: The Origins of Humanitarian Intervention* (New York: Alfred A. Knopf, 2008).

30. Jean-Luc Blondel, "Getting Access to the Victims: Role and Activities of the ICRC," *Journal of Peace Research* 24, no. 3 (1987): 307–14.

31. Fiona Terry, *Condemned to Repeat? The Paradox of Humanitarian Action* (Ithaca, NY: Cornell University Press, 2002), 28.

ing reports, maintaining only a limited presence inside authoritarian regimes and relying on public opinion to force changes. Mainstream humanitarian relief agencies often worked in camps outside the main conflict zones. "During the Cold War respect for norms of state sovereignty usually relegated aid organizations to refugee camps on the periphery of conflicts and few ventured inside a country at war."[32] Agencies aided refugees from Cambodia in Thailand, and refugees from Nicaragua in Honduras, for example.

MSF in that period worked in places others did not go to; for example, it famously provided services behind mujahideen lines in Afghanistan. MSF combines providing medical services with appealing to states' responsibilities to uphold their obligations vis-à-vis civilians. But MSF initially did not envision it to be its role to protect civilians beyond the power of its witnessing.

After the end of the Cold War, suffering populations became accessible in a new way. Agencies found themselves working within war zones. Operation Lifeline Sudan in 1989 began a period during which the United Nations negotiated access for aid agencies in ongoing civil conflicts.[33] After 1990 there was also a change in the way the international community responded to refugee flows, shifting to an effort to provide aid in source countries.[34] Aid workers found themselves in situations where they had to confront the question of violence. Safety became something that affected their work and something that they thought they ought to do something about.

In Rwanda and in Bosnia, refugee camps became targets of attacks. Aid workers feared they were irrelevant or, worse, sharing some responsibility for the violence that occurred. What use was their work if they delivered food in the context of violence they could do nothing about? Fiona Terry recalls MSF's experience in Bosnia: "The failure of the UN Protection Force (UNPROFOR) to protect the 'safe area' of Srebrenica in Bosnia in 1995 forced MSF to consider to what extent its presence in the enclave contributed to the illusion of protection that encouraged the population to stay and hence what share of responsibility it ought to assume for the tragedy."[35]

32. Ibid., 143.
33. Mark Duffield, *Global Governance and the New Wars: The Merging of Development and Security* (London: Zed Books, 2001), 77.
34. Bill Frelick, "Paradigm Shifts in the International Responses to Refugees," in *Fear of Persecution: Global Human Rights, International Law, and Human Well-Being*, ed. James White and Anthony J. Marsella (Lanham, MD: Lexington Books, 2007), 33–59.
35. Terry, *Condemned to Repeat?*, 18.

In this context, many relief workers felt it was no longer enough to provide material assistance. A guide on protection for relief agencies published by the professional association ALNAP begins: "Agencies realize they have an obligation to work with communities, mandated agencies, and responsible authorities to ensure people's safety as well as providing assistance to those in need."[36]

In 1996 the ICRC began to host a series of conversations in Geneva that brought humanitarian and human rights workers together for discussions around protection.[37] Protection also became a fundable issue and thus an opportunity for programming. But states were under pressured to "do something" about violence against civilians. States have been ambivalent about intervening in faraway crises. The US experience in Somalia further dampened enthusiasm for intervention.[38] Donor governments thus welcomed NGOs' contributions in crises and their framing of protection projects.

Some practices are shared between relief and human rights agencies in this area. Human rights standards inform the assessment that is part of protection programming. However, relief agencies have reservations about giving public testimony because it might affect their ability to operate in an area. In some cases they will pass on information to an organization that can better present findings to a public.[39]

Agencies consider a broad range of activities to be within the framework of protection. A practical guide for agencies on the issue recommends objectives including the following:

Women and girls will have safe access to water and move freely to collect it without intimidation.

Families will have sufficient and appropriately designed shelter in IDP camps that enables them to balance privacy with freedom of movement and association.

All children in IDP camp X will have access to good quality primary education.[40]

In some cases, agencies think about the protection implications of activities that have long been part of the repertoire of relief agencies in the

36. Hugo Slim and Andrew Bonwick, "Protection: An ALNAP Guide for Humanitarian Agencies" (Oxford: Oxfam Publications, 2006), 3.

37. Sylvie Giossi Caverzasio, *Strengthening Protection in War: A Search for Professional Standards, Summary of Discussions among Human Rights and Humanitarian Organizations—Workshops at the ICRC, 1996-2000* (Geneva: ICRC, 2001).

38. Mark Cutts, "Politics and Humanitarianism," *Refugee Survey Quarterly* 17, no. 1 (1998): 1-15; Samantha Power, *A Problem from Hell: America and the Age of Genocide* (New York: Basic Books, 2002).

39. Brennan and Martone, "Evolving Role of Relief Organizations."

40. Slim and Bonwick, "Protection," 73.

sectors of water and sanitation, shelter, or education. These are cases of what Peter Uvin calls "rhetorical packaging."[41] In other cases, as the example above shows, protection simply means trying to reduce the risks that populations incur by being part of a relief program: if water points or latrines are located at the edge of the camp, women and girls are in danger of assaults and rape. This does add a new layer of reflexiveness to humanitarian work, but it does not fully confront the external threats to populations in need.

A tension remains between protection as an end in itself, protection as a precondition for meaningful humanitarian relief, and protection as a basis for broader political transformations. What is new about the protection agenda is that it claims the authority to intervene provisioned for in international humanitarian law, for a range of actors, on a range of issues to which international humanitarian law, refugee law, or human rights law may apply. This agenda was to come to full fruition with the new legal doctrine of a "responsibility to protect."[42]

For agencies, concerns about protection are linked to their own projects. Agencies have taken up protection as an area of programming. In extreme cases, they use the protection agenda to further their existing programming. De Waal reports on an extreme case of this in Rwanda. In this case, de Waal explains, agencies "insisted on awarding refugee status to people who were refugees from justice. . . . Agencies interpreted IHL— and their own elaboration of it, called humanitarian principles—to mean that it was not legitimate for one belligerent to attack another simply because the former were based in a populated area receiving relief aid. . . . They compounded the error by calling for an international military intervention to protect their aid programs."[43]

Human Rights as an Attitude: Rights-Based Relief

Some humanitarian relief workers have looked to the concept of human rights as a new basis for the work they have already been doing. In this

41. Peter Uvin, quoted in Tammie O'Neil, *Human Rights and Poverty Reduction: Realities, Controversies, and Strategies* (London: Overseas Development Institute, 2006), 51; Sara Pantuliano and Sorcha O'Callaghan, "'The Protection Crisis': A Review of Field-Based Strategies for Humanitarian Protection in Darfur," HPG Discussion Papers (London: ODI, 2006); Marc Dubois, "Protection—The New Humanitarian Fig-Leaf," n.d., accessed November 18, 2012, http://www.urd.org/IMG/pdf/Protection_Fig-Leaf_DuBois.pdf.

42. Gareth Evans and Mohamed Sahnoun, "The Responsibility to Protect," *Foreign Affairs* 81, no. 6 (2002): 99–110; Thomas Weiss, "The Sunset of Humanitarian Intervention? The Responsibility to Protect in a Unipolar Era," *Security Dialogue* 35, no. 2 (2004): 135–53; David Chandler, "The Responsibility to Protect? Imposing the Liberal Peace," *International Peacekeeping* 11, no. 1 (2004): 59–81.

43. De Waal, "Human Rights, Institutional Wrongs," 257.

tradition, humanitarians argue that people not only *need* food, water, health care, and shelter but have a *right* to food, water, health care, and shelter. By adopting rights language, officials have hoped that they could help take relief beyond charity, and that the concept of human rights could serve as the basis for a new relationship to the populations agencies work with, shaping an encounter with beneficiaries as rights holders rather than primarily people in need.

We have discussed the Sphere Project as an attempt to ground humanitarian work in the concept of human rights. In this context, the concept of human rights is used in a way that emphasizes basic material needs, not civil or political rights. Regarding those material needs the Sphere Handbook covers a broad range of issues. The Humanitarian Charter speaks of the right of people to an adequate standard of living, and the Sphere standards give aid workers an indication of what an adequate standard of living might mean concretely.

But as the Declaration of Human Rights gets translated into the Sphere Handbook, and the Sphere Handbook gets translated into agency practice, a subtle shift can take place. The right of every human being to a life with dignity becomes the right of targeted beneficiaries to goods and services offered by unspecified third parties. The Sphere Handbook is already explicit about this: "Sphere is based on two core beliefs: first, that all possible steps should be taken to alleviate human suffering arising out of calamity and conflict, and second, that those affected by disaster have a right to life with dignity and therefore *a right to assistance*."[44]

The document goes on to say: "We understand an individual's right to life to entail the right *to have steps taken to preserve life* where it is threatened, and a corresponding duty on others to take such steps."[45] Agencies have interpreted the rights-based approach as a mandate to increase their lobbying with states to encourage them to ensure that rights are fulfilled, rather than to provide relief themselves. Yet agencies also use the language of rights-based relief to argue for the rights of beneficiaries or potential beneficiaries to relief offered by them; to the extent that agencies chose the beneficiaries, the right to assistance can become the agency's right to assist within its areas of expertise.

44. Sphere Project, *Humanitarian Charter and Minimum Standards in Disaster Response* (Geneva: The Sphere Project, 2003), 17 (my emphasis).
45. Sphere Project, *Humanitarian Charter and Minimum Standards*, 17.

Human Rights as Political Consequences

Humanitarianism is supposed to focus on the relief of suffering as an end in itself. It is an important part of the definition of humanitarian relief in its pure form that those who pursue it must not have any other benefits of their actions in mind, and that they must act on their principles—to some extent without regard for the consequences. Despite this emphasis on humanitarian relief as an end in itself—and indeed partly because of this emphasis—reflection on the possible effects of relief—both desirable and undesirable effects—has haunted the field.[46]

In this context, relief workers have used the language of human rights to express concern regarding the consequences of their own work. We could call these consequences political, but relief workers and commentators often prefer to use the language of human rights. These consequences could be immediate or long-term consequences of humanitarian action; they could be negative or positive consequences, desired or undesired consequences.

Framing "political consequences" in terms of "human rights" has analytical costs. David Kennedy, an experienced international human rights lawyer and scholar, has pointed out that the concept of rights deals only in absolute rights and wrongs and makes it hard to weigh costs and benefits in a practical way.[47] This feature is part of what makes the concept so attractive for those in humanitarian relief. The language of human rights has become fashionable in a variety of fields, but there are specific reasons why humanitarians find it appealing. Because humanitarian authority is built on an opposition to politics, relief workers have a particular difficulty conceiving of their work in political terms. When the ideology of pure relief fails in confrontation with the real world, the concept of human rights provides an alternative alternative to the profane world of politics.

Agencies' experience in the refugee camps in Goma in the aftermath of the genocide in Rwanda is also often framed as a dilemma of pure relief versus "human rights consequences." The camps in Zaire provided refuge

46. Mary B. Anderson, *Do No Harm: How Aid Can Support Peace-or War* (Boulder, CO: Lynne Rienner Publishers, 1999); Terry, *Condemned to Repeat?*; Peter Uvin, *Aiding Violence: The Development Enterprise in Rwanda* (West Hartford, CT: Kumarian Press, 1998); Sarah K. Lischer, *Dangerous Sanctuaries: Refugee Camps, Civil War, and the Dilemmas of Humanitarian Aid* (Ithaca, NY: Cornell University Press, 2006).

47. David Kennedy, *The Dark Sides of Virtue: Reassessing International Humanitarianism* (Princeton, NJ: Princeton University Press, 2004).

to people who had fled Rwanda as the Rwandan army advanced, with the power structures of entire villages largely intact. The refugees thus included the perpetrators of the genocide, and the violence continued. As recalled by Fiona Terry, then head of MSF France in Rwanda, on one side of the dilemma was conventional medical ethics demanding treatment for "anyone who needed it regardless of their history."[48] On the other side was what many termed an issue of "human rights," with the concept being used to label a complex set of concerns regarding the worthiness of patients, the social structure of the camp, and the killings that relief could not prevent and may have enabled.

In this way, a debate about principles took the place of what could have been a very complicated debate about evidence, politics, and responsibility, on the one hand, or a complicated calculation of the consequences of either course of action, on the other hand. This understanding of the relevance of human rights within relief is in tension with rights-based relief, which would claim that every human being has a right to these services. It is contested among relief workers whether humanitarian action can or should address these long-term concerns—and if so, how.

Relief workers also use human rights to evoke possible positive consequences of humanitarian relief. Donor agencies have increasingly emphasized the links between relief and longer-term strategic goals.[49] Some agencies hold that relief can and should be linked to long-term human rights targets, as well as to peace, stability, security, and development. The International Rescue Committee, for example, an agency with a traditional focus on refugees and disasters, has developed an expertise regarding the integration of relief, reconstruction, and development, and human rights is used to make the link between these.

Human Rights as a Stage for Symbolic Divisions

If, as I have argued, it is important to examine how concepts like human rights are translated into practices, it is also worth noting that the practices in question might be symbolic ones. Some argue that human rights is the tool that can save humanitarianism from itself—that is, from pure charity.[50] Others suggest that the concept is threatening to corrupt the

---

48. Terry, *Condemned to Repeat?*, 3.
49. Duffield, *Global Governance and the New Wars*.
50. Slim, "Is Humanitarianism Being Politicised? A Reply to David Rieff" (paper presented at the Dutch Red Cross Symposium on Ethics in Aid, The Hague, October 8, 2003).

soul of the humanitarian enterprise.[51] The positions in these debates can be better understood when considering the practical logic of the symbolic structure of the field. Agencies on the autonomous pole of the field contest the discourse of human rights to demonstrate their independence. They are wary of the use of rights language, because they see it as introducing considerations that compete with the pure notion of the relief of immediate suffering. Their role is to insist on the distinctive role of relief. Others in the field value the concept precisely because it allows them to link humanitarianism to resources in the political field, both with claims to be on the side of the oppressed and with cooperation with donor agencies. "Human rights" provides an alternative source of the sacred that allows humanitarian actors to engage in struggles over political authority without getting too entangled in what they see as mere everyday politics.

There are many good reasons to feel that neutrality is limiting for humanitarian relief or for working with the war-affected or the poor more generally. In principle, going beyond neutrality might allow relief agencies to become a true ally of the poor, working for political change. That is certainly the hope associated with human rights among some agencies in the English socialist tradition, such as Oxfam and Save the Children. Hugo Slim, for example, claims that, though ambivalent, rights talk is a Trojan horse for those opposed to mainstream power.[52]

Rights talk allows relief agencies to link relief with longer-term efforts as well as with advocacy efforts. It also give agencies considerable flexibility beyond the narrow confines of international humanitarian law, and it allows them to err on the side of accessing additional resources in the name of populations in need: CARE, for example, has been championing a rights-based approach. When other organizations, notably MSF, left Afghanistan because of concerns about their ability to provide independent relief, CARE argued that the population there had a right to relief, and that that justified accepting contracts from the US government in a context in which that same government was one of the warring parties. When asked about the role of human rights in relief, one former CARE employee explained to me:

I think it's really helped them [CARE] in difficult situations such as post-conflict situations like Afghanistan. . . . MSF was saying we can't be assisting the government, and

51. David Chandler, *From Kosovo to Kabul: Human Rights and International Intervention* (London: Pluto Press, 2002).

52. Hugo Slim, "A Response to Peter Uvin: Making Moral Low Ground; Rights as the Struggle for Justice and the Abolition of Development," *Praxis: The Fletcher School Journal of Development Studies* 17 (2002): 491–94.

we can't be assisting in recovery efforts, because this could jeopardize our humanitarian standing. . . . Whereas CARE and others were starting to work in stability programs and in building the peace and helping the government sort of get on its feet, and it's because CARE and others are not just humanitarian, but they also do development, so they kind of make that transition. Paul O'Brien was able to use the rights-based approach for I thought a pretty clear explanation of how CARE was approaching this, and that once the acute needs have passed, it's within the beneficiaries' best interest to have peace and security and stability, and that's where CARE was going.[53]

For the purist pole of the field CARE's use of the language of human rights seems to confirm that the discourse of human rights provides an entry point for a variety of political agendas. Writers associated with ICRC or MSF worry that rights-based claims may threaten their ability to function as independent humanitarian agencies.[54]

MSF on Rights

MSF confuses its observers with regard to its stance on the question of human rights. MSF is sometimes understood to be close to a human rights–inspired approach.[55] Yet MSF representatives have been among those most critical of the integration of the language of human rights into relief work. Once we move beyond the misleading question of whether MSF, or anyone else for that matter, is "for" human rights, or "against," MSF's position can be understood as a coherent expression of its position vis-à-vis other actors and vis-à-vis funding sources in the humanitarian field.

MSF is not opposed to human rights in the abstract, but it insists on a very specific role for humanitarian agencies. MSF has insisted on speaking out, since its beginning in Biafra, and this could be likened to practices associated with human rights monitoring. Linked to the duty to speak is the famous *droit d'ingérence*, or right of intervention," which asserts the humanitarian imperative to relieve suffering over and above state sovereignty. But MSF's public observations focus on violations of international humanitarian law and are usually closely related to MSF's medical operations. MSF's campaign for access to essential medicines could be seen as

---

53. Reference is to Paul O'Brien, "Politicized Humanitarianism: A Response to Nicolas de Torrente," *Harvard Human Rights Journal* 17, no. 1 (2004): 31–40.

54. Chandler, "Road to Military Humanitarianism"; Rieff, *Bed for the Night.*

55. E.g., Renée C. Fox, "Medical Humanitarianism and Human Rights: Reflections on Doctors Without Borders and Doctors of the World," *Social Science & Medicine* 41, no. 12 (1995): 1607–16.

a human rights campaign, but it is largely framed around "need" and around "access" for the poor.

MSF critiques other agencies' attempts to use human rights language in order to draw on political authority. The agency thereby performs its own purist position in the humanitarian field. MSF sees the integration of relief and human rights as dangerous because human rights provides a docking point for various political projects. Donor states may use relief projects to further their own political ends in receiving countries by appealing to the notion of human rights. MSF rhetoric also paints the specter of a future in which donor governments make receipt of relief fully dependent on compliance with their political demands couched in human rights language.[56]

MSF has kept its distance from rights-based relief and the Sphere Project. In their criticism of the Sphere standards, MSF representatives have emphasized that it blurs the question of whose responsibility it is to make sure the standards for a life with dignity are fulfilled.[57] MSF insists that agencies should never assume a task that should be the government's. This would not only ease responsibility on governments to care for their populations; it would also reduce the noble vocation of relief to a mere technical task.

Conclusion

Standing between donors and activists on the one hand, and distant suffering on the other hand, "human rights," to begin with, is just two words. The concept of human rights cannot provide unity for humanitarian relief on an ideological level—it cannot even fulfill that role for human rights work. Neither can it provide a coherent alternative to humanitarian relief. Because of the indeterminacy of the concept, we need a detailed examination—for human rights as well—of how the different meanings it could have are selected by and mediated through various institutional forms.

In this chapter, I have focused on how the impact of human rights ideas has been mediated by fields of organizations. The field of human

56. Nicolas de Torrente, "Humanitarianism Sacrificed: Integration's False Promise," *Ethics* 18, no. 2 (2004): 3–12; De Torrente, "Humanitarian Action under Attack: Reflections on the Iraq War," *Harvard Human Rights Journal* 17 (2004): 1–29.

57. Peter Giesen, "Sphere and Accountability: A View from MSF," (n.d.) http://www.sphere project.org/about/guest_nl5.htm; Charlotte Dufour et al., "Rights, Standards, and Quality in a Complex Humanitarian Space: Is Sphere the Right Tool?," *Disasters* 28, no. 2 (2004): 124–41.

rights organizations has privileged specific practices over others; it has focused on research and reporting, for example, and has not engaged in the provision of goods and services or mass mobilization to the same extent. At the same time, despite this relative narrowing in meaning, human rights work remains contested within the field of human rights.

In the field of humanitarian relief, "human rights" means different things as well. Human rights means a variety of things to relief workers precisely because there is not a single natural way for it to be translated into practice or related to their work. Relief workers incorporate the concept in ways that fit with what they have already been doing; in its different meanings, it is mediated by practices of project management, and by practices of symbolic contestation.

Human rights becomes an accessory to the production of projects, albeit one that increases reflexivity about some concerns that are usually externalized. Relief workers have used the concept of human rights to confront the fact that the people they are serving are sometimes threatened by physical violence; they have used it to confront the fact that their agencies sometimes have a long-term relationship with populations they serve, and that broader consequences—both undesired ones, such as the continuation of war and violence, and desired ones, like reconstruction and development—should matter to relief work—though this is contested. Relief workers seem to prefer the language of human rights to a more straightforward conversation about violence, politics, and consequences because human rights is in some way an alternative candidate for a purer alternative to politics.

Conclusion

This book has focused on humanitarian relief NGOs. I have argued that these organizations inhabit a shared social space, the field of humanitarian relief organizations. I have argued that they share practices, and that we can specify and describe the logic of practice of this field. I have argued, first, that relief agencies share practices of project management, and second that agencies produce projects for a quasi market, in which donors are the consumers. The project is a commodity, and thus those helped, beneficiaries, become a commodity.

Agencies produce projects with a defined outcome and a defined budget or price. Agencies seek to make a difference and seek to do projects that "add value." When agencies consider adding value, they consider resources, access, and their own prior experience. This introduces a dynamic that is relatively independent of the values of humanitarian relief, the needs of the populations on the ground, and the interests of donor governments.

There are many different kinds of relief agencies. Some agencies work closely with government donor agencies, and others are fiercely independent. Humanitarian relief agencies have been engaged in highly charged debates about what it means to be a humanitarian, and these differences are themselves a product of the shared space of the field of humanitarian relief organizations. Differences among relief agencies become superimposed on shared assumptions about the project as the unit of relief and can form a part of the market for projects. Donors' relationship to distant suffering is mediated both by the practices shared among agencies and by the symbolic differentiation among them.

The form humanitarian relief takes today has a specific history and does not simply follow either from the content of humanitarian ideas or from the fact that there is suffering in the world, or that there are disasters or civil wars. I have taken a specific approach to the task of writing the history of humanitarian relief and to the task of explaining how we got to the present moment. My aim has not been to focus on one cause of change and then show that this cause is more important than all other causes. Nor have I simply aimed to tell a story that situates the present moment in larger contexts and processes. My approach has been to identify the elements of the logic of the field of humanitarian relief and then identify the conditions of possibility that have to be in place for relief to exist in the form in which it exists today. On a general level, this means being explicit about some of the conditions that we usually take for granted and therefore do not consider as causes of humanitarianism in its present form, and that we therefore also usually do not consider as possible leverage points for analysis and for political action. At its most general, the preconditions of the form of humanitarian relief are first that large populations on this planet lack access to basic provisions for their needs. And they do not lack access to these provisions only under exceptional circumstances. This lack of access has to do both with capitalism in general and with decades of restructuring policies that have attacked the poor. On the response side, the preconditions include, for example, the means of learning about suffering.[1] I have specifically emphasised a loss of hope in development, the transformation of the state through competitive contracting to for-profit and nonprofit private actors, and the emergence of a global scale of comparison for relief projects. I also trace the history of the authority specific to the humanitarian field. This authority draws on the authority of suffering produced by war, the authority of states responsible for that suffering, and the authority of the medical profession. In contrast to accounts that analyze and critique "humanitarian reason" based on a reconstruction that attributes coherence based on ideas or interests, I argue that the pattern we see is rather one of a fragmentation of reason.

In the remaining sections, I will revisit some of the expectations asso-

---

1. Thomas Haskell, "Capitalism and the Origins of the Humanitarian Sensibility, Part 1," *American Historical Review* 90, no. 2 (1985): 339–61; Haskell, "Capitalism and the Origins of the Humanitarian Sensibility, Part 2," *American Historical Review* 90, no. 3 (1985): 547–66.

ciated with humanitarian relief NGOs based on this analysis, and return to the implications of the indeterminacy of ideas, before raising some questions toward a politics vis-à-vis the specific form of mediation analyzed here.

International NGOs and Global Order beyond the Problem of Communication

When NGOs are associated with global civil society, defined as "the organized expression of the values and interests of society,"[2] or as a public sphere, commentators emphasize their potential for political representation or communication.[3] NGOs are then expected to facilitate communication between the Global South and the Global North; humanitarian relief NGOs, in particular, might be expected to channel the voices of populations in need into a global conversation.[4]

The literature on NGOs remains indebted to this problematic of communication in the questions it poses, even in critical work on advocacy organizations.[5] This work has modeled the way advocacy is structured by organizational interests, and has described advocacy itself as a kind of market. For the case of humanitarian relief NGOs, it is also important to note that advocacy is only one of the professed aims of humanitarian relief NGOs and that we would understand their role only incompletely if we focused only on their role as advocacy groups.

2. Manuel Castells, "The New Public Sphere: Global Civil Society, Communication Networks, and Global Governance," *Annals of the American Academy of Political Science* 616, no. 1 (2008): 78–93.

3. See Jürgen Habermas, *The Structural Transformation of the Public Sphere* (Cambridge, MA: MIT Press, 1989); Rudolf Stichweh, "The Genesis of a Global Public Sphere," *Development* 46, no. 1 (2003): 26–39; Nancy Fraser, "Transnationalizing the Public Sphere: On the Legitimacy and Efficacy of Public Opinion in a Post-Westphalian World," in *Identities, Affiliations, and Allegiances*, ed. Şeyla Benhabib, Ian Shapiro, and Danilo Petranović (Cambridge: Cambridge University Press, 2007), 45–67.

4. David Held, *Democracy and the Global Order: From the Modern State to Cosmopolitan Governance* (Stanford, CA: Stanford University Press, 1995): Margaret E. Keck and Kathryn Sikkink, *Activists beyond Borders: Advocacy Networks in International Politics* (Ithaca, NY: Cornell University Press, 1998); Paul Wapner, *Environmental Activism and World Civic Politics* (Albany: SUNY Press, 1996); Wapner, "The Normative Promise of Non-State Actors: A Theoretical Account of Global Civil Society," in *Principled World Politics: The Challenge of Normative International Relations*, ed. Lester Ruiz and Paul Wapner (Lanham, MD: Rowman & Littlefield, 2000), 261–74.

5. Aseem Prakash and Mary Kay Gugerty, eds., *Rethinking Advocacy Organizations: A Collective Action Perspective* (Cambridge: Cambridge University Press, 2010); Clifford Bob, *The Marketing of Rebellion: Insurgents, Media, and International Activism* (Cambridge: Cambridge University Press, 2005); Anna Holzscheiter, "The Representational Power of Civil Society Organisations in Global AIDS Governance: Advocating for Children in Global Health Politics," in *Power and Transnational Activism*, ed. Thomas Olesen (London: Routledge, 2010), 173–89. The focus on democratic outcome is also in Wendy Wong, *Internal Affairs: How the Structure of NGOs Transforms Human Rights* (Ithaca, NY: Cornell University Press, 2012).

I have argued that humanitarian relief is also a form of production, and, more specifically, that humanitarian relief NGOs share practices geared toward producing relief projects. This means, on the one hand, that communication, in the sense of a public sphere, is distracted and refracted by the practical logic of the field of humanitarian relief.[6] To the extent that the production of projects drives relief, populations in need come to the attention of global civil society only if they are perceived as an opportunity to add value by an organization.

This means more generally that we should discuss NGOs not just as (better or worse) players in a struggle for a fair conversation, or a struggle to influence policy, but that we also need to ask broader questions about different fields of practice and their role in constituting global order. NGOs can themselves be important sites of the distribution of resources.

The Politics of Humanitarianism beyond the Politics of Ideas

Humanitarian relief is often discussed with reference to abstract ideas, values, or meanings, by those who celebrate humanitarian NGOs as organizations pursuing their stated values, but also in accounts that provide a critical analysis of humanitarianism as a discourse. In the first perspective, commentators identify humanitarian NGOs by their commitment to easing suffering or to human solidarity in the face of war and disaster; in the second, critics might denounce humanitarian ideas as Western or colonial ideas, or criticize their focus on mere charity or the construction of bare life. They might also detect a tendency to patronize populations in need.

I have argued, however, that we need to look beyond the content of ideas toward the way they are interpreted in practice and implemented, and the way resources associated with them are allocated. I have argued that it is not so much anything in particular about the values or meanings of humanitarianism that leads to some of the limitations of humani-

6. Habermas already alerted us to the growing distortion of public communication by organized private interests in 1961 in *The Structural Transformation of the Public Sphere*. Oskar Negt and Alexander Kluge coined the term "public sphere of production" to highlight a similar danger; see Oskar Negt and Alexander Kluge, *Public Sphere and Experience: Toward an Analysis of the Bourgeois and Proletarian Public Sphere* (Minneapolis: University of Minnesota Press, 1993). One example of such a distortion or distraction of public communication is when journalists are influenced by the concerns of their employers about the bottom line—rather than about genuine communication. Another example is when a parliamentarian is looking not for reasoned dialogue with other parliamentarians but is playing to TV audiences and looking for political gains for his or her party. Organizational interests become a distraction or diversion from communication.

tarian relief; rather, it is their indeterminacy. From values very little follows by way of concrete instructions as to what to do, and it is organizational routines and practices that do the deciding. In thinking about approaches to distant suffering and global social problems, we should go beyond values and beyond a critique of ideology to also contend with the institutional dynamics, which mediate between "helpers" and "helped."

This does not mean that "culture" does not matter, as the mediating practices I focus on here are also meaningful practices. This does also not mean replacing a focus on values and ideas with a focus on organizational processes based on a model of how (all) organizations work. Rather, I would suggest it is important to explore the specific practices of different kinds of actors and fields of actors empirically.

Under similar structural conditions other sets of ideas for approaching distant suffering might be mediated by similar dynamics. Human rights activists, for example, might say that relief is mere charity, and not oriented toward the long term. Those who work in development work might say, similarly, that relief is too much oriented by the short term and has a too narrow a conception of what people need and want. It is an open question, however, in which way development or human rights work is more long-term than humanitarian relief if it is planned around similarly short-term contracts or campaigns in terms of the commitment of resources.

Indirect Domination and the Field of Humanitarian Relief NGOs

If most accounts of NGOs still see them as antithetical to power, most accounts of power in humanitarian relief imply a form of direct domination, exercised by those who are powerful over those who are not. This is clearest for theories of imperialism, but I would include here most accounts of governmentality inspired by Foucault—despite his protestations to the contrary—as I have discussed in more detail in chapter 2. I would include here also critiques of symbolic patterns that do not analyze institutional forms of mediation. We will only incompletely understand the role humanitarian relief NGOs play if we see humanitarian relief NGOs simply as agents of donor governments, of traditional colonialism or new imperialism, of a form of governmentality, or of an apolitical discourse. There is also a mechanism of indirect domination at work—a form of domination that is mediated through the practical logic of the field of humanitarian relief organization.

There are two preconditions for noticing indirect domination as well as direct domination. The first is to shift from a view of humans as threatened only by constraint and interference to one that acknowledges their needs and dependencies. The second is to include populations *not* served as well as populations served in the analysis of real-existing humanitarianism. Humanitarian relief NGOs allocate resources via projects. This means that some of the poorest populations in the world are in competition against each other—instead of against elites in their own countries or elsewhere, say—to become part of projects. Because populations in need are part of the product of relief and compete against each other as part of projects, symbolic value is extracted from them in exchange for some of them getting help some of the time.

The debate about the limits of relief has two positions at its extremes, the liberal and the cynical. Liberals might suggest that humanitarian relief is an incomplete system, where relief is not doing enough of what it is already doing. Cynics might suggest that it is a system that wholly serves some sinister purpose. The relationship of competition and exchange, which the market for projects introduces, suggests it is an incomplete system with perverse tendencies.

Toward a Politics vis-à-vis the Mediating Logic of the Field of Humanitarian Relief NGOs

In political discussions about aid, perhaps even more so than in other political discussion, it is very common to rail against the burdens of bureaucracy or the failures of planning,[7] but my account is not intended as a general critique of formal organizations or bureaucratic structures. Such a critique is often leveled in the name of the market, but markets themselves, as economic sociologists have taught us, are highly organized, and the specific form of organization usually called "the market" has already failed those targeted by humanitarian relief. It would also be too easy to offer a general critique of organizations in the name of "beneficiaries," "populations in need," or "the people"—people who usually cannot be seen or asked directly as to which critique specifically they would like to lend their authority to. As I have discussed, critique and self-critique in the name of beneficiaries or populations in need is a rather routine feature accompanying humanitarian relief, but it is a rhetorical

7. E.g., William Easterly, *The White Man's Burden: Why the West's Efforts to Aid the Rest Have Done So Much Ill and So Little Good* (London: Penguin Press, 2006).

move put to many different uses and cannot form the basis for deciding between different intellectual or political positions. The "people" will not suddenly stand up as one, and if there is a spontaneous voice of the people, it is unclear how it can be heard.

Organizations as relatively stable arrangements for doing things together are an essential feature of complex, mediated societies, and an ongoing achievement, essential for both democratic voice and physical well-being. The question seems to be not "Do we want organizations?" but "What kind of organization do we want?" I have not intended to dismiss bureaucracies in the name of the market or the people; I have focused in on one specific problematic mechanism, which is partly, in fact, the *result* of general critiques of planning and bureaucracies, as I have discussed in chapter 3.

Every organization may have the potential for an internal logic that is counterproductive in terms of its substantive aims. The sociologist Robert Michels, a student of Max Weber, claimed to have discovered the iron law of oligarchy, according to which in each organization power gravitates to the few.[8] In the terms of the argument developed in this book, we might say that any organization has a tendency to develop an instrumental attitude toward its beneficiaries. But there are differences in degree, and the specific difference I have wanted to highlight here is the difference between organizations for whom commitment to any particular population is optional, and those for whom it is not. There is a difference between attempts to self-organize that may be limited by oligarchic tendencies to some extent, and attempts to help mediated by the market in projects, which I describe here.

We face the issues of the market for projects the more people are dispossessed—that is, the more people are separated from what they need— and the more the commitment of the responding organizations to any particular population is optional for the organization. This optional commitment brings with it new forms of inequality and decreases people's power to engage service providers.

The case of humanitarian relief is an extreme case of the market for projects; but it is a case that has lessons for other, less extreme cases. Markets for projects also increasingly undermine forms of welfare provision within national boundaries, including within wealthy nation-states. Markets for projects arise in domestic provision whenever governments

8. Robert Michels, *Political Parties: A Sociological Study of the Oligarchical Tendencies of Modern Democracy* (1911; New York: Transactions Publishers, 1999).

invite applications for schemes, whose resourcing bears no relationship to the overall need across the territory, and whenever policies are not based on coverage of the population but on a competition among service providers that entails a competition among different populations.

The questions the book leaves us with are, then: What are all the different kinds of linkage to distant suffering we can observe once we pay attention to organizational and field dynamics? What are their implications? What conditions shape their distribution in the world? Which ones might we prefer under which circumstances? How might we get to one rather than the other? What could be strategies to try to circumvent the markets for projects?

I cannot answer these questions here, but it is worth noting that there *are* ways of organizing provision that are fundamentally different from the market for projects. Building state institutions that aim at guaranteeing rights, not results, has been one way to link forms of provision with forms of accountability. Self-organizing might be able to confront power directly in workplaces, communities, and households and might set limits on the amount of symbolic capital that can be extracted. Solidarity within the global labor movement, based on such attempts at self-organizing, is one example of a different form of linkage with distant suffering.

Within humanitarian relief there is, to my knowledge, not one initiative that addresses the specific aspect of the market for projects—the reform projects I discussed aim at slightly different targets. But there are many efforts by staff within agencies and by individuals across agencies that resist and subvert the market for projects and the kind of commitment it implies. There are a lot of practical choices that matter within everyday organizational practice. There are of course efforts within and across relief agencies to make projects meaningful and to sustain longer-term commitments within and sometimes despite the constraints of project funding. There are also efforts, both individual and collective, to abstain from the more extreme forms of symbolic profiteering at the expense of populations in need. There are voices, for example, that insist that more forms of local participation are recognized as labor and paid.[9]

Efforts to change the type of commitment that projects imply include those by local staff who protest the conditions under which they are engaged, such as the volunteers in a program to deliver eye medicine

9. On this see, for example, Paul Farmer, "Making Human Rights Substantial," in *Partner to the Poor: A Paul Farmer Reader*, ed. Haun Saussy (Berkeley: University of California Press, 2010), 545–61.

studied by Ari Samsky,[10] or the Liberian security guards who took MSF France to court over unfair labor practices in 2007.[11] We should also not be surprised if beneficiaries themselves at times refuse relief or seek to renegotiate its terms.

10. Ari Samsky, "Since We Are Taking the Drugs: Labor and Value in Two International Drug Donation Programs," *Journal of Cultural Economy* 30, no. 1 (2011): 27–43.
11. Sonpon D. Weah, *Aggrieved MSF-France Workers Demand Justice,* accessed November 9, 2010, http://www.analystliberia.com/civil_service_may03_07.html.

Appendix on Methods

Research Design

This book draws on different kinds of materials, including archival sources, reports, observations in training events for relief professionals, background interviews, and in-depth expert interviews. The research was carried out over a period of five years from 2005 to 2010.

I sought to understand the way relief agencies do their work, and I was interested in the everyday practices of managers. Formally speaking, the empirical research had two aims. First, I wanted to test the hypothesis that there is a practical logic shared by relief organizations that has an impact on allocation decisions and is relatively independent of absolute need on the ground or a donor agency's stated preferences. The hypothesis for this first aim can be stated as follows:

H0a: Allocation decisions are made according to need.
H0b: Allocation decisions are made according to donor agencies' interests.
H1: Practices shared across relief organizations mediate between needs and interests, on the one hand, and outcomes, on the other hand.

The discussion about relief sometimes proceeds as though H0a and H0b are meaningful possibilities, and because of this I think it is important to be precise about the basic claim I am making. But I also acknowledge that H0a and H0b are rather easy to argue against, sociologically speaking. The interest really lies in the details of H1. After establishing that practices do matter, the following questions arise: What kind of practices do these agencies share? Who exactly shares them? How do these practices matter? My second aim was thus to describe the practical logic of this space sociologically, and to explore the boundaries of this shared social space.

As part of this research, I interviewed people with a very specific role across different organizations, and I asked them about their everyday work practices. I interviewed fifty desk officers and directors of operations in sixteen of the world's largest relief NGOs. The people I interviewed—the desk officers and directors of operations—are not representative of all relief workers, and I did not aim to construct a representative sample of all relief workers. Rather, I spoke to this particular group of managers because they occupy a position that is of great practical relevance. Their offices are only one site to investigate as part of the sociology of humanitarianism—one could focus on the United Nations, for example, or on local organizations—and only one site for studying humanitarian relief NGOs—one could study specific interventions in the field, for example. But these offices are a very interesting site and a strategic site for studying the field of humanitarian relief organizations.

I interviewed desk officers and directors of operations because they play a key mediating role between strategic planning in the organizations' headquarters and the day-to-day management of operations in the field. In a relief organization, the operations department usually oversees work across the world in liaison with the agency's country directors. It is the center of the organization's outgoing flows. Humanitarian agencies' operational departments are divided into several regions or "desks." A desk officer is in charge of operations in at least one but usually several countries. Decisions are prepared and implemented here, and the most detailed knowledge of internal structures and events is located here, not at the highest level in the organizational hierarchy. Decisions on this level also set the frame for implementation on the ground.

I asked desk officers about their work, their everyday practices, probing for details wherever possible. I sought to uncover the shared practical knowledge and shared frames of interpretation of this group of managers. With this design, I stand in a specific tradition of interviewing experts with roots in the sociology of knowledge.[1]

Many interview studies place the encounter with the respondent in the context of his or her biography.[2] Expert-interviewing is different from these kinds of life-history interviews. In the kind of expert-interviews I conducted here, the experience and orientations of the respondent are not primarily placed in the context of his or her biography but are rather analyzed in the institutional context of his or her work. I was not only interested in the individual respondent but in assumptions and schemata of interpretations he or she might share with specific others. The target of the expert-interview is the practical knowledge and shared frames of interpretation of a group of experts.

1. Alexander Bogner, Beate Littig, and Wolfgang Menz, eds., *Interviewing Experts* (London: Macmillan, 2009); Michael Meuser and Ulrike Nagel, "ExpertInneninterviews—vielfach erprobt, wenig bedacht," in *Qualitativ-empirische Sozialforschung: Konzepte, Methoden, Analysen*, ed. Detlef Garz and Klaus Kraimer (Opladen: Westdeutscher Verlag, 1991), 441–71.

2. For interesting life-history research on related questions, see David Lewis, "Tidy Concepts, Messy Lives," in *Adventures in Aidland: The Anthropology of Professionals in International Development*, ed. David Mosse (New York: Berghahn Books, 2011), 177–98.

While sometimes experts are interviewed to give information about a subject area that they are knowledgeable about as an observer, I interviewed desk officers about their own practice. Their practical knowledge of organizational processes that respondents themselves are involved in was the target of my investigation. Their knowledge was not targeted so much because it is "better," but because it is especially practically relevant and full of consequences, as they have decision-making power.

I targeted the population of desk officers and directors of operations in an informed sample of relief organizations. I wanted to learn about the largest and most influential Western relief organizations. While there are many humanitarian organizations in many different parts of the world, in terms of the funding, this is a very concentrated sector. A significant share of the funding for humanitarian relief is channeled through the largest organizations, and thus it is important that we understand these organizations.[3]

I also wanted to probe the boundaries of this field of practice and thus included a range of organizations that we might assume to be different from each other. I included some religious and some nonreligious organizations, organizations of different national backgrounds and organizations with different technical expertise, and some organizations with affiliation to a larger family of organizations and some without. Respondents worked for various organizations, including ACF France, ACF UK, CAFOD UK, CARE International, CARE USA, Christian Aid (UK), ICRC, IFRC (International Federation of Red Cross and Red Crescent Societies), Lutheran World Federation, MSF Switzerland, MSF France, Oxfam UK, Oxfam US, Save the Children UK, Save the Children US, Tearfund UK, UMCOR, and World Vision International.

I contacted desk officers and directors of operations directly based on publicly available information, or as referred by other respondents. Semistructured interviews with desk officers were conducted in person to the extent at all possible. In two cases, where participation could not otherwise be secured, interviews were conducted by phone, and in one case by Skype. Interviews lasted between one hour and 100 minutes. With the participants' permission, all interviews were audio recorded.

The people I interviewed took a variety of routes into these positions. Many older workers had some initial background in development work and had moved into humanitarian relief because it seemed more immediately necessary and useful, or because the emphasis of funders had shifted. Some of the younger workers had specifically set out to become professional humanitarians. Some had a specific

3. See Peter Walker and Kevin Pepper, *Follow the Money: A Review and Analysis of the State of Humanitarian Funding.* (Medford, MA: Feinstein International Center, Tufts University, 2007); Kang Zhao et al., "Assortativity Patterns in Multi-Dimensional Inter-Organizational Networks: A Case Study of the Humanitarian Relief Sector," in *Advances in Social Computing: Third International Conference on Social Computing, Behavioral Modeling, and Prediction, SBP 2010, Bethesda, MD, USA, March 30–31, 2010; Proceedings*, ed. Sun-Ki Chai, John J. Salerno, and Patricia L. Mabry, Lecture Notes in Computer Science 6007 (New York: Springer, 2010), 265–72.

technical background as doctors, nurses, water engineers, or experts in nutrition; some had joined from management positions in the private sector; and some had joined from the military. When I met them, these workers were based in New York, Atlanta, London, Paris, Geneva, or Brussels; but they all had previous experience in delivering programs in the field, and they all still travel to visit the field in the Global South regularly. Staff spoke with remarkable openness and reflexivity about a work they knew well and had thought a lot about.

In analyzing the interview transcripts my aim was to identify shared categories and assumptions. Each interview was first analyzed with regard to codes or headings emerging from it. While in the narrative interview, the priority is on sequence or the inviolable logic of the single interview, here the focus was also on the search for common themes and unifying codes and headings. Results of thematic comparison were tested against the text and the full data set. Commonalities were probed, but deviations, contradictions, and particulars were also identified.

In this research design, reliability and validity depend on the shared social position of the respondents and on the interview guidelines. The method produces reliable results (that is, results replicable by another researcher) and valid results (that is, meaningful with regard to the underlying reality) if the selected respondents are a relevant group to be targeted for this research, if there is some form of shared practical knowledge, and if the questions are meaningful in relation to this practical knowledge.

My early experiences in this project underlined, on the one hand, that one cannot take these conditions of reliability and validity for granted, but also that the assumptions that the design is built on are falsifiable. As I began designing this project, I did pilot interviews with people in humanitarian relief in a range of roles, and asking a range of questions; in other words, my sample was unfocused, and my questions not well targeted. If the respondents' answers are strongly divergent, if they do not reveal any shared assumptions about routines and procedures, or if the terms of the questions do not make sense to respondents, the conditions for validity are not fulfilled.

In the early stages of the interviewing, I also observed 100 hours of training sessions on professional standards and needs assessment. Attending these sessions allowed me to participate in simulations of relief planning and to observe experienced professionals interacting with each other in simulations of disaster scenarios. These observations informed my research design and interview questions.

The questions I asked targeted decision-making processes; tacit, practical knowledge; structures of relevance; and unwritten procedures. I include a list of questions below—it is not an exhaustive list. Rather, I used opportunities provided to probe for examples and further explication.

Interview research sometimes raises questions about whether respondents are telling the truth and how what the respondent is telling us relates to the underlying reality. It is important to note that different kinds of research design relate to this problematic in different ways. If we ask respondents about facts, values, or opinions, we face a different challenge than if we ask about practices and stories. Asking about practices and processes does not solve the problem of validity, but it does go some way toward addressing it. Interviews about practices create a set of engagements between interviewer and respondent that are meaningful beyond the factual and make the researcher less dependent on factual correctness. Respondents might lie about their income if asked in a survey, so that if we ask about income, and that information is false, we have not gained much information. Respondents will find it harder to make up a whole alternative everyday work life with concrete stories. If we ask about processes and practices, and some factual details are omitted or relayed in a tendentious way, we still have gained valuable insights.

In that sense, asking for stories is more similar to direct observation than it is to survey research or questions about values, ideas, or views, though it may never reach direct observation's closeness to practice because it takes respondents out of the context of their work. We also lose, of course, in depth compared to ethnographic observation; on the other hand, we gain by being able to obtain insights across a set of organizations.

In addition to in-depth interviews and observations, I also conducted background interviews and used reports, documents, evaluation studies, and position papers. These provided accounts of humanitarian practice that I could compare to the findings of my interview data. They also provided insights into some of the sites my interviews did not target, such as the official presentations of humanitarian work, the work of independent consultants, and the practices in field offices. I also worked in the Lyndon B. Johnson and John F. Kennedy presidential archives to explore the history of results-based management in US government.

Interview Guidelines

What is your current role?
What does a typical day in the office look like?
How did you originally get involved in humanitarian work?
Why did you stay in it? Why did you make a career out of it?
What would you say makes your organization different from other organizations?
What considerations go into opening a project somewhere?
What do you think constitutes an emergency?
How do you decide on the size of a project?
How do you decide what kind of services you are going to provide?
What considerations go into choosing a site?
What considerations go into targeting an intervention?
What considerations go into closing a project somewhere?
(as applicable) What considerations go into choosing a partner?
How do you determine your strategic priorities?
How have they changed?

I am interested to hear what you think makes a good project. So I would ask you to tell me about a project you thought was especially good, and why this was so.

I am interested to hear what you think makes a good funding proposal. So I would ask you to tell me about a project you thought was especially good, and why this was so.

(as applicable) I am interested to hear what you think makes a good partner organization. So I would ask you to tell me about a project you thought was especially good, and why this was so.

Can you tell me about a project that did not go so well?

Can you tell me about disagreements you had with colleagues about particular decisions?

Would you say your organization has changed? If so, how?

Would you say relief has changed? If so, how?

What changes would you like to see?

Bibliography

Abbott, Andrew. "Linked Ecologies: States and Universities as Environments for Professions." *Sociological Theory* 23, no. 3 (2005): 245–74.

———. *The System of Professions: An Essay on the Division of Expert Labor*. Chicago: University of Chicago Press, 1988.

———. "Transcending General Linear Reality." *Sociological Theory* 6, no. 2 (1988): 169–86.

Agamben, Giorgio. *Homo Sacer: Sovereign Power and Bare Life*. Translated by Daniel Heller-Roazen. Stanford, CA: Stanford University Press, 1998.

Ager, Alastair, and Joey Ager. "Faith and the Discourse of Secular Humanitarianism." *Journal of Refugee Studies* 24, no. 3 (2011): 456–72.

Allmand, Christopher T. "War and the Non-Combatant in the Middle Ages." In *Medieval Warfare*, edited by Maurice Keen, 253–72. Oxford: Oxford University Press, 1999.

Anderson, Mary B. *Do No Harm: How Aid Can Support Peace or War*. Boulder, CO: Lynne Rienner Publishers, 1999.

Andreoni, James. "Giving with Impure Altruism: Applications to Charity and Ricardian Equivalence." *Journal of Political Economy* 97, no. 6 (1989): 1447–58.

———. "Impure Altruism and Donations to Public Goods: A Theory of Warm-Glow Giving." *Economic Journal* 100, no. 401 (1990): 464–77.

———. "Toward a Theory of Charitable Fund-Raising." *Journal of Political Economy* 106, no. 6 (1998): 1186–213.

Appadurai, Arjun. *Modernity at Large: Cultural Dimensions of Globalization*. Minneapolis: University of Minnesota Press, 1996.

Arendt, Hannah. *The Human Condition*. Chicago: University of Chicago Press, 1958.

Atlani-Duault, Laëtitia. *Au bonheur des autres: Anthropologie de l'aide humanitaire.* Paris: Armand Collins, 2009.

Attawell, Kathy, and Jackie Mundy. *Provision of Antiretroviral Therapy in Resource Limited Settings: A Review of Experience up to August 2003.* London: DFID Health Systems Resource Centre in Collaboration with the World Health Organisation, 2003.

Aune, Jens B. "Logical Framework Approach and PRA—Mutually Exclusive or Complementary Tools for Project Planning?" *Development in Practice* 10, no. 5 (2000): 687–90.

Barman, Emily. "An Institutional Approach to Donor Control: From Dyadic Ties to a Field-Level Analysis." *American Journal of Sociology* 112, no. 5 (2007): 1416–57.

Barnett, Michael. *Empire of Humanity: A History of Humanitarianism.* Ithaca, NY: Cornell University Press, 2011.

———. *Eyewitness to a Genocide: The United Nations and Rwanda.* Ithaca, NY: Cornell University Press, 2002.

———. "Faith in the Machine? Humanitarianism in an Age of Bureaucratization." In *Sacred Aid: Faith and Humanitarianism,* edited by Michael Barnett and Janice Gross Stein, 188–211. New York: Oxford University Press, 2011.

———. "Humanitarianism Transformed." *Perspectives on Politics* 3, no. 4 (2005): 723–40.

Barnett, Michael, and Janice Gross Stein, eds. *Sacred Aid: Faith and Humanitarianism.* New York: Oxford University Press, 2011.

Barnett, Michael, and Thomas G. Weiss, eds. *Humanitarianism in Question: Politics, Power, Ethics.* Ithaca, NY: Cornell University Press, 2008.

Bartley, Tim. "Certifying Forests and Factories: States, Social Movements, and the Rise of Private Regulation in the Apparel and Forest Products Fields." *Politics & Society* 31, no. 3 (2003): 433–64.

———. "Corporate Accountability and the Privatization of Labor Standards: Struggles over Codes of Conduct in the Apparel Industry." *Research in Political Sociology* 14 (2005): 211–44.

———. "Institutional Emergence in an Era of Globalization: The Rise of Transnational Private Regulation of Labor and Environmental Conditions." *American Journal of Sociology* 113, no. 2 (2007): 297–351.

Bass, Gary. *Freedom's Battle: The Origins of Humanitarian Intervention.* New York: Alfred A. Knopf, 2008.

Beasley-Murray, John. "Value and Capital in Bourdieu and Marx." In *Pierre Bourdieu: Fieldwork in Culture,* edited by Nicholas Brown and Imre Szeman, 100–119. Lanham, MD: Rowman & Littlefield, 2000.

Becker, Gary S. "A Theory of Social Interactions." *Journal of Political Economy* 82, no. 6 (1974): 1063–93.

Becker, Howard S. *Art Worlds.* Berkeley: University of California Press, 1982.

Becker, Penny Edgell. *Congregations in Conflict: Cultural Models of Religious Local Life.* Cambridge: Cambridge University Press, 2000.

Bender, Thomas, ed. *The Antislavery Debate: Capitalism and Abolitionism as a Problem in Historical Interpretation.* Berkeley: University of California Press, 1992.

Benthall, Jonathan. "Financial Worship: The Quranic Injunction to Almsgiving." *Journal of the Royal Anthropological Institute* 5, no. 1 (1999): 27–42.

———. "Islamic Humanitarianism in Adversarial Contexts. In *Forces of Compassion: Humanitarianism between Ethics and Politics*, edited by Erica Bornstein and Peter Redfield, 99–121. Santa Fe, NM: School for Advanced Research Press.

Benthall, Jonathan, and Jerome Bellion-Jourdan. *The Charitable Crescent: Politics of Aid in the Muslim World.* London: I. B. Tauris, 2003.

Best, Geoffrey Francis Andrew. *Humanity in Warfare.* London: Weidenfeld and Nicolson, 1980.

Biberson, Philippe, and Ronny Brauman. "Le 'droit d'ingérence' est un slogan trompeur." *Le Monde Internationale*, 23 October 1999.

Bierschenk, Thomas, Jean-Pierre Chauveau, and Jean-Pierre Olivier de Sardan. *Courtiers en développement: Les villages africains en quête de projets.* Paris: Karthala, 2000.

Binder, Andrea, and Claudia Meier. "Opportunity Knocks: Why Non-Western Donors Enter Humanitarianism and How to Make the Best of It." *International Review of the Red Cross* 93, no. 884 (2011): 1135–49.

Blau, Peter M. *The Dynamics of Bureaucracy: A Study of Interpersonal Relations in Two Government Agencies.* Chicago: University of Chicago Press, 1963.

Blondel, Jean-Luc. "Getting Access to the Victims: Role and Activities of the ICRC." *Journal of Peace Research* 24, no. 3 (1987): 307–14.

Bob, Clifford. *The Marketing of Rebellion: Insurgents, Media, and International Activism.* Cambridge: Cambridge University Press, 2005.

———. "The Market in Human Rights." In *Advocacy Organizations and Collective Action*, edited by Aseem Prakash and Mary Kay Guggerty, 133–55. Cambridge: Cambridge University Press, 2010.

Bockman, Johanna, and Gil Eyal. "Eastern Europe as a Laboratory for Economic Knowledge: The Transnational Roots of Neoliberalism." *American Journal of Sociology* 108, no. 2 (2002): 310–52.

Bogner, Alexander, Beate Littig, and Wolfgang Menz, eds. *Interviewing Experts.* Basingstoke, UK: Palgrave Macmillan, 2009.

Boissier, Pierre. *Histoire du Comité international de la Croix-Rouge: De Solférino à Tsoushima.* Paris: Plon, 1963.

Boltanski, Luc. *Distant Suffering: Morality, Media, and Politics.* Translated by Graham Burchell. Cambridge: Cambridge University Press, 1999.

Boltanski, Luc, and Eve Chiapello. *The New Spirit of Capitalism.* London: Verso, 2007.

Bornstein, Erica. *Disquieting Gifts: Humanitarianism in New Delhi.* Stanford, CA: Stanford University Press, 2012.

———. *The Spirit of Development: Protestant NGOs, Morality, and Economics in Zimbabwe.* Stanford, CA: Stanford University Press, 2005.

Bornstein, Erica, and Peter Redfield, eds. 2011. *Forces of Compassion: Humanitarianism between Ethics and Politics*. Santa Fe, NM: School for Advanced Research.

Boston, Jonathan, John Pallot, June Martin, and Pat Walsh. *Reshaping the State: New Zealand's Bureaucratic Revolution*. Auckland: Oxford University Press, 1991.

Bourdieu, Pierre. "The Force of Law." *Hastings Law Journal* 38 (1987): 805–53.

———. "Genesis and Structure of the Religious Field." *Comparative Social Research* 13 (1991): 1–44.

———. *Outline of a Theory of Practice*. Cambridge Studies in Social Anthropology 16. Cambridge: Cambridge University Press, 1977.

———. *The Rules of Art: Genesis and Structure of the Literary Field*. Stanford, CA: Stanford University Press, 1996.

Brand, Ulrich, Achim Brunnengräber, Lutz Schrader, Christian Stock, and Peter Wahl. *Global Governance: Alternative zur Neoliberalen Globalisierung? Eine Studie von Heinrich-Böll-Stiftung und WEED*. Münster: Westfälisches Dampfboot, 2000.

Brand, Ulrich, Alex Demirovic, Christoph Görg, and Joachim Hirsch, eds. *Nicht-regierungsorganisationen in der Transformation des Staates*. Münster: Westfälisches Dampfboot, 2001.

Brennan, Richard J., and Gerald Martone. "The Evolving Role of Relief Organizations in Human Rights and Protection." In *Fear of Persecution: Global Human Rights, International Law, and Human Well-Being*, edited by James D. White and Anthony J. Marsella, 75–92. Lanham, MD: Lexington Books, 2007.

Buchanan-Smith, Margie. *How the Sphere Project Came into Being: A Case Study of Policy-Making in the Humanitarian Aid Sector and the Relative Influence of Research*. London: Overseas Development Institute, 2003.

Calabresi, Guido, and Philip Bobbitt. *Tragic Choices: The Conflicts Society Confronts in the Allocation of Tragically Scarce Resources*. New York: Norton, 1978.

Calhoun, Craig. "Habitus, Field, and Capital: The Question of Historical Specificity." In *Bourdieu: Critical Perspectives,* edited by Craig Calhoun, Edward Lipuma, and Moishe Postone, 61–88. Chicago: University of Chicago Press, 1993.

———. "The Idea of Emergency: Humanitarian Action and Global (Dis)Order." In *Contemporary States of Emergency: The Politics of Military and Humanitarian Interventions*, edited by Didier Fassin and Mariella Pandolfi, 59–79. New York: Zone Books, 2011.

———. "A World of Emergencies: Fear, Intervention, and the Limits of Cosmopolitan Order." *Canadian Review of Sociology and Anthropology* 41, no. 4 (2004): 373–95.

CARE Human Rights Initiative. "Basic Introduction to Human Rights and Rights-Based Programming." N.p.: CARE Human Rights Initiative, n.d.

Carroll, Glenn R., and Anand Swaminathan. "Why the Microbrewery Movement? Organizational Dynamics of Resource Partitioning in the US Brewing Industry." *American Journal of Sociology* 106, no. 3 (2000): 715–62.

Casper, Steven, and Bob Hanckj. "Global Quality Norms within National Production Regimes: ISO 9000 Standards in the French and German Car Industries." *Organization Studies* 20, no. 6 (1999): 961–85.

Castells, Manuel. "The New Public Sphere: Global Civil Society, Communication Networks, and Global Governance." *Annals of the American Academy of Political Science* 616, no. 1 (2008): 78–93.

Catholic Relief Services. "Real-Time Evaluation of CRS' Flood Response in Pakistan: Jacobabad and Kashmore, Sindh." Baltimore: Catholic Relief Services, 2010.

Chambers, Robert. *Rural Development: Putting the Last First*. London: Longman, 1983.

———. *Whose Reality Counts? Putting the First Last*. London: Intermediate Technology, 1997.

Chandler, David. *From Kosovo to Kabul: Human Rights and International Intervention*. London: Pluto Press, 2002.

———. "The Responsibility to Protect? Imposing the Liberal Peace." *International Peacekeeping* 11, no. 1 (2004): 59–81.

———. "The Road to Military Humanitarianism: How the Human Rights NGOs Shaped a New Humanitarian Agenda." *Human Rights Quarterly* 23, no. 3 (2001): 678–700.

Checchi, Francesco, and Les Roberts. *Interpreting and Using Mortality Data in Humanitarian Emergencies: A Primer for Non-Epidemiologists*. Humanitarian Practice Network Paper 52. London: Overseas Development Institute, 2005.

Chomsky, Noam. "Humanitarian Imperialism: The New Doctrine of Imperial Right." *Monthly Review* 60, no. 4 (2008).

———. *The New Military Humanism: Lessons from Kosovo*. Monroe, ME: Common Courage Press, 1999.

Chouliaraki, Lilie. *The Spectatorship of Suffering*. London: Sage, 2006.

Chwastiak, Michele. "Taming the Untamable: Planning, Programming, and Budgeting and the Normalization of War." *Accounting, Organizations and Society* 26, no. 6 (2001): 501–19.

Clarke, John, Janet Newman, Nick Smith, Elizabeth Vidler, and Louise Westmarland. *Creating Citizen-Consumers: Changing Publics and Changing Public Services*. London: Sage Publications, 2007.

Cockayne, James, and International Peace Institute. *Commercial Security in Humanitarian and Post-Conflict Settings: An Exploratory Study*. New York: International Peace Institute , 2006.

Coeckelbergh, Mark. "Regulation or Responsibility? Autonomy, Moral Imagination, and Engineering." *Science, Technology & Human Values* 31, no. 3 (2006): 237–60.

Cohen, Stanley. *States of Denial: Knowing about Atrocities and Suffering*. Cambridge: Polity Press, 2000.

Collins, Janet, Deborah Rugg, Laura Kann, Stephen Banspach, Lloyd Kolbe, and Beth Pateman. "Evaluating a National Program of School-Based HIV Prevention." *Evaluation and Program Planning* 19, no. 3 (1996): 209–18.

Collmann, Jeff. "Clients, Cooptation, and Bureaucratic Discipline." In *Administrative Frameworks and Clients*, edited by Jeff Collmann and Don Handelman, 48–62. Social Analysis 9. Adelaide: University of Adelaide, 1981.

Comaroff, Jean, and John L. Comaroff. *Of Revelation and Revolution: Christianity, Colonialism, and Consciousness in South Africa*. Chicago: University of Chicago Press, 1991.

Cooke, Bill, and Uma Kothari, eds. *Participation—The New Tyranny?* London: Zed Books, 2001.

Cooley, Alexander, and James Ron. "The NGO Scramble: Organizational Insecurity and the Political Economy of Transnational Action." *International Security* 27, no. 1 (2002): 5–39.

Cooper, Frederick, and Randall M. Packard, eds. *International Development and the Social Sciences: Essays on the History and Politics of Knowledge*. Berkeley: University of California Press, 1997.

Coser, Lewis, Charles Kadushin, and Walter W. Powell. *Books: The Culture and Commerce of Publishing*. New York: Basic Books, 1982.

Cosgrave, John, Celia Gonçalves, Daryl Martyris, Riccardo Polastro, and Muchimba Sikumba-Dils. "Inter-agency Real-Time Evaluation of the Response to the February Floods and Cyclone in Mozambique." New York: United Nations Office for the Coordination of Humanitarian Affairs, 2007.

Csáky, Corinna. "No One to Turn To: The Under-Reporting of Child Sexual Exploitation and Abuse by Aid Workers and Peacekeepers." London: Save the Children, 2008.

Cutts, Mark. "Politics and Humanitarianism." *Refugee Survey Quarterly* 17, no. 1 (1998): 1–15.

Darcy, James. "Locating Responsibility: The Sphere Humanitarian Charter and Its Rationale." *Disasters* 28, no. 2 (2004): 112–23.

Darcy, James, and Charles-Antoine Hofmann. *According to Need? Needs Assessment and Decision-Making in the Humanitarian Sector*. Humanitarian Policy Group Report 15. London: Overseas Development Institute, 2003.

Dauvin, Pascal, and Johanna Siméant. *Le travail humanitaire: Les acteurs des ONG, du siège au terrain*. Paris: Presses de Sciences Po, 2002.

Davidson, Sara. *People in Aid: Code of Best Practice in the Management and Support of Aid Personnel*. London: Overseas Development Institute, 1997.

Davis, David. *The Problem of Slavery in the Age of Revolution, 1770–1823*. Ithaca, NY: Cornell University Press, 1975.

De Certeau, Michel. *The Practice of Everyday Life*. Berkeley: University of California Press, 1984.

De Cordier, Bruno. "Faith-Based Aid, Globalisation and the Humanitarian Frontline: An Analysis of Western-Based Muslim Aid Organisations." *Disasters* 33, no. 4 (2009): 608–28.

De Silva, Soma, Kayoko Gotoh, Andre Griekspoor, Iain Hall, Claude Hilfiker, Jeff Labovitz, Gerald Martone, and Mohamed Zejjari. "Real-Time Evaluation of the Cluster Approach—Pakistan Earthquake: Application of the IASC Cluster Approach in the South Asia Earthquake." Geneva: IASC, 2006.

De Torrente, Nicolas. "Humanitarian Action under Attack: Reflections on the Iraq War." *Harvard Human Rights Journal* 17 (2004): 1–29.

———. "Humanitarianism Sacrificed: Integration's False Promise." *Ethics* 18, no. 2 (2004): 3–12.

Development Initiatives. *Global Humanitarian Assistance Report, 2013*. London: Development Initiatives, 2013.

———. *Public Support for Humanitarian Crisis through NGOs*. London: Development Initiatives, 2009.

de Ville de Goyet, Claude, and Lezlie C. Morinière. "The Role of Needs Assessment in the Tsunami Response." London: Tsunami Evaluation Coalition, 2006.

de Waal, Alex. *Famine Crimes: Politics and the Disaster Relief Industry*. London: James Currey, 1997.

———. "Human Rights, Institutional Wrongs." In *Rethinking International Organizations: Pathology and Promise*, edited by Dennis Dijkzeul and Yves Beigbeder, 234–60. New York: Berghahn, 2003.

Dezalay, Yves, and Bryant Garth. "From the Cold War to Kosovo: The Rise and Renewal of the Field of International Human Rights." *Annual Review of Law and Social Science* 2 (2006): 231–55.

———. *The Internationalization of Palace Wars: Lawyers, Economists, and the Contest to Transform Latin American States*. Chicago: University of Chicago Press, 2002.

Dijkzeul, Dennis, and Markus Moke. "Public Communication Strategies of International Humanitarian Organizations." *International Review of the Red Cross*, n.s. 87 (2005): 673–92.

DiMaggio, Paul J., and Walter W. Powell. "The Iron Cage Revisited: Institutional Isomorphisms and Collective Rationality in Organisational Fields." *American Sociological Review* 48, no. 2 (1983): 147–60.

Donini, Antonio, Larry Minear, and Peter Walker. "The Future of Humanitarian Action: Mapping the Implications of Iraq and Other Recent Crises." *Disasters* 28, no. 3 (2004): 190–204.

Douzinas, Costas. "Humanity, Military Humanism, and the New Moral Order." *Economy and Society* 32, no. 2 (2003): 159–83.

Drucker, Peter F. *The Practice of Management*. New York: Harper and Brothers, 1954.

Dubois, Marc. "Protection—The New Humanitarian Fig-Leaf." N.d. Accessed November 18, 2012. http://www.urd.org/IMG/pdf/Protection_Fig-Leaf_DuBois.pdf.

Dudai, Ron. "'Can You Describe This?' Human Rights Reports and What They Tell Us about the Human Rights Movement." In *Humanitarianism and Suffering*, ed Richard Ashby Wilson and Richard D Brown, 245–65. Cambridge: Cambridge University Press, 2009.

Duffield, Mark. *Development, Security, and Unending War: Governing the World of Peoples*. Cambridge: Polity Press, 2007.

———. *Global Governance and the New Wars: The Merging of Development and Security*. London: Zed Books, 2001.

Dufour, Charlotte, Veronique de Geoffroy, Hugues Maury, and François Grunewald. "Rights, Standards, and Quality in a Complex Humanitarian Space: Is Sphere the Right Tool?" *Disasters* 28, no. 2 (2004): 124–41.

Dunant, Henry. *The Origin of the Red Cross: Un souvenir de Solferino*. Philadelphia: John C. Winston Co, 1911.

Easterly, William. *The White Man's Burden: Why the West's Efforts to Aid the Rest Have Done So Much Ill and So Little Good*. London: Penguin Press, 2006.

Ebersole, Jon M. "Mohonk Criteria for Humanitarian Assistance in Complex Emergencies." *Disaster Prevention and Management* 4, no. 3 (1993): 14–24.

Edwards, Michael, and David Hulme. "Too Close for Comfort? The Impact of Official Aid on Nongovernmental Organizations." *World Development* 24, no. 6 (1996): 961–73.

Engel, Gloria V. "The Effect of Bureaucracy on the Professional Autonomy of the Physician." *Journal of Health and Social Behavior* 10, no. 1 (1969): 30–41.

———. "Professional Autonomy and Bureaucratic Organization." *Administrative Science Quarterly* 15, no. 1 (1970): 12–21.

Enthoven, Alain. Papers. LBJ Presidential Library, Austin, TX.

Eriksson, John, Howard Adelman, John Borton, Hanne Christensen, Krishna Kumar, Astri Suhrke, David Tardif-Douglin, Stein Villumstad, and Lennart Wohlgemuth. *The International Response to Conflict and Genocide: Lessons from the Rwanda Experience*. Copenhagen: Steering Committee of the Joint Evaluation of Emergency Assistance to Rwanda, 1996.

Evans, Gareth, and Mohamed Sahnoun. "The Responsibility to Protect." *Foreign Affairs* 81, no. 6 (2002): 99–110.

Farmer, Paul. "Making Human Rights Substantial." In *Partner to the Poor: A Paul Farmer Reader*, edited by Haun Saussy, 545–61. Berkeley: University of California Press, 2010.

Farmer, Paul, Fernet Léandre, Joia S. Mukherjee, Marie Sidonise Claude, Patrice Nevil, Mary C. Smith-Fawzi, Serena P. Koenig, Arachu Castro, Mercedes C. Becerra, Jeffrey Sachs, Amir Attaran, and Jim Yong Kim. "Community-Based Approaches to HIV Treatment in Resource-Poor Settings." *The Lancet* 358, , no. 9279 (August 2001): 404–9.

Farrington, John, and Anthony Bebbington. *Reluctant Partners? Non-governmental Organizations, the State, and Sustainable Agricultural Development*. London: Psychology Press, 1993.

Fassin, Didier. "Humanitarianism as a Politics of Life." *Public Culture* 19, no. 3 (2007): 499–520.

———. *Humanitarian Reason: A Moral History of the Present*. Berkeley: University of California Press, 2012.

Fassin, Didier, and Mariella Pandolfi, eds. *Contemporary States of Emergency: The*

Politics of Military and Humanitarian Interventions. New York: Zone Books, 2012.

Favez, Jean-Claude. *The Red Cross and the Holocaust*. Cambridge: Cambridge University Press, 1999.

Fearon, James D. "The Rise of Emergency Relief Aid." In *Humanitarianism in Question: Politics, Power, Ethics*, edited by Michael Barnett and Thomas G. Weiss, 49–73. Ithaca, NY: Cornell University Press, 2008.

Feldman, Ilana, and Mirian Ticktin. *In the Name of Humanity: The Government of Threat and Care*. Durham, NC: Duke University Press, 2012.

Ferguson, James. *The Anti-Politics Machine: "Development," Depoliticization, and Bureaucratic Power in Lesotho*. Cambridge: Cambridge University Press, 1990.

Fink, Guenther, and Silvia Redaelli. *Determinants of International Emergency Aid—Humanitarian Need Only?* Policy Research Working Paper 4839. Washington, DC: World Bank, 2009.

Finnemore, Martha. "Redefining Development at the World Bank." In *International Development and the Social Sciences: Essays on the History and Politics of Knowledge*, edited by Frederick Cooper and Randall Packard, 203–27. Berkeley: University of California Press, 1997.

Fligstein, Neil. "Social Skill and the Theory of Fields." *Sociological Theory* 19, no. 2 (2001): 105–25.

Foucault, Michel. *Discipline and Punish: The Birth of the Prison*. New York: Pantheon Books, 1977.

———. *The History of Sexuality*. Vol. 1, *An Introduction*. Translated by Robert Hurley. New York: Pantheon Books, 1978.

Fourcade, Marion. *Economists and Societies: Discipline and Profession in the United States, Britain, and France, 1890s to 1990s*. Princeton, NJ: Princeton University Press, 2009.

Fox, Renée C. "Medical Humanitarianism and Human Rights: Reflections on Doctors Without Borders and Doctors of the World." *Social Science & Medicine* 41, no. 12 (1995): 1607–16.

Franks, Suzanne. "The CARMA Report: Western Media Coverage of Humanitarian Disasters." *Political Quarterly* 77, no. 2 (2006): 281–84.

Fraser, Nancy. "Transnationalizing the Public Sphere: On the Legitimacy and Efficacy of Public Opinion in a Post-Westphalian World." In *Identities, Affiliations, and Allegiances*, edited by Şeyla Benhabib, Ian Shapiro, and Danilo Petranović, 45–67. Cambridge: Cambridge University Press, 2007.

Fredrikson, Aurora. "Making Humanitarian Spaces Global: Coordinating Crisis Response through the Cluster Approach." PhD diss., Columbia University, 2012.

Frelick, Bill. "Paradigm Shifts in the International Responses to Refugees." In *Fear of Persecution: Global Human Rights, International Law, and Human Well-Being*, edited by James White and Anthony J. Marsella, 33–59. Lanham, MD: Lexington Books, 2007.

Friedland, Roger, and Robert R. Alford. "Bringing Society Back In: Symbols,

Practices, and Institutional Contradictions." In *The New Institutionalism in Organizational Analysis,* edited by Walter W. Powell and Paul J. DiMaggio, 232–63. Chicago: University of Chicago Press, 1991.

Frohardt, Mark, Diane Paul, and Larry Minear. *Protecting Human Rights: The Challenge to Humanitarian Organizations.* Occasional Paper 35. Providence, RI: Thomas J. Watson Jr. Institute for International Studies, 1999.

Furedi, Frank. *The New Ideology of Imperialism: Renewing the Moral Imperative.* London: Pluto Press, 1994.

Gabriel, Richard, and Karen Metz. *A History of Military Medicine.* New York: Greenwood Press, 1992.

Gasper, Des. "Evaluating the 'Logical Framework Approach' towards Learning-Oriented Development Evaluation." *Public Administration and Development* 20, no. 1 (2000): 17–28.

Giesen, Peter. "Sphere and Accountability: A View from MSF." N.d. http://www.sphereproject.org.

Giossi Caverzasio, Sylvie. *Strengthening Protection in War: A Search for Professional Standards, Summary of Discussions among Human Rights and Humanitarian Organizations—Workshops at the ICRC, 1996-2000.* Geneva: ICRC, 2001.

Glazer, Amihai, and Kai A. Konrad. "A Signaling Explanation for Charity." *American Economic Review* 86, no. 4 (1996): 1019–28.

Glazer, Nona Y. "Servants to Capital: Unpaid Domestic Labor and Paid Work." *Review of Radical Political Economics* 16, no. 1 (1984): 60–87.

Go, Julian. "Global Fields and Imperial Forms: Field Theory and the British and American Empires." *Sociological Theory* 26, no. 3 (2008): 201–29.

Green, Maia. "Calculating Compassion: Accounting for Some Categorical Practices in International Development." In *Adventures in Aidland: The Anthropology of Professionals in International Development,* edited by David Mosse, 33–47. New York: Berghahn Books, 2011.

Greenberg, Stephen. "Plague, the Printing Press, and Public Health in Seventeenth-Century London." *Huntington Library Quarterly* 67, no. 4 (2004): 508–27.

Griekspoor, André, and Egbert Sondorp. "Enhancing the Quality of Humanitarian Assistance: Taking Stock and Future Initiatives." *Prehospital and Disaster Medicine* 16, no. 4 (2001): 209–15.

Gross, Bertram M. "McNamaran Management." *Public Administration Review* 25, no. 3 (1965): 259–61.

———. "The New Systems Budgeting." *Public Administration Review* 29, no. 2 (1969): 113–37.

Gross Stein, Janice. "Humanitarian Organizations: Accountable—Why, to Whom, for What, and How?" In *Humanitarianism in Question: Politics, Power, Ethics,* edited by Michael Barnett and Thomas G. Weiss, 124–42. Ithaca, NY: Cornell University Press, 2008.

Guggenheim, Michael. "Organisierte Umwelt: Umweltdienstleistungsfirmen zwischen Wissenschaft, Wirtschaft und Politik." Bielefeld: Transcript, 2005.

Guilhot, Nicolas. *The Democracy Makers*. New York: Columbia University Press, 2005.

―――. "Limiting Sovereignty or Producing Governmentality? Two Human Rights Regimes in U.S. Political Discourse." *Constellations* 15, no. 4 (2008): 502–16.

Guillory, John. "Bourdieu's Refusal." *Modern Language Quarterly* 58, no. 4 (1997): 367–98.

Habermas, Jürgen. *The Structural Transformation of the Public Sphere*. Cambridge, MA: MIT Press, 1989.

Hacking, Ian. *The Taming of Chance*. Ideas in Context 17. Cambridge: Cambridge University Press, 1990.

Haerting, Heike. "Global Humanitarianism, Race, and the Spectacle of the African Corpse in Current Western Representations of the Rwandan Genocide." *Comparative Studies of South Asia Africa and the Middle East* 28 (2008): 61–77.

Hall, Peter D. *Inventing the Nonprofit Sector and Other Essays on Philanthropy, Voluntarism, and Nonprofit Organizations*. Baltimore: Johns Hopkins University Press, 1992.

Hammond, Paul Y. "A Functional Analysis of Defense Department Decision-Making in the McNamara Administration." *American Political Science Review* 62, no. 1 (1968): 57–69.

Hannan, Michael T., and John Freeman. "The Population Ecology of Organizations." *American Journal of Sociology* 82, no. 5 (1977): 929–64.

Hansmann, Henry B. "The Role of Nonprofit Enterprise." *Yale Law Journal* 89, no. 5 (1980): 835–901.

HAP: Humanitarian Accountability Partnership. *HAP 2007 Standard in Humanitarian Accountability and Quality Management*. Geneva: HAP International, 2007.

―――. *The 2010 HAP Standard in Accountability and Quality Management*. Geneva: HAP International, 2010.

―――. "Principles of Accountability." Accessed September 8, 2011. http://www.hapinternational.org/projects/standard/development/principles-of-accountability.aspx.

Harper, Edwin L., Fred A. Kramer, and Andrew M. Rouse. "Implementation and Use of PPB in Sixteen Federal Agencies." *Public Administration Review* 29, no. 6 (1969): 623–32.

Harries, A. D., D. S. Nyangulu, N. J. Hargreaves, O. Kaluwa, and F. M. Salaniponi. "Preventing Antiretroviral Anarchy in Sub-Saharan Africa." *The Lancet* 358, no. 9279 (August 2001): 410–14.

Harvey, Paul. *Towards Good Humanitarian Government: The Role of the Affected State in Disaster Response*. HPG Report 29. London: ODI, 2009.

Haskell, Thomas L. "Capitalism and the Origins of the Humanitarian Sensibility, Part 1." *American Historical Review* 90, no. 2 (1985): 339–61.

―――. "Capitalism and the Origins of the Humanitarian Sensibility, Part 2." *American Historical Review* 90, no. 3 (1985): 547–66.

Healy, Kieran. "Altruism as an Organizational Problem: The Case of Organ Pro-
curement." *American Sociological Review* 69, no. 3 (2004): 387–404.
———. *The Last Best Gifts: Altruism and the Market for Human Blood and Organs.*
Chicago: University of Chicago Press, 2006.
Heins, Volker. *How to Meet the First Public Obligation: Contending Discourses in
Humanitarian Organizations.* KSG Carr Center Working Paper. Cambridge,
MA: KSG Carr Center, n.d.
Held, David. *Democracy and the Global Order: From the Modern State to Cosmopolitan
Governance.* Stanford, CA: Stanford University Press, 1995.
Henkel, Heiko, and Roderick Stirrat. "Participation as Spiritual Duty; Empower-
ment and Secular Subjection." In *Participation—The New Tyranny?*, edited by
Bill Cooke and Uma Kothari, 168–84. London: Zed Books, 2001.
Hilhorst, Dorothea. "Being Good at Doing Good? Quality and Accountability of
Humanitarian NGOs." *Disasters* 26, no. 3 (2002): 193–212.
———. *The Real World of NGOs: Discourses, Diversity, and Development.* London:
Zed Books, 2003.
Hilhorst, Dorothea, and Maliana Serrano. "The Humanitarian Arena in Angola,
1975–2008." *Disasters* 34, no. 2 (2010): 183–201.
Hitchens, Christopher. *The Missionary Position: Mother Teresa in Theory and Prac-
tice.* London: Verso, 1995.
Hoffman, Peter. "When Hired Guns Guard Humanitarian Spaces: Norms and
Humanitarian Agency-Security Contractor Interactions." PhD diss., CUNY
Graduate Center, 2008.
Holzscheiter, Anna. "The Representational Power of Civil Society Organisations
in Global AIDS Governance: Advocating for Children in Global Health Poli-
tics." In *Power and Transnational Activism,* edited by Thomas Olesen, 173–89.
London: Routledge, 2010.
Hood, Christopher. *The Art of the State: Culture, Rhetoric, and Public Management.*
Oxford: Clarendon Press, 1998.
———. "Exploring Variations in Public Management Reform of the 1980s." In
Civil Service Systems in Comparative Perspective, edited by Hans A. G. M. Bekke,
James L. Perry, and Theo A. J. Toonen, 268–87. Bloomington: Indiana Univer-
sity Press, 1996.
Hopgood, Stephen. *Keepers of the Flame: Understanding Amnesty International.*
Ithaca, NY: Cornell University Press, 2006.
Hopgood, Stephen, and Leslie Vinjamuri. "Faith in Markets." In *Sacred Aid: Faith
and Humanitarianism,* edited by Michael Barnett and Janice Stein, 37–54.
Oxford: Oxford University Press, 2012.
Hopwood, Anthony G., and Peter Miller, eds. *Accounting as Social and Institutional
Practice.* Cambridge Studies in Management 24. Cambridge: Cambridge
University Press, 1994.
Hulme, David. "Projects, Politics, and Professionals: Alternative Approaches for
Project Identification and Project Planning." *Agricultural Systems* 47, no. 2
(1995): 211–33.

Hulme, David, and Michael Edwards. *NGOs, States, and Donors: Too Close for Comfort?* New York: St. Martin's Press, 1997.

Humphrey, Christopher, Peter Miller, and Robert W. Scapens. "Accountability and Accountable Management in the UK Public Sector." *Accounting, Auditing & Accountability Journal* 6, no. 3 (1993): 7–29.

Hunt, Lynn. *Inventing Human Rights: A History.* New York: Norton, 2007.

Hunt, Matthew. R. "Moral Experience of Canadian Health Care Professionals in Humanitarian Work." *Prehospital and Disaster Medicine* 24, no. 6 (2009): 518–24.

Hutchinson, John. *Champions of Charity: War and the Rise of the Red Cross.* Boulder, CO: Westview Press, 1996.

Hyndman, Jennifer. *Managing Displacement: Refugees and the Politics of Humanitarianism.* Minneapolis: University of Minnesota Press, 2000.

Ignatieff, Michael. *The Lesser Evil: Political Ethics in an Age of Terror.* Princeton, NJ: Princeton University Press, 2004.

International Council of Voluntary Agencies. "Proceedings: Workshop on the Development of Human Rights Training for Humanitarian Actors, Geneva, 29–30 November 2001." http://www.icva.ch/doc00000748.html.

International Federation of Red Cross and Red Crescent Societies. *The Code of Conduct for The International Red Cross and Red Crescent Movement and NGOs in Disaster Relief.* Geneva: International Federation of Red Cross and Red Crescent Societies, 1994.

———. "Guidelines for Emergency Assessment." Geneva: International Federation of Red Cross and Red Crescent Societies, 2005.

INTRAC and South Research. "Recent Developments in GTZ's Use of the ZOPP." In *A Tool for Project Management and People-Driven Development: Proceedings of the INTRAC and South Research Workshop on LFA and OOIP, Leuven, Belgium, 16–18 May 1994*, pt. 1, *Main Report*, 28–29. Oxford: INTRAC, 1994.

Jablonsky, Stephen F., and Mark W. Dirsmith. "The Pattern of PPB Rejection: Something about Organizations, Something about PPB." *Accounting, Organizations and Society* 3, no. 3/4 (1978): 215–25.

Jean, François. *From Ethiopia to Chechnya: Reflections on Humanitarian Action.* New York: MSF, 2008.

Kaldor, Mary. *New and Old Wars: Organized Violence in a Global Era.* Cambridge: Polity Press, 2006.

Kalpagam, Umamaheswaran. "Colonial Governmentality and the 'Economy.'" *Economy and Society* 29, no. 3 (2000): 418–38.

Kant, Immanuel. *Perpetual Peace, and Other Essays on Politics, History, and Morals.* Translated by Ted Humphrey. Indianapolis: Hackett, 1983.

Keck, Margaret E., and Kathryn Sikkink. *Activists beyond Borders: Advocacy Networks in International Politics.* Ithaca, NY: Cornell University Press, 1998.

Kennedy, David. *The Dark Sides of Virtue: Reassessing International Humanitarianism.* Princeton, NJ: Princeton University Press, 2004.

Kieserling, André. *Selbstbeschreibung und Fremdbeschreibung.* Frankfurt: Suhrkamp, 2004.

Kirmani, Nida, Ajaz A. Khan, and Victoria Palmer. *Does Faith Matter? An Examination of Islamic Relief's Work with Refugees and Internally Displaced Persons*. London: Islamic Relief, 2008.

Korf, Benedict, Shahul Habullah, Pia Hollenbach, and Bart Klem. "The Gift of Disaster: The Commodification of Good Intentions in Post-tsunami Sri Lanka." *Disasters* 34, no. 2 (2010): 60–77.

Kurasawa, Fuyuki. *The Work of Global Justice: Human Rights as Practices*. Cambridge Cultural Social Studies. New York: Cambridge University Press, 2007.

Latour, Bruno. *Science in Action: How to Follow Scientists and Engineers through Society*. Cambridge, MA: Harvard University Press, 1987.

Latour, Bruno, and Steve Woolgar. *Laboratory Life: The Social Construction of Facts*. Princeton, NJ: Princeton University Press, 1986.

Law, John. *After Method: Mess in Social Science Research*. International Library of Sociology. London: Routledge, 2004.

Lewis, David. "Tidy Concepts, Messy Lives: Defining Tensions in the Domestic and Overseas Careers of U.K. Non-Governmental Professionals." In *Adventures in Aidland: The Anthropology of Professionals in International Development*, edited by David Mosse, 177–98. New York: Berghahn Books, 2011.

Lewis, David, and David Mosse, eds. *Development Brokers and Translators: The Ethnography of Aid and Agencies*. Bloomfield, CT: Kumarian Press, 2006.

Lindenberg, Mark, and Coralie Bryant. *Going Global: Transforming Relief and Development NGOs*. Bloomfield, CT: Kumarian Press, 2001.

Lipsky, Martin. *Street-Level Bureaucracy: Dilemmas of the Individual in Public Services*. New York: Russell Sage Foundation Publications, 2010.

Lischer, Sarah K. *Dangerous Sanctuaries: Refugee Camps, Civil War, and the Dilemmas of Humanitarian Aid*. Ithaca, NY: Cornell University Press, 2006.

Long, Norman, and Ann Long. *Battlefields of Knowledge: The Interlocking of Theory and Practice in Social Research and Development*. London: Routledge, 1992.

Loundsbury, Michael. "Institutional Rationality and Practice Variation: New Directions in the Institutional Analysis of Practice." *Accounting, Organizations and Society* 33, nos. 4–5 (2008): 349–61.

———. "Institutional Sources of Practice Variation: Staffing College and University Recycling Programs." *Administrative Science Quarterly* 46, no. 1 (2001): 29–56.

Luhmann, Niklas. "Differentiation of Society." *Canadian Journal of Sociology* 2, no. 1 (1977): 29–53.

———. *The Differentiation of Society*. Translated by Stephen Holmes and Charles Larmore. European Perspectives. New York: Columbia University Press, 1982.

Major, Aaron. "Hanging in the Balance: Global Capitalism and the American Welfare State." PhD diss., New York University, 2008. ProQuest (AAT 3330156).

Manzo, Kate. "Africa in the Rise of Rights-Based Development." *Geoforum* 34, no. 4 (2003): 437–56.

Martin, John Levi. "What Is Field Theory?" *American Journal of Sociology* 109, no. 1 (2003): 1–49.

Marx, Karl, and Friedrich Engels. *The Communist Manifesto.* London: Penguin, 1967.

Maury, Hugues, and Rémi Russbach. "The Quality Compass—A New Tool to Manage and Evaluate Humanitarian Assistance." *International Journal of Disaster Medicine* 2, no. 3 (2004): 106–10.

Mauss, Marcel. *The Gift: The Form and Reason for Exchange in Archaic Societies.* London: Routledge, 1990.

Mayr, Ernst. *The Growth of Biological Thought: Diversity, Evolution, and Inheritance.* Cambridge, MA: Belknap Press, 1982.

McGerr, Michael. *A Fierce Discontent: The Rise and Fall of the Progressive Movement in America, 1870–1920.* Oxford: Oxford University Press, 2003.Médecins Sans Frontières. *International Financial Report 2011.* Geneva: MSF International, 2012.

Medvetz, Thomas. *Think Tanks in America.* Chicago: University of Chicago Press, 2012.

Merry, Sally Engle. "Rights Talk and the Experience of Law: Implementing Women's Human Rights to Protection from Violence." *Human Rights Quarterly* 25, no. 2 (2003): 243–381.

———. "Transnational Human Rights and Local Activism: Mapping the Middle." *American Anthropologist* 108, no. 1 (2006): 38–51.

Merry, Sally, and Mark Goodale. *The Practice of Human Rights: Tracking Law between the Global and the Local.* Cambridge Studies in Law and Society. Cambridge: Cambridge University Press, 2007.

Meuser, Michael, and Ulrike Nagel. "ExpertInneninterviews—vielfach erprobt, wenig bedacht." In *Qualitativ-empirische Sozialforschung: Konzepte, Methoden, Analysen,* edited by Detlef Garz and Klaus Kraimer, 441–71. Opladen: Westdeutscher Verlag, 1991.

Meyer, John W., and Brian Rowan. "Institutionalized Organizations: Formal Structure as Myth and Ceremony." *American Journal of Sociology* 83, no. 2 (1977): 340–63.

Michels, Robert. *Political Parties: A Sociological Study of the Oligarchical Tendencies of Modern Democracy.* 1911. New York: Transactions Publishers, 1999.

Miller, Hannah. "From 'Rights-Based' to 'Rights-Framed' Approaches: A Social Constructionist View of Human Rights Practice." *International Journal of Human Rights* 14, no. 6 (November 2010): 915–31.

Miller, Peter. "Governing by Numbers: Why Calculative Practices Matter." *Social Research* 68, no. 2 (2001): 379–96.

Miller, Peter, and Ted O'Leary. "Mediating Instruments and Making Markets: Capital Budgeting, Science, and the Economy." *Accounting, Organizations and Society* 32, no. 7/8 (2007): 701–34.

Millwood, David, ed. 1996. *The International Response to Conflict and Genocide: Lessons from the Rwanda Experience.* Geneva: Steering Committee of the Joint Evaluation of Emergency Assistance to Rwanda.

Minear, Larry, and Thomas G. Weiss. *The Humanitarianism and War Project*. Boulder, CO: Lynne Rienner Publishers, 1993.

Mitchell, Timothy. "Fixing the Economy." *Cultural Studies* 12, no. 1 (1998): 82–101.

———. "The Limits of the State: Beyond Statist Approaches and Their Critics." *American Political Science Review* 85, no. 1 (1991): 77–96.

Moon, Claire. "What One Sees and How One Files Seeing: Human Rights Reporting, Representation, and Action." *Sociology* 46, no. 5 (2012): 876–90.

Morgenthau, Hans J. *Politics among Nations: The Struggle for Power and Peace*. New York: A. A. Knopf, 1948.

Mosse, David, ed. *Adventures in Aidland: The Anthropology of Professionals in International Development*. New York: Berghahn Books, 2011.

———. *Cultivating Development: An Ethnography of Aid Policy and Practice*. London: Pluto Press, 2005.

———. "The Making and Marketing of Participatory Development." In *A Moral Critique of Development: In Search of Global Responsibilities*, edited by Philip Quarles van Ufford and Ananta Kumar Giri, 43–75. London: Routledge, 2003.

———. "People's Knowledge, Participation, and Patronage: Operations and Representations in Rural Development." In *Participation—The New Tyranny?*, edited by Bill Cooke and Uma Kothari, 16–35. London: Zed Press, 2001.

Moyn, Samuel. *The Last Utopia: Human Rights in History*. Cambridge, MA: Harvard University Press, 2012.

Nakabayashi, Saeko. "The Japanese Version of Project Cycle Management: Adoption, Adaptation and Application of Zopp—A Comparative Analysis of Methods and Methodologies." ISS Working Paper Series/General Series, Working Paper 319. The Hague: Institute of Social Studies, 2000.

Nash, Kate. *The Cultural Politics of Human Rights*. Cambridge: Cambridge University Press, 2009.

———. "Human Rights, Movements, and Law: On Not Researching Legitimacy." *Sociology* 46, no. 5 (2012): 797–812.

Negt, Oskar, and Alexander Kluge. *Geschichte und Eigensinn*. Frankfurt am Main: Zweitausendeins, 1981.

———. *Public Sphere and Experience: Toward an Analysis of the Bourgeois and Proletarian Public Sphere*. Minneapolis: University of Minnesota Press, 1993.

Neiman, Susan. *Evil in Modern Thought: An Alternative History of Philosophy*. Princeton, NJ: Princeton University Press, 2002.

Newhouse, Joseph P. "Toward a Theory of Nonprofit Institutions: An Economic Model of the Hospital." *American Economic Review* 60, no. 1 (1970): 64–74.

Niditch, Susan. *War in the Hebrew Bible: A Study in the Ethics of Violence*. Oxford: Oxford University Press, 1993.

O'Brien, Paul. "Politicized Humanitarianism: A Response to Nicolas de Torrente." *Harvard Human Rights Journal* 17, no. 1 (2004): 31–40.

O'Flynn, Maureen, and International Save the Children Alliance. *Child Rights*

Programming: How to Apply Rights-Based Approaches in Programming; A Hand-book for International Save the Children Alliance Members. Stockholm: Save the Children Sweden, n.d.

O'Malley, Pat, Lorna Weir, and Clifford Shearing, "Governmentality, Criticism, Politics." *Economy and Society* 26, no. 4 (1997): 501–17.

O'Neil, Tammie. *Human Rights and Poverty Reduction: Realities, Controversies, and Strategies.* London: Overseas Development Institute, 2006.

Pantuliano, Sara, and Sorcha O'Callaghan. "'The Protection Crisis': A Review of Field-Based Strategies for Humanitarian Protection in Darfur." HPG Discussion Papers. London: ODI, 2006.

Paras, Andrea, and Janice Gross Stein. "Bridging the Sacred and the Profane in Humanitarian Life." In *Sacred Aid: Faith and Humanitarianism,* edited by Michael Barnett and Janice Stein, 211–40. Oxford: Oxford University Press, 2012.

Parsons, Talcott. "The Professions and Social Structure." *Social Forces* 17, no. 4 (1939): 457–67.

———. "A Sociologist Looks at the Legal Profession." In *Essays in Sociological Theory,* by Talcott Parsons, 370–85. New York: Simon and Schuster, 1954.

PARTICIP GmbH. *Introduction to the Logical Framework Approach (LFE) for GEF-Financed Projects—Reader.* Berlin: Deutsche Stiftung für Internationale Entwicklung, 2004.

Pauly, Mark V. "Nonprofit Firms in Medical Markets." *American Economic Review* 77, no. 2 (1987): 257–62.

Petras, James. "NGOs: In the Service of Imperialism." *Journal of Contemporary Asia* 29, no. 4 (1999): 429–40.

Pigg, Stacey Leigh. "Investing Social Categories through Place: Social Representations and Development in Nepal." *Comparative Studies in Society and History* 34, no. 3 (1992): 491–513.

Polastro, Riccardo, Aatika Nagrah, Nicolai Steen, and Farwa Zafar. "Inter-agency Real-Time Evaluation of the Humanitarian Response to Pakistan's 2010 Flood Crisis." DARA International, 2011. http://daraint.org/wp-content/uploads/2011/03/Final-Report-RTE-Pakistan-2011.pdf.

Porter, Dorothy. *Health, Civilization, and the State: A History of Public Health from Ancient to Modern Times.* London: Routledge, 1999.

Postone, Moishe. *Time, Labor, and Social Domination: A Reinterpretation of Marx's Critical Theory.* Cambridge: Cambridge University Press, 1993.

Powell, Walter, and Paul DiMaggio. *The New Institutionalism in Organizational Analysis.* Chicago: University of Chicago Press, 1991.

Power, Michael. *The Audit Society: Rituals of Verification.* Oxford: Oxford University Press, 1997.

Power, Samantha. *A Problem from Hell: America and the Age of Genocide.* New York: Basic Books, 2002.

Prakash, Aseem, and Mary Kay Gugerty, eds. *Rethinking Advocacy Organizations: A Collective Action Perspective.* Cambridge: Cambridge University Press, 2010.

Preston, Alistair M., David J. Cooper, and Rod W. Coombs. "Fabricating Budgets: A Study of the Production of Management Budgeting in the National Health Service." *Accounting, Organizations and Society* 17, no. 6 (1992): 561–93.

Pupavac, Vanessa. "Between Compassion and Conservativism: A Genealogy of Humanitarian Sensibilities." In *Contemporary States of Emergency: The Politics of Military and Humanitarian Intervention,* by Didier Fassin and Mariella Pandolfi, 129–53. New York: Zone Books, 2011.

Quine, Willard Van Orman. *Word and Object.* Cambridge, MA: MIT Press, 1960.

Rajaram, Prem Kumar. "Humanitarianism and Representations of the Refugee." *Journal of Refugee Studies* 15, no. 3 (2002): 247–64.

Ramalingam, Ben, John Mitchell, John Borton, and Kristin Smart. *Counting What Counts: Performance and Effectiveness in the Humanitarian Sector.* London: ALNAP, 2009.

Redfield, Peter. "Doctors, Borders, and Life in Crisis." *Cultural Anthropology* 20, no. 3 (2005): 328–61.

———. "The Impossible Problem of Neutrality." In *Forces of Compassion: Humanitarianism between Ethics and Politics,* edited by Erica Bornstein and Peter Redfield, 53–70. Santa Fe, NM: School for Advanced Research Press, 2011.

———. "A Less Modest Witness: Collective Advocacy and Motivated Truth in a Medical Humanitarian Movement." *American Ethnologist* 33, no. 1 (2006): 3–26.

———. "Sacrifice, Triage, and Global Humanitarianism." In *Humanitarianism in Question: Politics, Power, Ethics,* edited by Michael Barnett and Thomas G. Weiss, 196–214. Ithaca, NY: Cornell University Press, 2008.

Rieff, David. *A Bed for the Night: Humanitarianism in Crisis.* New York: Simon & Schuster, 2003.

Risse, Thomas, Steve C. Ropp, and Kathryn Sikkink, eds. *The Power of Human Rights: International Norms and Domestic Change.* Cambridge: Cambridge University Press, 1999.

Ritzer, George, and David Walczak. "Rationalization and the Deprofessionalization of Physicians." *Social Forces* 67, no. 1 (1988): 1–22.

Rootes, Chris, ed. *Environmental Movements: Local, National, and Global.* London: Frank Cass, 1999.

———, ed. *Environmental Protest in Western Europe.* Oxford: Oxford University Press, 2003.

———. "Global Civil Society and the Lessons of European Environmentalism." In *Creating a Better World,* edited by Rupert Taylor, 147–69. Bloomfield, CT: Kumarian Press, 2004.

Rosen, George. *A History of Public Health.* Baltimore: Johns Hopkins University Press, 1993.

Rosenberg, Leon J., and Larry D. Posner. *The Logical Framework: A Manager's Guide to a Scientific Approach to Design and Evaluation.* Washington, DC: Practical Concepts Incorporated, 1979.

Rossi, Benedetta. "Aid Policies and Recipient Strategies in Niger: Why Donors and Recipients Should Not Be Compartmentalized into Separate 'Worlds of Knowledge.'" In *Development Brokers and Translators: The Ethnography of Aid and Agencies*, edited by David Lewis and David Mosse, 27–50. Bloomfield, CT: Kumarian Press, 2006.

Rottenburg, Richard. "Accountability for Development Aid." In *Facts and Figures: Economic Representations and Practices*, edited by Herbert Kalthoff, Richard Rottenburg, and Hans-Juergen Wagener, 143–73. Marburg: Metropolis Verlag, 2000.

———. *Far-Fetched Facts: A Parable of Development Aid*. Cambridge, MA: MIT Press, 2009.

Rubenstein, Jennifer. "The Distributive Commitments of International NGOs." In *Humanitarianism in Question: Politics, Power, and Ethics*, edited by Michael Barnett and Thomas G. Weiss, 215–35. Ithaca, NY: Cornell University Press, 2008.

Ryfman, Philippe. *Une histoire de l'humanitaire*. Paris: La Découverte, 2008.

Saint-Martin, Denis. "Management Consultants, the State, and the Politics of Administrative Reform in Britain and Canada." *Administration & Society* 30, no. 5 (1998): 533–68.

Samsky, Ari. "'Since We Are Taking the Drugs': Labor and Value in Two International Drug Donation Programs." *Journal of Cultural Economy* 30, no. 1 (2011): 27–43.

Sassen, Saskia. *Territory, Authority, Rights: From Medieval to Global Assemblages*. Princeton, NJ: Princeton University Press, 2006.

Saussy, Haun. *Partner to the Poor: A Paul Farmer Reader*. Berkeley: University of California Press, 2010.

Save the Children. *From Camp to Community: Liberia Study on Exploitation of Children*. Monrovia, Liberia: Save the Children, 2006.

Schaar, Johan. "The Birth of the Good Humanitarian Donorship Initiative." In *The Humanitarian Response Index 2007: Measuring Commitment to Best Practice*, edited by Silvia Hidalgo and Augusto Lopez-Claros, 37–45. London: Macmillan, 2008.

Schick, Allen. "The Budget as an Instrument of Presidential Policy." In *The Reagan Presidency and the Governing of America*, edited by Lester M. Salamon and Michael S. Lund, 91–125. Washington, DC: Urban Institute Press, 1985.

———. "A Death in the Bureaucracy: The Demise of Federal PPB." *Public Administration Review* 33, no. 2 (1973): 146–56.

———. "The Road to PPB: The Stages of Budget Reform." *Public Administration Review* 26, no. 4 (1966): 243–58.

———. "Systems Politics and Systems Budgeting." *Public Administration Review* 29, no. 2 (1969): 137–51.

———. *USAID Program and Operations Assessment Report No. 4: A Performance-Based Budgeting System for the Agency for International Development*. Arlington, VA: USAID Development Information Services Clearinghouse, 1993.

Schmitz, Constance C. *Leaders against Family Violence: A Fictionalized Account of a*

W. K. Kellogg Foundation-Sponsored Cluster Evaluation. Battle Creek, MI: W. K. Kellogg Foundation, 1998.

Schwartz, Robert A. "Personal Philanthropic Contributions." *Journal of Political Economy* 78, no. 6 (1970): 1264–91.

Scott, James C. *Seeing Like a State: How Certain Schemes to Improve the Human Condition Have Failed.* New Haven, CT: Yale University Press, 1998.

———. *Weapons of the Weak: Everyday Forms of Peasant Resistance.* New Haven, CT: Yale University Press, 1985.

Scott, W. Richard. "Professionals in Bureaucracies—Areas of Conflict." In *Professionalization*, edited by Howard M. Vollmer and Donald L. Mills, 265–75. Englewood Cliffs, NJ: Prentice Hall, 1966.

Scott, W. Richard, and John W. Meyer. *Institutional Environments and Organizations: Structural Complexity and Individualism.* Thousand Oaks, CA: SAGE Publications, 1994.

Sending, Ole, and Iver B. Neumann. "Governance to Governmentality: Analyzing NGOs, States, and Power." *International Studies Quarterly* 50, no. 3 (2006): 651–72.

Sewell, William H., Jr. "Ideologies and Social Revolutions: Reflections on the French Case." *Journal of Modern History* 57, no. 1 (1985): 57–85.

Shapiro, Stuart. "Degrees of Freedom: The Interaction of Standards of Practice and Engineering Judgment." *Science, Technology & Human Values* 22, no. 3 (1997): 286–316.

Shaw, Martin. *Civil Society and Media in Global Crises: Representing Distant Violence.* New York: Pinter, 1996.

Silber, Ilana F. "Bourdieu's Gift to Gift Theory: An Unacknowledged Trajectory." *Sociological Theory* 27, no. 2 (2009): 173–90.

Siméant, Johanna. "What Is Going Global? The Internationalization of French NGOs 'Without Borders.'" *Review of International Political Economy* 12, no. 5 (2005): 851–83.

Singer, Amy. *Charity in Islamic Societies.* Themes in Islamic History. Cambridge: Cambridge University Press, 2008.

Skocpol, Theda. "Cultural Idioms and Political Ideologies in the Revolutionary Reconstruction of State Power: A Rejoinder to Sewell." *Journal of Modern History* 57, no. 1 (1985): 86–96.

———. *States and Social Revolutions: A Comparative Analysis of France, Russia, and China.* Cambridge: Cambridge University Press, 1979.

Slim, Hugo. "Dissolving the Difference between Relief and Development: The Making of a Rights-Based Solution." *Development in Practice* 10, no. 3 (2000): 491–94.

———. "Is Humanitarianism Being Politicised? A Reply to David Rieff." Paper presented at the Dutch Red Cross Symposium on Ethics in Aid, The Hague, 8 October 2003.

———. "Not Philanthropy but Rights: The Proper Politicisation of Humanitarian Philosophy." *International Journal of Human Rights* 6, no. 2 (2002): 1–22.

———. "A Response to Peter Uvin: Making Moral Low Ground; Rights as the Struggle for Justice and the Abolition of Development." *Praxis: The Fletcher School Journal of Development Studies* 17 (2002): 491–94.

———. "Why Protect Civilians? Innocence, Immunity, and Enmity in War." *International Affairs* 79, no. 3 (2003): 481–501.

Slim, Hugo, and Andrew Bonwick. "Protection: An ALNAP Guide for Humanitarian Agencies." Oxford: Oxfam Publications, 2006.

Smillie, Ian. *Patronage or Partnership: Local Capacity Building in a Humanitarian Crisis*. Bloomfield, CT: Kumarian Press, 2001.

Smith, Jackie, Ron Pagnucco, and George A. Lopez. "Globalizing Human Rights: The Work of Transnational Human Rights NGOs in the 1990s." *Human Rights Quarterly* 20, no. 2 (1998): 379–412.

Smith, Kerry. *Non-DAC Donors and Humanitarian Aid: Shifting Structures, Changing Trends*. Global Humanitarian Assistance Briefing Paper. Somerset, UK: Development Initiatives, 2011.

Smythe, Dallas Walker. "On the Audience Commodity and Its Work." In *Media and Cultural Studies: KeyWorks*, edited by Meenakshi Gigi Durham and Douglas Kellner, 230–56. Oxford: Blackwell, 2001.

Sparrow, Bartholomew. *Uncertain Guardians: The News Media as a Political Institution*. Baltimore: Johns Hopkins University Press, 1999.

Speich, Daniel. "Der Blick von Lake Success: Das Entwicklungsdenken der frühen UNO als 'lokales Wissen.'" In *Entwicklungswelten: Globalgeschichte der Entwicklungszusammenarbeit*, edited by Hubertus Büschel and Daniel Speich, 143–74. Frankfurt: Campus, 2009.

———. "The Use of Global Abstractions: National Income Accounting in the Period of Imperial Decline." *Journal of Global History* 6, no. 1 (2011): 7–28.

Sphere Project. *Humanitarian Charter and Minimum Standards in Disaster Response*. Geneva: The Sphere Project, 2003.

———. *Humanitarian Charter and Minimum Standards in Disaster Response*. Geneva: The Sphere Project, 2011.

———. *The Sphere Project Training Package: Humanitarian Charter and Minimum Standards in Disaster Response*. Geneva: The Sphere Project, 2003.

Stichweh, Rudolf. "The Genesis of a Global Public Sphere." *Development* 46, no. 1 (2003): 26–39.

———. "Professionen und Disziplinen: Formen der Differenzierung zweier Systeme beruflichen Handelns in modernen Gesellschaften." In *Wissenschaft, Universität, Professionen*, by Rudolf Stichweh, 278–336. Frankfurt a. M.: Suhrkamp, 1994.

———. "Professions in Modern Society." *International Review of Sociology* 7, no. 1 (1997): 95–102.

———. *Wissenschaft, Universität, Professionen*. Frankfurt a. M.: Suhrkamp, 1994.

Stinchcombe, Arthur L. "Third Party Buying: The Trend and the Consequences." *Social Forces* 62, no. 4 (1984): 861–84.

Stirrat, Roderick L., and Heiko Henkel. "The Development Gift: The Problem of

Reciprocity in the NGO World." *Annals of the American Academy of Political and Social Science* 554 (1997): 66–80.

Stoddard, Abby. "Humanitarian NGOs: Challenges and Trends." In *Humanitarian Action and the "Global War on Terror": A Review of Trends and Issues*, edited by Joanna Macrae and Adele Harmer, 25–36. Humanitarian Policy Group Report 14. London: Overseas Development Institute, 2003.

Stoddard, Abby, Adele Harmer, and Katherine Haver. "Providing Aid in Insecure Environments: Trends in Policy and Operations." London: Center on International Cooperation/Overseas Development Institute Humanitarian Policy Group, 2006.

Strathern, Marilyn, ed. *Audit Cultures: Anthropological Studies in Accountability, Ethics, and the Academy*. London: Routledge, 2000.

Stroup, Sarah S. *Borders among Activists: International NGOs in the United States, Britain, and France*. Ithaca, NY: Cornell University Press, 2012.

Taithe, Bertrand. "Pyrrhic Victories? French Catholic Missionaries, Modern Expertise, and Secularizing Technologies." In *Sacred Aid: Faith and Humanitarianism*, edited by Michael Barnett and Janice Stein, 166–87. Oxford: Oxford University Press, 2012.

Tarp, Finn, and Peter Hjertholm, eds. *Foreign Aid and Development: Lessons Learnt and Directions for the Future*. London: Routledge, 2000.

Tassie, Jean-Michel, Elisabeth Szumilin, Alexandra Calmy, and Eric Goemaere. "Highly Active Antiretroviral Therapy in Resource Poor Settings: The Experience of Médecins Sans Frontières." *AIDS* 17, no. 13 (2003): 1995–97.

Taylor, Harold. "Insights into Participation from Critical Management and Labour Process Perspectives." In *Participation—The New Tyranny?*, edited by Bill Cooke and Uma Kothari, 122–38. London: Zed Press, 2001.

Tearfund. *Accountability to Beneficiaries in Kashmir*. Teddington, UK: Tearfund, 2008.

Terranova, Tiziana. "Free Labor: Producing Culture for the Digital Economy." *Social Text* 63.18, no. 2 (2000): 33–58.

Terry, Fiona. *Condemned to Repeat? The Paradox of Humanitarian Action*. Ithaca, NY: Cornell University Press, 2002.

Thaut, Laura C. "The Role of Faith in Christian Faith-Based Humanitarian Agencies: Constructing the Taxonomy." *Voluntas: International Journal of Voluntary and Nonprofit Organizations* 20, no. 4 (2009): 319–50.

Thompson, John B. *Books in the Digital Age: The Transformation of Academic and Higher Education Publishing in Britain and the United States*. Cambridge: Polity Press, 2005.

Thorbecke, Erik. "The Evolution of the Development Doctrine and the Role of Foreign Aid, 1950–2000." In *Foreign Aid and Development: Lessons Learnt and Directions for the Future*, edited by Finn Tarp and Peter Hjertholm, 17–47. London: Routledge, 2000.

Thornton, Patricia H., and William Ocasio. "Institutional Logics and the Historical Contingency of Power in Organizations: Executive Succession in the Higher Education Publishing Industry." *American Journal of Sociology* 105, no. 3 (1999): 801–43.

Thucydides. *The Peloponnesian War*. London: Hackett, 1998.

Tong, Jacqui. "Questionable Accountability: MSF and Sphere in 2003." *Disasters* 28, no. 2 (2004): 176–89.

Tuckman, Alan. "The Yellow Brick Road: Total Quality Management and the Restructuring of Organizational Culture." *Organization Studies* 15, no. 5 (1994): 727–51.

Ufford, Philip Quarles van, and Ananta Kuma Giri, eds. *A Moral Critique of Development: In Search of Global Responsibilities*. London: Routledge, 2003.

Uvin, Peter. *Aiding Violence: The Development Enterprise in Rwanda*. West Hartford, CT: Kumarian Press, 1998.

Vallaeys, Anne. *Médecins Sans Frontières: La biographie*. Paris: Fayard, 2004.

Van Dyke, Marci, and Ronald Waldman. *The Sphere Project Evaluation Report*. New York: Mailman School of Public Health, 2004.

Vaux, Tony. *The Selfish Altruist: Relief Work in Famine and War*. London: Earthscan/James & James, 2001.

Vidler, Elizabeth, and John Clarke. "Creating Citizen-Consumers: New Labour and the Remaking of Public Services." *Public Policy and Administration* 20, no. 2 (2005): 19–37.

Walker, Peter. "Cracking the Code: The Genesis, Use, and Future of the Code of Conduct." *Disasters* 29, no. 4 (2005): 323–36.

Walker, Peter, and Daniel G. Maxwell. *Shaping the Humanitarian World*. London: Taylor & Francis, 2008.

Walker, Peter, and Kevin Pepper. *Follow the Money: A Review and Analysis of the State of Humanitarian Funding*. Briefing Paper. Medford, MA: Feinstein International Center, Tufts University, 2007.

Walker, Peter, and Susan Purdin. "Birthing Sphere." *Disasters* 28, no. 2 (2004): 100–111.

Walker, Peter, and Catherine Russ. *Professionalising the Humanitarian Sector: A Scoping Study*. Cardiff: Enhanced Learning and Research for Humanitarian Assistance, 2010.

Wallace, Tina, Sarah Crowther, and Andrew Shepherd. *Standardising Development: Influences on UK NGOs' Policies and Procedures*. Oxford: WorldView Publishing, 1997.

Waltz, Kenneth N. *Theory of International Politics*. Boston: McGraw-Hill, 1979.

Wapner, Paul. *Environmental Activism and World Civic Politics*. Albany: SUNY Press, 1996.

———. "The Normative Promise of Non-State Actors: A Theoretical Account of Global Civil Society." In *Principled World Politics: The Challenge of Normative International Relations*, edited by Lester Ruiz and Paul Wapner, 261–74. Lanham, MD: Rowman & Littlefield, 2000.

Warner, Daniel. "The Politics of the Political/Humanitarian Divide." *International Review of the Red Cross* 833 (1999): 109–18.

Waters, Tony. *Bureaucratizing the Good Samaritan: The Limitations to Humanitarian Relief Operation*. Boulder, CO: Westview Press, 2001.

Watkins, Susan Cotts, Ann Swidler, and Thomas Hannan. "Outsourcing Social Transformation: Development NGOs as Organizations." *Annual Review of Sociology* 38 (2012): 285–315.

Weah, Sonpon D. *Aggrieved MSF-France Workers Demand Justice*. 2008. Accessed November 9, 2008. http://www.analystliberia.com/civil_service_may03_07 .html.

Weiss, Thomas. "Principles, Politics, and Humanitarian Action." *Ethics and International Affairs* 13 (1999): 1–22.

———. "The Sunset of Humanitarian Intervention? The Responsibility to Protect in a Unipolar Era." *Security Dialogue* 35, no. 2 (2004): 135–53.

White, Harrison C. *Markets from Networks: Socio-Economic Models of Production*. Princeton, NJ: Princeton University Press, 2002.

Wholey, Joseph S. *Evaluation: Promise and Performance*. Washington, DC: Urban Institute, 1979.

Whooley, Owen. "Diagnostic Ambivalence: Psychiatric Workarounds and the Diagnostic and Statistical Manual of Mental Disorders." *Sociology of Health & Illness* 32, no. 3 (2010): 452–69.

Wiebe, Robert H. *The Search for Order, 1877–1920*. New York: Hill and Wang, 1967.

Wilder, Andrew. *Perceptions of the Pakistan Earthquake Response: Humanitarian Agenda 2015 Pakistan Country Study*. Medford, MA: Feinstein International Center, Tufts University, 2008.

Wilson, Richard. *Human Rights, Culture, and Context: Anthropological Perspectives*. London: Pluto, 1997.

Wilson, Richard, and Richard Brown. *Humanitarianism and Suffering*. Cambridge: Cambridge University Press, 2009.

Wong, Wendy. *Internal Affairs: How the Structure of NGOs Transforms Human Rights*. Ithaca, NY: Cornell University Press, 2012.

Wright, Susan, ed. *Anthropology of Organizations*. London: Routledge, 1994.

———. *Parish to Whitehall: Administrative Structure and Perceptions of Community in Rural Areas*. Gloucestershire Papers in Local and Rural Planning 16. Gloucester: Gloucestershire College of Arts and Technology, 1982.

Yaylaci, Ismael. "Communitarian Humanitarianism: The Politics of Islamic Humanitarian Organizations." Paper presented at the Workshop on Humanitarism and Religion, American University, Cairo, 3–5 June 2008.

Young, Helen, Abdul Monim Osman, Yacob Aklilu, Rebecca Dale, Babiker Badri, and Abdul Jabbar Abdullah Fuddle. *Darfur—Livelihoods under Siege*. Medford, MA: Feinstein International Center, Tufts University, 2005.

Zhao, Kang, Louis-Marie Ngamassi, John Yen, Carleen Maitland, and Andrea Tapia. "Assortativity Patterns in Multi-Dimensional Inter-Organizational Networks: A Case Study of the Humanitarian Relief Sector." In *Advances in*

Social Computing: Third International Conference on Social Computing, Behavioral Modeling, and Prediction, SBP 2010, Bethesda, MD, USA, March 30–31, 2010; Proceedings, edited by Sun-Ki Chai, John J. Salerno, and Patricia L. Mabry, 265–72. Lecture Notes in Computer Science 6007. New York: Springer, 2010.

Žižek, Slavoj. "Against Human Rights." *New Left Review* 34 (July/August 2005).

Index

Abby Stoddard, 52, 110–11
abolitionism, 17, 138
acceptance, discourse of and labor by beneficiaries, 52
accountability: ALNAP and, 109; beneficiary labor and, 56–57; clarity in planning and management and, 86; definitions of, 141–42; donor demand for, 130; performing to the test and, 36; rights versus results and, 80–81, 175. *See also* Humanitarian Accountability Partnership
accounting, critical studies of, 76
Action against Hunger. *See* Action Contre la Faim
Action Contre la Faim, 95, 111
Afghanistan: Action Contre la Faim and, 95; CARE and, 164; donor governments and, 116; *Eigensinn* ("obstinacy") in, 67–68; Médecins sans Frontières and, 106, 117–18, 158, 164; mobilization of Islamic public in, 108; NGOs as part of US "combat team" in, 18; polarization within relief and, 117
Africa: decolonization of, 85; treatment of HIV-AIDS in, 123. *See also specific countries*
Agamben, Giorgio, 17
aid-aware, populations in need as, 66
allocation of resources: agency expertise and, 26–28, 31–32, 35; beneficiaries' redistribution of

aid and, 66; desk officers and, 9, 23–26; direct and indirect domination and, 62–63; disparities in, 31, 37, 48n15; logistical considerations and, 32–34, 37; interests and ideas and, 16–21; populations competing against each other and, 37, 41, 59, 60, 61; public versus official donors and, 49n16; as a specific problem for relief agencies, 14–16; symbolic differentiation in the field and, 121–23; worthy beneficiaries and, 61. *See also* selection of projects
ALNAP (Active Learning Network for Accountability and Performance), 109, 129, 159
altruism, 62
Americares, 111
Amnesty International, 152, 153, 153n18, 154, 156
anthropology, concept of community and culture in, 43; of policy, 76
Appadurai, Arjun, 80
Appia, Louis, 101
art for art's sake, humanitarian purity and, 105–6
Asia, decolonization of, 85. *See also specific countries*
assessment. *See* needs assessment
assessment fatigue, 53, 64
Association Internationale des Juristes Democrates, 152
audience commodity, 40–41

Made in the USA
Columbia, SC
08 January 2018